good
girl

A MEMOIR

SARAH TOMLINSON

G

GALLERY BOOKS

New York   London   Toronto   Sydney   New Delhi

Gallery Books
An Imprint of Simon & Schuster, Inc.
1230 Avenue of the Americas
New York, NY 10020

Copyright © 2015 by Sarah Tomlinson

Names and some identifying details of some of the people portrayed in this book have been changed.

First Gallery Books hardcover edition April 2015

GALLERY BOOKS and colophon are registered trademarks of Simon & Schuster, Inc.

For information about special discounts for bulk purchases, please contact Simon & Schuster Special Sales at 1-866-506-1949 or business@simonandschuster.com.

The Simon & Schuster Speakers Bureau can bring authors to your live event. For more information or to book an event contact the Simon & Schuster Speakers Bureau at 1-866-248-3049 or visit our website at www.simonspeakers.com.

Interior design by Jaime Putorti

Manufactured in the United States of America

10 9 8 7 6 5 4 3 2 1

Library of Congress Cataloging-in-Publication Data

Tomlinson, Sarah.
  Good girl / Sarah Tomlinson. — First Gallery Books hardcover edition.
     pages cm
(ebook) 1. Fathers and daughters—Biography. 2. Interpersonal relations. 3. Parental acceptance.
4. Fatherhood. I. Title.
  HQ755.85.T66 2015
  306.874'2—dc23
                                        2014039356

ISBN 978-1-4767-4896-2
ISBN 978-1-4767-4898-6 (ebook)

This book is dedicated to Simon's Rock,
where I was first encouraged and supported
to discover and become the writer and
person I am.

And to my mom, whose decision to send me
there was yet another example of the great
imagination, courage, and love with which
she raised me.

good
girl

chapter one

BACK TO THE LAND

We were building the house we would live in forever. The two-by-fours rose like a ship's mast against the still, blue New England sky. I squinted into the sun watching, feeling the adults' anticipation swell. It was our house. We were making it ourselves: my mom, her boyfriend, Craig, and me. Helping us were members of the community we'd formed with three other families in the woods of midcoast Maine that spring of 1979.

Where there had been nothing but forest and swamp, there was now a clearing, a home. Dressed in denim and flannel, the men called back and forth to one another beneath the wooden skeleton. I stood nearby, clutching my Raggedy Ann doll, trying not to get in the way. At three and a half, I was tall for my age, unathletic and pale, with crimson-brown hair and heavy, reddish freckles across my cheeks and the bridge of my nose.

One by one, the men removed their hands from the beams and stepped away. The timber stood straight and true. Everyone relaxed and laughed and paused to have a drink of water. Even with just the outline drawn, it already looked like a house.

At day's end, we camped in a tent. This little orange triangle felt like home, as we had begun staying there on weekends the previous year, clearing trees and brush to prepare for the build, and then pouring cement for the foundation. After that, Craig went by himself to pound nails on weekday afternoons, until we were ready for the group effort of the house raising. During the week, we lived in an apartment an hour away.

When she'd left my dad the previous spring, Mom had moved us up to Augusta and taken a job at her friend Lou's health food store. She soon reunited with her college boyfriend, Craig, who had been living at home on the Jersey Shore, working at his family's flower shop and as a carpenter. He joined us in our new life.

The idea to go back to the land had first taken root among a small circle of my mom and dad's like-minded friends, including Lou and Dot, whom my parents had met before I was born. Mom had inherited a little money from her grandmother and wanted to buy a piece of the hundred-acre plot the group had found in Maine. But my father, who had become a compulsive gambler soon after my birth, would not agree to the plan. Believing deeply in the chance to create a better way to live, and realizing she would end up on welfare if she stayed with my dad, my mom left him in Boston.

My mom and dad had met at the Trenton Public Library in 1973, where Mom worked after graduating from the West Virginia liberal arts college Davis & Elkins. My dad had recently washed up at his mom's apartment after hitchhiking back and forth across the country, emulating the Beat writers he adored and dropping acid 120 times. He was tall and loud, with a thick, dark beard and a shambling laugh, and he smelled musky and exotic, like sandalwood and myrrh.

A photo of my parents appeared in the 1973 year-end issue of *LIFE* magazine. They're kissing in the crowd at the Summer Jam at Watkins Glen, a music festival with performances by the Grateful Dead and the Band. One of only two photos that exist of them together, it sums up their union. Blown together by a frenzied cultural moment, they had a passionate relationship that could not be sustained. And they had me.

Their connection was already troubled when Mom became pregnant. When my dad proposed, she said no, later telling me that she refused him because she believed in marriage. When my dad learned I was on the way, he redoubled his focus on est, a seminar devoted to personal transformation, hoping to become the man and father he knew he was not. I was born in January 1976 at a farmhouse in Freedom, Maine. My dad said I came to him in a dream during Mom's pregnancy, and I was born two weeks late so I could be an Aquarius. Mom took my name from Bob Dylan's song "Sara," which, tellingly, was written for his wife during their divorce. My father insisted I have a home birth, having read how important it is to ease a child into the world gently and with love.

That summer my dad left Mom and me alone at the farmhouse with no car, miles from the nearest town, and hitchhiked to Boston to attend a review seminar of the est training. Although he had never been drawn to gambling before, he went to the track and won a hundred dollars. And then he lost a hundred dollars.

When he hitchhiked back to Maine and told Mom, she was devastated. He was not otherwise working, and they had almost no money. In lieu of paying rent, my dad had agreed to paint the farmhouse, but the owners weren't happy with his work and we had to leave in a hurry. We lived in a big domed tent in the yard of some friends, and my dad worked for Lou, helping him break down a stone wall for a masonry project.

That fall my parents relocated us to Boston. My dad drew on the connections he'd made through rebirthing to find a sublet in Somerville and a job driving a cab. Rather than being warned off gambling by his first failure, my father had stirred up a fierce compulsion. Mom held on, staying home with me while my dad lost money and drove extra shifts to allow him to spend more time attempting to make up for his loss. And then, realizing he would never change, she left.

After we had been in Augusta for a few months, Mom told me that my dad was coming to stay with me while she and Craig went camping in Baxter State Park with college friends. The anticipation built and built, and then, he was there. The moments I remember of my father—like this one—are vivid with detail and emotion because I saw him so infrequently and cherished our time together. It was overwhelming, almost too much, but I moved toward him anyway. When he bent down to hug me, I pulled back before he did, knowing even at three not to seem needy or provoke his guilt.

My dad took me to St. Augustine's, the Catholic church across the street from our apartment, because he wanted to check it out. I felt very small as we crossed the road, which sloped steeply down toward the river.

I let my father lead as we climbed a flight of steps carved from the same pale stone as the building's exterior. It was so big and fancy that I held my breath as we went inside. I didn't understand what it was, but I didn't dare ask.

My dad paused and surveyed the scene. "Far out," he said.

He looked down at me. I smiled, uncertain, but happy to be with him.

"We're going to visit all the churches of the world," he said.

"Okay," I replied.

Okay was my response to whatever my dad said or did. I could tell how hard it was for him to be around Mom and Craig, and even me, although I had no idea why. It seemed as if he were about to spook and bolt like one of the horses at his beloved racetrack, and I knew that if he did, there was a good chance he was never coming back.

Before it seemed like the visit had really begun, he was headed home to Boston. There was no stopping his leaving, nothing to be done. As soon as the door closed behind him, my attention became fixed on the next time I would see him, and on how we would do, together, all the things he had promised.

A few months later, I was coloring a picture on the floor of our apartment. My real focus, though, was on my father, who was coming to visit me that day. He would be there any minute. The phone rang in the other room. My mom's face grew clouded. But she had become a master at the smooth facade, and she smiled at me as she went to answer. I could hear the low murmur of her voice, but not her words. Anxiety bloomed inside of me. When she returned, she sat next to me on the floor, down at my level.

"Sarah, your dad can't come up this weekend," she said.

I didn't look at her, intent as I was on coloring absolutely within the lines, controlling my exterior even more rigidly as my feelings began to riot.

"Why?" I said.

She paused for a long moment. Still, I kept my eyes down, holding on tight.

"He has to work."

"But why?"

"He's going to come see you as soon as he can."

Soon was not now. Anything beyond now was impossibly far away. I wasn't hearing her anymore. I was running to my bed, taken over by the flash flood of tears I only allowed myself when he was not there. Mom let me cry until I had exhausted my tears. There was nothing she could say to comfort me, or to explain, but she never spoke badly of my father, either. She let it be between him and me.

In the fall of 1979, when I was three and a half, I was invited down to Boston to visit my dad in the big city where he lived, where I wanted to live, too. I was taking stock from the moment he parked his cab. His apartment was on a short, dead-end street in Somerville. I studied the drab vinyl exterior. So this was where my father spent his time instead of with me. I followed him up the dark, narrow stairwell to his second-floor apartment, absorbing every detail as he swung the door wide, revealing a life that was as strange and wondrous as I'd always imagined it to be.

He turned on the kitchen light, upending my sense of reality. The lightbulb was red and bathed us in an intense, surreal glow like Christmas gone crazy. The kitchen wall above the table was a giant collage of newspaper clippings and health food store greeting cards with photos of sacred locales in India and Asia, and illustrations of mandalas and the Buddha. I drew close. I'd seen these images on the cards my dad sent Mom, sometimes with forty or sixty dollars, more often with an excuse, only mentioning the track when he'd won, always blaming his lack of money on his taxi shifts.

He was already bopping into the next room, lighting incense. I followed him, breathing in his particular scent of essential oils and the musty paper from his many notebooks and the racing forms and new age magazines he read. I followed him into the living room. He pulled the chain dangling from the lightbulb. Even though I was prepared this time, the blue light that bathed everything in an aquatic chill was still startling.

With my gaze, I traced the yellowing Scotch tape on a crack in the living room window. Although I'd been too little to remember it, we'd all lived here together, the family I wanted us to still be, Dad and Mom, and me. But now my dad lived here alone. I lived far away with Mom and Craig, who struggled to mask how little he thought of my dad. He wasn't like my father, who focused on me with flattering wonder during our brief visits. Instead, he could be aloof and short with me, as if he didn't know what to do with this intense little girl he'd suddenly found himself helping to raise.

My dad took me out for Japanese food, the tempura batter crunchy on the broccoli and carrots—unlike anything I'd ever eaten. I fumbled with the chopsticks but didn't ask for help. Instead, I did my best to mimic how my dad balanced his on a little dish of soy sauce, which had the magical feel of a child-size tea party.

My father leaned in.

"Do you like Joni?" he asked, inquiring about one of my parents' friends.

I looked at him with surprise.

"Daddy, I like everyone," I said.

My dad laughed his big, shuffling laugh, and I puffed up with joy.

After dinner, my dad walked me through the city streets. I marveled at each cab and building and person. We arrived at a big lurking structure, which shimmered inside with twinkling lights and the salty allure of hot popcorn. It was a revival movie house. Sitting beside my father, I thrilled at the bright, happy chatter of *Singing in the Rain*, loving how the characters spun around light posts and twirled their umbrellas.

The next day, my dad took me to the place he had, in a way, chosen over Mom and me—Suffolk Downs racetrack, or Suffering Downs, as he later told me it is called by those in Boston wise enough to avoid its grinding gears. My father was easy amid the frantic sea of strangers, who jostled each other as they hurried back and forth across the wide, barren space—like a city train station without the excitement of an impending trip. He ran into a friend and, barely introducing me, bent down to listen eagerly as the tiny man spoke. I trailed behind him as he made his way to place a bet at the window, his racing form folded under his arm. During our visits before, he'd been intent on me, and I didn't like how far he seemed from me now. There was no magic in the horses, or the jockeys' bright satin uniforms, or the pomp and circumstance of the announcer's voice over the loudspeaker. Everything was gray and dark and cold.

Not long after I returned to Augusta, Mom called me to her one day. "Your dad sent us a letter," she said.

I leaned against her as she read it out loud in her soft, clear voice:

"Halo Lovelies, Oh Sue I'm so sorry, I'm finally in touch with my irresponsibility, it's what I've wanted to feel lately, because I have been doing things all along and not feeling them, and I kept thinking I know I do these things, but I don't feel it like I used to and now I do, it's great, and I get the only one I really hurt is me. So now I am living and breathing and digging (loving) everything. I know it will take a while to straighten everything out, but it will be easier now, now that I'm here doing it, instead of wanting to do it and feeling sorry that I wasn't."

The message ended with a description of how charmed he was by our conversation over dinner. "She's such a blessing and I'll be up as soon as I can."

The majority of his letter had been way beyond my understanding. But I felt like my efforts to behave well had been rewarded, and I was happy to have made a positive impression. Even if he hadn't realized he couldn't stand to be away from me, which was my ultimate goal. And that meant more waiting.

As much as my separation from my father pained me, the life my mom and I were leading in his absence was actually running smoother than ever. After our house raising, the building had come together in fits and starts. By 1980, the construction site was our home, and we lived on the land with three other families, whose six kids were my first friends. The seven of us were given free reign to run back and forth through the woods between the houses, where our parents could rest assured that all of the snacks would be healthy and vegetarian, and we'd be encouraged to play outside whenever possible and only watch educational TV. The men had jobs off the land, but there was always a mom home some-where, and I remember a safe feeling of being watched over.

Designed to heat itself with sunlight during the day, our house had four big skylights across its roof and four big windows in front. They looked out onto the yard Mom and Craig had cleared. It seemed I was always standing at one of the windows, careful not to get too close because the glass was chilly, even in summer, and I had been warned not to smudge it. My father's promise of a visit "soon" had extended into more than a year, but today he was really coming to see me. I watched intently for the flash of yellow through the sun-dappled trees that would signal my father's taxicab, doing math in my mind—it took three and a half hours to drive from Boston to midcoast Maine. If he'd left at nine, then he would be there by twelve thirty, or maybe one, depending on how many stops he made. I hummed with anticipation and joy. His cab should appear any minute, and he'd be there with me, just like he'd said.

Our house was like my sibling. We grew up together, intertwined. A ladder of two-by-fours nailed to the wall gave way to stairs, which were pitched at a steep angle and crossed by a low beam that held up the two bedrooms. When I was little, I fell down those stairs constantly. By the time I was old enough not to fall, I was also tall enough to hit my head on the beam, never quite adjusting to the house's quirks. Our only source of heat was a pretty maroon woodstove, and we chopped our own firewood. From an early age, I knew how to use a small ax and feed logs into a wood splitter we rented from town, and one of my regular chores was to stack firewood in the summer, and bring in armloads of wood after school in the winter.

The house was what we did as a family when other kids and their parents were sailing or playing Ping-Pong or watching TV. Though, eventually there was a television with rabbit ears that sort of got a few channels, and a record player for the hours Mom and Craig spent listening to music—the Beatles, Bob Dylan, Bruce Springsteen, Linda Ronstadt, Joan Armatrading, the Pretenders, the Police. I knew how to pound nails (not well) and spackle (which wasn't hard enough for me to be bad at it) and sand and stain wood (which was forgiving enough to hide the flaws in my work). I knew how to get a banked fire going again. I knew how almost every item of food I ate was made or where it came from. I knew how to weed and water the organic vegetables we grew in raised beds Craig built for Mom. The garden was like my refrigerator. I pulled up carrots, wiped the soil on the grass, and ate them standing in the sun. My childhood motto, probably learned from Mom, was "A little dirt never hurt."

But still, my dad was the one who I thought held the wisdom. As I waited for him to arrive, I rested my fingertips on the wood of the windowsill, staving off my fear of disappointment by redoing the numbers in my mind. At two, when he still had not come, I held on to the logic of my math problem: if he left at eleven, he'd be there by two thirty. But no, just to be safe, maybe he hit traffic, or got his cab serviced, or grabbed a fish sandwich on Route 1.

When four o'clock arrived and the phone rang, I felt a heavy knowing inside of me, like being aware of my own powerlessness. But I did not lose faith, not even then. I still believed in my dad, even when Mom summoned me to the phone, her face so devoid of any emotion it was scarier than if she were crying or raging with fury. In the absence of any signal from her, I didn't know how to behave.

I knew how I felt—bereft—but I didn't let it show. I took the cold plastic receiver and turned away from Mom, preferring to be alone within the sliver of personal space I wanted to believe I could control.

"Hi, Sarah," my dad said.

My heart went sweet and sour like marmalade. I loved his voice, the languor of his slightly nasal New Jersey twang, like he couldn't be bothered to close up the syllables. He flattened out the *a*'s in "Sarah," saying my name as no one else could, his tone giving me value. He retained the dropped consonants of the teenage hoodlum who sang doo-wop in the Trenton projects, where he was one of the only white kids and got kicked out of ninth grade for his bad grades and truancy. His words were separated by spaced-out pauses, the synapses of his brain—and his world vision—altered by those 120 acid trips.

"Bernie couldn't lend me a cab for the weekend," he said. Or maybe it was . . .

"My cab broke down on Ninety-Five, and it won't be fixed until next week." Or . . .

"I couldn't get the money together to come this weekend." Or . . .

"My back is acting up. I can't make it this weekend. But I'll try to come next weekend. And if I can't get up then, I'll be up as soon as I can."

Never that he *wouldn't* come to see me; always that he *couldn't,* as if there were a barrier between Boston and Maine that made it impossible for him to reach me. Of course there was an obstacle, only I didn't understand what it was at the time.

I listened to him very closely, careful not to do anything to scare him off. I did not cry or yell or lie down on the pine floorboards and kick my feet. I did not tell him I had been standing at the window all day, believing in him, when even he did not believe, not really, in himself, and Mom did not believe, and Craig did not believe, and my cat, Molasses, did not believe. "I'm sorry, Sarah," he said.

"It's okay," I said, not quite convinced of the lie myself but pretty sure he was.

"It'll be great when I can get the cab," he said in a rush, relieved to be on to the fun promises that were always really, truly going to happen next time. "We'll go for a long drive. And we'll stop at McClellan's on Route 1 and get a fish sandwich. And we'll drive up to Rangeley and go camping. I have a little tent we can use."

"Okay," I said, clutching the phone, willing myself to hold on, just hold on.

I never asked for an explanation of what was keeping us apart or pressed him to tell me why I should trust him. I simply believed him, the way my dad believed, insanely, after losing everything hundreds and thousands of times at the track, he would suddenly win one day, and it would be transcendent, everything he'd ever dreamed of on all of those sad, losing days. Next time he would win, he managed to believe. Yes, next time we would win, I, too, believed.

My dad's great, lumbering laugh erupted from him; he was glad to be free of his earlier anxiety about disappointing me, and to have gotten exactly what he needed from me. I was happy, too, because even though I hadn't gotten what I'd wanted, I'd made him happy.

If I didn't say anything to scare him off, and I made myself smart enough and funny enough and pleasant enough, maybe I could keep him on the phone just a while longer, and maybe, just maybe, he would come see me soon. I would be a good girl whose father wouldn't stay away for any reason in the world.

But long distance was expensive, and money was always an issue.

"I gotta go, Sarah," he said. "This call's costing a fortune, and I missed a shift this week because my back was acting up."

"Okay," I said, pushing down the panic rising within me.

"Tell Mommy I'm gonna send yous the money for last month as soon as I can. I'll figure out when I can get up again, and I'll send a letter with the dates."

"When?" I asked, trying to sound casual.

"I don't know, Sarah, as soon as I can. I have to go."

"Okay."

When I was sure he had hung up, I returned the receiver to its cradle and tried to fold myself back into reality, which seemed flat and stale compared to even just his voice on the phone. Around me were the roughly built counters, which were nothing more than open wooden boxes, really, topped with plywood, containing the big glass jars in which Mom stored brown rice and dried beans. This was my real life, but it felt like a cheap substitute for what I most wanted: my dad.

When we moved to the land full-time in the winter of 1980, Mom gave up her job at the health food store in Augusta. I loved having her at home with me. Her days were largely devoted to the never-ending tasks by which we shaped the house into a home and stayed warm and fed. Throughout the morning, she would return to the kitchen and punch down her rising bread, a job I enjoyed helping her with, my small fists sinking into the dough, which was soft and sticky, pliant in a way that felt very much alive.

Once the bread was in the oven, Mom could usually be convinced to play a game or do a puzzle with me. Craig didn't like to play games or do puzzles, and he could be impatient with my little-girl whimsy, so we were not close. Instead, we were joined by a shared adoration of my mom. She made me a game out of small pieces of paper, each printed with a letter, which had a match hidden in the stack of squares. After we had played a few times, I knew my letters. I begged Mom to teach me to read, which fascinated me because I saw her doing it all the time. I wanted to be just like her, because she was beautiful and good at so many things.

Mom and Craig had met at Davis & Elkins in 1969 and maintained the bohemian habits of their generation, growing a few pot plants for occasional consumption during our first few years on the land. From an early age, I knew the plants were illicit and sometimes snuck other kids back to the clearing where they sprouted. Briefly, during Nancy Reagan's Just Say No campaign, I worried Mom and Craig would get arrested and be taken away. But, overall, the pot intrigued me, as did everything on the land. It was something the grown-ups did, and I was interested in everything the grown-ups did.

My only issue with them smoking together in the evenings was that I wanted to watch TV like other kids, and instead, Mom and Craig preferred to listen to music and talk. They sometimes let me watch *The Waltons* as a compromise.

One night, Craig turned off the television after my show was over, and a small orb of light hung in the center of the darkened screen for a long moment. When that faded, it seemed to sever any tie we had to the outside world. A rattling sound scattered across one of the skylights. My head jerked up, even though I was always terrified I would see a face looking down at me through the glass. There was nothing there, just more darkness.

"It was only an acorn," Mom said, smiling at me.

Craig kneeled and slid out a record, handling it carefully the way he had showed me, even though my own hands were too small, and I wasn't allowed to play the records yet. There was a faint staticky hiss and the album began: Peter Gabriel's *Security*.

I sat next to Craig on the floor and pored over the album cover for Pink Floyd's *Wish You Were Here*, with its image of two suit-clad men shaking hands, one of them on fire. Craig lit a small purple glass bong. The room filled with sweet, musty smoke. He passed it to Mom. Her long hair fell around her face as she leaned down to inhale. Craig's stereo speakers were large and powerful, and Peter Gabriel wailed amid a wash of electronic instruments. I became very aware of our place in the world, just the three of us alone together, tucked away in a small house amid a big forest on the edge of the immense ocean, and felt a deep melancholy I didn't quite know what to do with.

I loved the music deeply, consuming it as if it were food, tasting its flavors of genius, of madness, and of the vast, magic world just beyond the land. When I got bored of listening, Mom played Parcheesi with me, always letting me be the red player, because that was my favorite, even when I gave her first pick.

Every night, Mom slid into my twin bed with me and read me a chapter or two from the books I already loved like family—*Little Women* and *The Secret Garden*, or my favorite book from my childhood, *The Year of Mr. Nobody*, the story of a discontented middle child who feels alien-ated from his family and so invents an imaginary friend.

With my Sesame Street comforter pulled up to my chin, my mom lanky beside me in jeans and her Guatemalan slippers, her bangles mak-ing their familiar music as she turned the page, I felt safe and content, maybe not entirely happy, but at least full of an uneasy peace that was a relief from my normal waiting state. Inside the world of the book, I could forget my own longing and lack. A few months into our new life on the land, I could read the easy authors kids learn first—Dr. Seuss and Shel Silverstein.

Mom got a job and put me in a local day care. My only real, vivid memory of the place is how much I hated naptime, already eager for a life filled with constant activity and excitement. The heavy claustrophobia of insomnia rising, I knew I would not be able to sleep. But I was a perfectionist and a rule follower, never tantruming in front of anyone but Mom and Craig, and so I willed myself still.

When I couldn't stand it anymore, I quietly reached for a book. The adults who found me reading couldn't really be angry since I hadn't disturbed anyone. My mutiny was permitted. Reading became a reward for me, and finally, something I could control.

As much as I loved reading, I would have preferred to be at home playing with my own toys, on the land with the other kids who were like me. Being out in the world was always a little fraught. We didn't live like other people. We didn't watch the same TV programs or eat the same food, and as much as my instinct was to fit in, I mostly liked how we lived. It was familiar, and it had an aura of old-timey adventure, like living in *Little House on the Prairie*. Going back and forth between the two realities—carob at home versus chocolate at day care, wooden blocks and tinker toys versus plastic, plastic, plastic—was like being bilingual.

From an early age, I had a list of chores I was expected to complete each week. Instead, I was often hiding away upstairs, tearing through a library book. I hated getting in trouble, but I was like a drunk at the bar in the final minutes before last call, trying to squeeze in a few more precious sips.

The one chore I didn't have to be harassed about was checking the mail. As I stood on the side of the country road that passed by our house, I willed myself to yank open the wooden mailbox. Usually, it was just bills and seed catalogs for Mom.

But sometimes, there was an envelope that smelled exotic yet familiar, its exterior marked with my dad's distinctive handwriting, which I adored and tried to copy for a time in my teens—my name rendered with lowercase *a*'s nestled between a capital *S,* capital *R,* and capital *H.* When I was little, these cards were mostly addressed to Mom. I clutched the envelope to my chest and ran all the way back, always a little surprised when our house came into view amid the unrelenting trees, the skylights glinting in the mellow New England sun. Mom was making a stained-glass window at the table, bent down over the pattern of blue and yellow flowers she'd laid out, her hair falling forward.

"Mom, Mom, you got a letter from Dad," I said.

She looked up, her face tense, then smiled at me. "Here, I'll open it," she said.

I held my hand on her bare arm, freckled like mine, as she tilted the card so I could see the painting of an old-fashioned woman holding a brown dog, and read:

"Hi Sue and Sarah, Hope/Intend this catches up with yous. How does bringing Sarah down Sun the 21st or Mon. the 22nd sound and I'll probably bring her back up on the bus, cause I just don't have enough confidence in my bomb."

My heart leapt in my chest. *I was going to see my dad. I was, wasn't I?* I looked at Mom, but she was focused on reading, not giving anything away: "If it sounds good to you call me collect from the land or otherwise I'll call you Weds. morning. Good luck, good weather with your house, tell everyone I love them, John."

Mom gave me the card, picked up her soldering iron, and went back to work.

"Am I going to Boston?" I asked.

"We'll see," she said.

It was like Christmas, Easter, and Halloween all put together, but better, because it was a wonderful surprise I hadn't dared to let myself hope for. Now I just had to wait until his phone call to make sure it was really happening.

"Why don't you go outside and play?" Mom said.

Ever since I'd learned to read, I wasn't so into playing in the woods. I'd outgrown the idea that a little dirt didn't hurt, and I always seemed to be afflicted with a sunburn, even when I'd barely been outside. But this was the refrain of my childhood, and I wanted to behave so nothing would get in the way of my time with my dad. I took my book—its constant presence like an extension of my body—out to the front yard.

Everything on the land had a strong smell; the air never seemed to warm up completely, except for a few weeks in late summer, and in the short, cool afternoons, the earth's odor was sharp and tangy with minerals. I lay on the grass, which was sweet and clean like the aftertaste of milk. It was so quiet I could hear the wind in the trees, a gentle whooshing noise that became hypnotic. There was something supremely lonely about the sound. In order to hear it, there must be no evidence of human life anywhere—no car engines or horns, no television laugh tracks, no human voices talking about the price of potatoes, no electric guitar solo from a classic rock song drifting over from someone's radio. There was nothing and no one, a feeling like the end of the world, an absence and emptiness that created an early, unformed dread; I was all alone, as we were all alone, with nothing but the wind in the trees.

chapter Two

JOHN LENNON'S COMING BACK

Every sixth or seventh time my dad vowed to visit, as I stood waiting at the window, my vigilance paid off. There was a flash of yellow through the trees. He was coming. He was really coming this time. It had been more than a year since his last visit, six months since I'd last been down to Boston. He had promised to see me at least half a dozen times in between. But I had believed, and now he was here. Joy and terror filled me in equal parts. I ran outside to greet him, but then held back at the last moment, paralyzed with shyness and the sheer overwhelming fact that my father was there, suddenly, in the flesh. After I had gotten over my initial anxiety, I met him in the driveway.

"Hi, Sarah," he said, his lazy enunciation of my name familiar and beloved.

"Hi," I said, watching him closely for guidance.

He squatted down to my height, and I breathed him in and felt his worn green T-shirt under the skin of my bare arms, his little notebook poking at me from his chest pocket. I tried to hold him tight, but my reach didn't go all the way around.

"My back's been acting up all day," he said, pushing himself to stand.

His bad back was the number one reason he gave for canceling our visits, and I watched him closely now, afraid it would cause him to leave abruptly.

"Are you okay?" I asked.

"Yeah, I'm fine, Sarah," he said. "How are you?"

"Good," I said, scurrying ahead of him toward the house, which I felt proud of, as if it were a drawing I'd made and now had the chance to show off.

He held back a little, and I slowed my steps to match his. When he caught up, I led him inside. Mom was chopping chickpeas in the blender for fresh hummus. She turned off the loud whirring blades when we came through the door.

"Hi, John," she said.

"Hi, Sue," he said, barely able to look at her. "How are yous?"

"We're good," Mom said. "Sarah's glad you're here."

He reached into his back pocket and pulled out a bent envelope.

"I'm sorry it isn't more," he said.

She didn't say anything, didn't reach for the envelope. All of us were silent. He held it out to her. Finally, she took it from him, and I exhaled.

"Thank you," she said. "Do you want some lunch?"

"Nah, I stopped and got a fish sandwich at McClellan's on the way up. I think we're gonna take a drive."

"Sarah, have some lunch first," Mom said.

"I'm not hungry," I said, even though I loved to eat, hungry or not.

All I wanted was to be alone with my dad. I thought he was some- how more special than the other dads who were a regular part of life on the land, because he lived in a faraway city, and he drove a cab, which was glamorous, big-city work, and if he could only be with me once every six to eighteen months, then his time must be more valuable than that of the other fathers, who shoveled the driveways and ate the tabbouleh at the potlucks during our regular day-to-day. He was like a touring rock star that only rolled into town when his adoring public and exciting lifestyle allowed him to get away.

When my dad was with me, I was greedy about his time. His visits with the other families on the land—Lou and Dottie, who'd been my parents' friends when they were together, and Penny, who lived in the house behind ours and shared similar interests and beliefs with my dad—made me restless. As we sat together on the bench in Dottie's kitchen, where he sipped herbal tea from a chunky ceramic mug, I hated losing him to adult conversations I could barely follow. Nevertheless, I stayed close by his side.

"Do you wanna go play?" he said, looking down at me.

I shook my head, determined to wait it out. But as the afternoon dragged on, I became frustrated that his attention wasn't on me. I reached up onto the table and pulled on his big, dad hand, trying to hurry him up. He looked down at me and laughed.

"All right, Sarah, let's go," he said, making my heart leap.

My dad's visits always found us indulging in one of his greatest passions—driving. He'd held jobs he'd loved delivering auto parts to mechanic shops up and down the Delaware River and parking cars, not to mention his cab driving. I would think of this when I later read Kerouac, because of my dad, of course, always picturing Neal Cassady as my dad during the scenes in which he parked cars with maniacal zeal. My dad's idealization of Kesey and Cassady and all of his counterculture heroes was the cover story for why he couldn't get a real job with the "squares" or be anything like a steady father to me.

I'm sure my dad's long rambles on the narrow coastal roads were due in part to his eagerness to stay out of the house, which must have been oppressive for him, even though Mom was remarkably good at keeping her anger in check, and Craig merely rolled his eyes.

Dad didn't know any other form of parenting, so what was he supposed to do anyhow? His father was a World War II sailor who never acknowledged his paternity and has never been more to our family than a name on a piece of paper. My grandmother Betty, an alcoholic model and hatcheck girl at mobster clubs in the New Jersey Palisades, lost her children to foster care when my dad was three and my aunt Mimi was eleven. After Betty got out of prison for child neglect, my dad's family time was limited to the few weekends when Betty convinced one boyfriend or another to ferry her out to the home of his foster parents, and take him on Sunday drives.

Among the few clear memories my dad has of me as a child is from when I was three: we are in one of his cabs, driving up the coast. He is looking down at me, and he is so happy to be there because, as he says, it is so "far out" to talk to me. I am listening to every word he says in the most intense way possible, creating a feeling within him that he sums up like this: "It's always nice if you can find one other person in the world who listens to you." Of course I was happy to listen to him. He had shaped me to be his best listener, ever. Grocery store clerks still tell me their secrets to this day.

My father did all of the usual dad pranks of driving with no hands, until I was sure we would crash, barely righting the car at the last minute, or sometimes driving with his knees. All of which made me shriek and giggle and feel as if we were two merry pranksters. Until my dad began pinching his waistline.

My dad had this habit, which he used to distract himself from his severe back pain. I anxiously watched his hand sneak down to the fabric of his shirt. This pain was my enemy. I didn't want it to make him go away. I always wanted to spend as much time with him as possible, and I would have done anything to keep him with me forever.

But I had to make do with his visits. When my dad came up to Maine, he couldn't afford a motel. Our house was small—only 740 square feet, including the bedrooms upstairs—and the only two rooms with doors were the bathroom and Mom and Craig's room. There was no guest room. For the first few years, we didn't have a couch. And so he stayed in my room with me.

As we settled in at bedtime, I rolled away from him into the crack between my bed and the wall, calming myself with my stuffed lamby and the familiar cool of the Sheetrock against my skin. I loved him more than anything else, but I was scared by the intensity of the love I felt for him, and how it bloomed when I was near him, because he was largely a stranger to me.

He shifted next to me, trying to compact his adult frame into my tiny bed, and I held myself tightly together, careful not to let our skin touch, overwhelmed by everything. I could feel the adult tension like a held breath in the house and couldn't stand that what I wanted most was obviously so hard on everyone else.

As the inevitable end of his visit drew near, I felt a rising dread. He had raced up the driveway in a flurry of yellow, and now he must drive away. He squatted down and hugged me good-bye with a scent of sandalwood and a scratch of beard. From my post at the window, I watched his cab flicker through the trees, away from me again.

A few months later, when I was five, my dad got a girlfriend: Phyllis. She smelled like essential oils and had long, brown hair and an intense bothered air that perplexed and upset me. When he visited that summer, she came with him. Not only did I now have to share my father with this person, but she seemed not to like me. Everyone else in my life had always rolled with my constant chatter, laughing and encouraging my insights. Even Craig, who could sometimes be harsh, was more likely to school me with sarcasm than scolding, and once I was old enough to master a cutting remark myself, I often earned laughs from him. Phyllis was different.

My father and Phyllis camped in our front yard and, ever eager to be near my dad, I slept in their tent with them. The three of us were close together—she was brushing her hair; he was stretched out on his sleeping bag; I was chattering away like a chickadee.

"Sometimes we play that we're squirrels, and we each have a house in a tree, but it's not a real house, it's make-believe. Or sometimes my house is that big rock over there. That's also our picnic rock. Sometimes Mom has a picnic on it with me. I want to have potato chips like in a restaurant. But we don't have potato chips. We have carrot sticks. And when I'm a squirrel, I gather nuts and berries for the winter. Because—"

"Will you ever stop talking?" Phyllis snapped at me.

I froze, paralyzed.

I looked at my dad. He didn't speak or even seem to register what was happening. I was on my own. I shut up and stayed that way.

The next day, the three of us got into my dad's cab and went on our version of a family vacation. We drove inland to a picturesque waterfall and swimming hole called Smalls Falls, just south of Rangeley Lake. My dad threw himself into an impassioned reverie—over what was essentially a roadside pit stop—about the beauty of Maine and the greater simplicity of life in a place where people still lived close to the land. After we had admired the falls, the woods, and the good, simple people, we returned to the car.

In a show of good-natured naïveté, my father had left the doors unlocked, and everything had been stolen—Phyllis's expensive camera, all of the luggage, and worst of all, my little overnight bag with my brand-new gold lamé bathing suit, which I adored, and my most beloved stuffed bear of the moment. I was devastated. I looked at my dad. He had deflated like a kid who'd just dropped the pop fly and cost his team the game.

"What is wrong with you?" Phyllis lit into him. "How could you be so stupid?"

I remained silent and looked away, embarrassed for my father. It was the only one of my dad's few visits that I did not want to last forever.

✦

That fall, it was time for me to go to school. I had been in kindergarten for a week or two when I settled into my seat on the floor with my classmates one morning. I became aware of a hushed shadowy conversation being held just beyond my perception, but clearly about me. A woman turned and smiled at me.

"Come with me, please," she said.

I didn't know much about school yet, but I could tell this wasn't the way things were normally done. As the other kids stared at me, looking glad they hadn't been singled out, I obediently followed her into the hallway and down the corridor.

A smiling teacher with short salt-and-pepper hair, Mrs. Falagario, gestured to an empty desk near the back of an orderly row. I faced another wall of staring eyes.

"Why don't you sit there?" Mrs. Falagario said.

Embarrassed, but also curious, as I was always interested in going someplace new, I walked silently to the desk and awkwardly slid in, uncertain through and through.

"If you look inside, you'll find all of your supplies for the year," she said. "They're your responsibility, so you have to take good care of them, okay?"

I nodded and glanced down at the opening of the desk and my own box of crayons and small plastic ruler. We had all of this at my house, sure, but something about being given my own little corner of the world at school felt special to me; I immediately determined my desk and supplies would be impeccable and stay that way.

Just like that, I was in the first grade. They hadn't known what to do with me in kindergarten because I could already read and was mature for my age, so they had skipped me a grade ahead. There it was: I was good at school. But I wasn't just going to be good. As with my maintenance of my school supplies, I was going to be perfect.

I had been in day care a few hours a week, but this was my first extended exposure to kids off the land. Most of them came from generations of locals. As with all transplants to Maine, those of us on the land were known as "from away," even though it'd been several years since we'd moved. Their dads hunted. The land had written bylaws that included no pesticides and no shooting of guns. They had heard of the Beatles, but they were more into Lynyrd Skynyrd.

At least I was attending elementary school in a mostly poor lobstering community in the early eighties, so no one had much of anything I didn't. Kids weren't brand conscious yet, so the fact that Mom sewed some of my clothes wasn't noticeable to them.

The only stressful part of the school day was lunch. I brownbagged it like most everyone else. Only, the other kids ate Jif and Fluff on Wonder Bread, with a Ho Ho for dessert. The whole wheat bread I loved helping Mom bake was often dry and had to be sliced thick to hold together. Paired with peanut butter and honey, this made for a cementlike sandwich. When I grew old enough to understand that making fun of myself first was the best way to ensure other kids didn't tease me, I dubbed them "suicide sandwiches." I didn't even try to get anyone to trade lunches with me.

Around the time I started first grade, in mid-October, we drove down to my grammy's house in Pennsylvania for Mom and Craig's wedding. Craig's family, who owned a flower shop in nearby Ocean Grove, New Jersey, had arrived early to set up the flowers—potted chrysanthemums that formed an aisle in the sloping grass of Grammy's front yard, leading to a trellis woven through with flowers—every little girl's dream. Even better, Mom had made me a special lace-trimmed dress to wear as I scattered rose petals down the aisle. I adored the fact that I looked like a littler version of her.

Because there is only a scattering of photos before Mom and Craig's wedding, it has always felt like our family began then. But my heart rebelled against these wedding photos because my father was not in them. As much as I was a part of this family in reality, I did not entirely feel like I was. Even worse, I suspected that to accept membership here was to betray my father.

I went down to Boston, early the next year, to visit my dad at his apartment in Somerville, where he and Phyllis now lived together. At bedtime on the first night of my visit, I completely lost my shit, the one and only occasion on which I have ever done so in front of my father. There was something so unsettling about going to sleep in this strange place with my dad and this woman I'd only met once, and Mom nowhere nearby, that was just too much for me. He held me as I kicked and shrieked in panic and frustration. Nothing was the way I wanted it to be, and I was too little to do anything about it, and I hated being so sad, and I was fed up with being left lacking, again and again and again. The meltdown went on and on, until I collapsed into exhausted sleep.

My meltdown seemed to make an impression on Phyllis, who softened toward me. We had planned a picnic for the next day. But of course we awoke to find the sky unleashing a torrential downpour—even when my father was trying, things never seemed to go his way. I was despondent until they saved the day with the kind of magical thinking that made time with my father such a treat. We would have an indoor picnic. Phyllis let me help make the picnic lunch, teaching me how to peel a hard-boiled egg for egg salad, while we listened to an old record of *Babes in Toyland* that had belonged to her as a child, the day and the visit rescued by her kindness.

I didn't see my dad for a few years after that. He was present so infrequently in my childhood that it's illogical to link his absence to my emotional display. But I was careful not to behave so badly again. And not only because I feared scaring him off, but because my freak-out had frightened me. When I had an overload of feelings around Mom and Craig, they formed a stable adult wall that confined my tumult—

maybe it was uncomfortable to smack up against them, but it also felt safe to know I was contained. My father offered no such stability. I had to constantly stretch myself to handle the unknown just to be with him.

The next summer when I was six, my dad's mother, Betty, began taking an active interest in me. I was not to call her Grammy or Bubby, or even Grandmother, all of which she felt would have aged her inconceivably. Instead, I was to address her by her given name, Betty. My mother and I took to calling her "the Big B," a homage to the grandiose *B* with which she signed the constant cards she sent.

Her own stab at parenting made my dad seem worthy of an award by comparison, but now that she was sober and earning a good living as a practical nurse to rich clients in Manhattan, she had taken to grandparenting with a vengeance. I was very lucky to have her, and not just because of the severe lack in her son, which she was probably trying to make up for, but because we were kindred spirits in many ways.

Betty represented everything I aspired to and feared I didn't deserve. She lived in Manhattan, and her temple was the Macy's in Midtown, her patron saint Estée Lauder, the only cosmetics worth wearing, according to her. And wear them she did, reapplying her bright red or coral lipstick at the table after every meal I ever ate with her.

Although she had never really made it as a model, she had been beautiful enough, and enjoyed adequate success with men because of it, that she hung on to a haughty pride about her looks. This would have been startling enough in the wilds of Maine. It was compounded by the fact that I was the kind of country girl who was sprinkled with freckles and had thick, frizzy hair with a tendency to tangle and snarl.

Like other little girls, I adored pink and dolls and ballet. But I was hopeless at girly things. I spent all of my time reading or playing in the woods. And Mom, who sewed most of my clothes and believed that girls should be as free as boys to enjoy their childhood fancies without concern for their appearance, was in exact opposition to Betty. It wasn't a problem, exactly. I adored Betty's posh ways and lapped up the many precious dresses she sent me in beautiful boxes from Macy's and Lord & Taylor, encased in diaphanous sheets of tissue paper that smelled like spun sugar. But even with the gifts, Betty frequently observed me with a critical eye.

That first summer, the Big B sent her commandment up from New York City for Mom to find us suitable lodging. She then arrived by Greyhound bus. Mom dutifully picked her up and took us to the cottage she'd rented, where Betty and I proceeded to sit for the next week. Betty couldn't drive, didn't cook, and outside of the city, she only seemed interested in reading the paper and smoking cigarettes.

Betty didn't like to discuss her past, which I later learned had been painful. She didn't speak much of my father, who seemed uneasy about her role in my life, if grateful for her generosity toward me. And when she did speak of him, she could be cutting, as she was regarding just about everyone, including me. My father later told me how she'd been orphaned by age eighteen and swindled by a lawyer out of a piece of family property in Cleveland; how her husband, a theater actor, had abandoned her and their daughter for Hollywood; how her boyfriends had led her to become an alcoholic; how when he was a teenager it seemed likely she'd started drinking again in secret, and had some- times been a kept woman, if not an outright whore; how she'd used food to control him as a boy, and let him smoke and drink in the apart- ment as a teen, hiding him when he went AWOL from the US Navy, all, he believed, in an attempt to manipulate him, but also, he had to grudgingly admit, as a kind of twisted unconditional love, as was the fact that she gave him money and a place to stay, no matter how bad his gambling was.

Betty would sometimes talk about how she'd taken my father to the Jersey Shore with this or that boyfriend when he was young. I loved her anecdotes because they were so exotic to me and contained the character of my dad as a child, which I had trouble wrapping my mind around, just as I did with the stories Grammy told me about Mom.

The people in Betty's stories—not just boyfriends, but also the friends who took her on car trips or rode out to Atlantic City with her on senior bus outings that included a roll of quarters—always dropped out of her life at some point in the tales. Even at an early age, I had a feeling that her strong personality had driven them away.

Betty had a loud voice that carried, and she felt entitled to speak unpleasant truths because of her age. At the same time, she was deeply paranoid. Once when I spoke Betty's name too loudly in a store, she glared at me.

"They'll hear you," she hissed.

I froze, unused to being addressed so harshly.

"Who?" I dared to ask.

"I can't have everyone knowing my name," she said, looking around her.

Now I was afraid, but for a different reason. This strange woman was my caretaker for the week.

Betty relished eating out, and she especially liked the kind of fatty, decadent food that was forbidden in my household. As she sat dousing her French fries in salt, I watched, wide-eyed, until my inner Good Samaritan got the better of me.

"You shouldn't eat so much salt," I said. "It's not good for you."

"I'm old," she crowed with a big, hearty laugh. "I want to enjoy myself."

Mostly, her visit had the hushed, stopped-time languor of a hospital waiting room. I watched Betty read the paper, apply her lipstick, and smoke. Our rented cottage was a drab, simple affair that was supposed to be within walking distance of the beach. It might have been, but I don't remember us going to the beach even once.

The next summer, Betty returned. Our rental this year was one of a half dozen neat white cottages with dark green shutters that matched a larger house with rocking chairs on its porch. My fear at what embarrassing thing Betty might say to the other guests as we sat in these chairs was trumped by my relief from the constant boredom of sitting in the cabin with her, and we spent long hours rocking together while she smoked.

Our new cabin was within walking distance of one of my favorite places in the world—the Pemaquid Point Lighthouse. Betty and I walked to the lighthouse every day, me prattling along as I did. "Why is that little building by the lighthouse red?" I asked.

"How should I know?" Betty laughed.

"Do they still have lighthouse keepers?" I asked, my commentary eventually puttering along on its own when I got no response from Betty.

Like my father, Betty wasn't accustomed to children, and so she didn't take the usual parental approach of trying to make every moment into a lesson. Instead, she laughed at me, not feeling the need to pretend to be polite.

She was old. I amused her. She didn't care how I felt or what anyone thought. She was going to laugh. She was on the vacation she had earned, and she was going to read her paper and smoke her cigarettes and eat as much salt as she wanted.

This second cabin was also near a restaurant that held an epic place of honor in my mind: the Gosnold Arms. It was across the road from the New Harbor Co-op, where Mom and Craig took visitors to eat fresh lobsters served on paper trays at picnic tables overlooking the harbor. At that age, and with our strict health food diet, I loved any excuse to eat out. I fancied myself a bit of a sophisticate, though, and looked longingly across the road at the Gosnold Arms, located in a regal building with a long front porch.

I'm not sure whether Betty and I arrived as the restaurant opened in an attempt to be thrifty, or because we'd both been waiting for dinner for hours, as it was one of the day's only distractions. But we happened to hit the early bird special.

I braced myself as the server approached. Who knew what Betty would say? She had a habit of demanding sliced lemon at the end of a seafood meal and rubbing it over her fingers to erase the fishy smell she imagined to be lingering there.

"We have two options for the early bird special tonight," the server happily chirped. "Lamb and veal."

Mom was raising me as a strict vegetarian. Although I enjoyed breaking the rules when I stayed with Grammy, eating one of her dry hamburgers was one thing. It was quite another thing to consume one of the cutest animals I'd ever seen. I had to have the alternative. I waited for the waitress to leave.

"What's veal?" I asked.

"Baby cow," Betty said without a second thought.

When the waitress came back to take our order, she beamed down at me.

"And what would you like?" she asked.

"Veal," I said, the word sticking in my throat.

As much as I was eager to join the big world and saw Betty as a means to get there, I was uncertain of my ability to handle the vast options it included. And yet, my longing only grew.

That summer, my dad visited again. As usual, it had been more than a year since I'd last seen him, so I was shy but eager. It didn't take long for him to win me over with his special way of talking, as if he were picking up our great ongoing conversation. I sat with him in his cab, which he had parked by Mom's garden, where the nasturtiums rioted red, orange, and yellow blooms over her wooden beds, the beans and peas in orderly rows.

Inside my dad's taxi, it smelled of his essential oils and something clean and healthy, like a natural food store, and also the incense he burned in the ashtray, a habit I took up when I got my first car. It was orderly, like everything about my father, with a slightly eccentric attention to detail. He always had at least one notebook going—pocket size with a Bic pen in the spiral binding, containing pages and pages of affirmations.

For each visit, he'd borrow a different cab. Some were generic modern sedans, but at least once he got an old Checker cab. All of the cabs had bulletproof glass between the backseat and driver—a scary detail I thankfully didn't have the mental sophistication to comprehend. I loved nothing more than to climb in back and push pennies through the money slot, pretending I was one of his fares. But today I was sitting next to him, his ever loyal copilot.

"John Lennon's coming back," he said in a conspiratorial tone of voice that suggested I was the only person in tune enough to get the message.

I nodded sagely, as if I knew exactly what he was talking about.

"There's this woman who's been channeling him, and he's gonna give a television interview, and tell us all about where he's been, and what we need to do."

I knew it was sad that John Lennon had died. I was interested in this TV appearance, but I think I was also looking for proof it was safe to believe my dad—that he knew truths about the world in the way adults were supposed to, and he could be trusted in his explanation of them. I watched for that TV special for years. In my mind, it's as if it actually happened.

The next summer, Betty's visit took a turn for the glamorous. She asked Mom to rent us a room at a bed-and-breakfast in Portland, sixty miles south and metropolitan by comparison. It had city buses, which Betty soon mastered. It had a department store, Porteous, which she waltzed us through as if I were Annie in a Daddy Warbucks montage.

At the bed-and-breakfast, as always, I feared Betty's interactions with the owners and other guests, but I was glad for an alternative to the tedium of past summers. Coffee was served in the salon. I loved the accompanying Hydrox cookies, which I washed down with the sugary coffee I began drinking as part of my endless bid to seem grown-up.

It wasn't always easy to fold myself back into regular life after my time with my dad or Betty. I was being raised to be disciplined and hardworking. But I was a kid, and one with a natural affinity for the big life—big cities, big meals, big emotions. I learned to live treat to treat, the way the orphans in after-school specials put all of their faith in that big Christmas miracle. When I was occasionally allowed one of the indulgences I loved—putting flowered barrettes in my hair for a restaurant outing when family visited, riding the roller coaster for hours at an amusement park during my summer stay with Grammy, or even just the delicious sensory overload of seeing a movie at the theater, rather than viewing public television on our staticky little TV, I savored every moment, abuzz with joy.

As much as I was desperate to go everywhere, and do everything, a part of me never wanted to leave the safe, perfect oasis Mom and Craig had carved out for us in the wild woods of Maine. Melancholy with longing, I became aware early on that wherever I was, a part of me would always want to be somewhere else.

chapter three

I STILL DREAM OF ORGONON

On Christmas Eve when I was nine, Mom and Craig sat down across from me, looking solemn. Christmas has always been sacred for me. Growing up without organized religion, and naturally drawn to ritual, I elevated the holiday to a holy place. I loved the Christmas tree with its sparkly glam-rock decorations. I loved the schmaltzy music. I loved the television specials, most of all *It's a Wonderful Life* with its seasonally palatable existential angst. Not to mention it was one of the few occasions we were allowed to eat sugar. In a sugar-soused reverie, I stared back at Mom as she spoke. "What if Santa brought you a little brother or sister for Christmas?"

I took this in—was it possible? This was the first I was hearing of it, and Santa was due in just a few short hours. Even I could do the math on this.

"What do you mean?" I asked.

"Well, I'm going to have a baby, so you're going to have a little brother or sister."

She and Craig looked at each other, and then Mom smiled and looked at me.

I got it now. My nine-year reign as the castle's sole princess was about to end.

"Noooooooo," I shrieked, as I ran upstairs to throw myself onto my bed.

Just as our house had grown up around the unit we had been, now that Mom and Craig were expanding their family, the house had to expand, too. Plans were made for an addition that would double the size of our living space and create a room for the baby. For months and months, as Mom's stomach grew with the baby inside of her, we were once again living in a construction site. But there was an upside; I would have my own room, with a door that closed, and I could paint it whatever color I wanted (pink, of course), and even install wall-to-wall carpeting, which Betty financed.

That summer, when I was ten, just before we found out whether Santa had chosen a boy or a girl, my dad took me on our second, and final, dad-daughter vacation. It had been several years since he'd taken me on a camping trip to Rangely Lake. We didn't go to Disneyland, or even Palace Playland, the white-trash amusement park an hour away. Instead, he took me to Orgonon, the home and laboratory of the late psychoanalyst Wilhelm Reich.

My father and Phyllis had broken up, and he was all mine again. I did not waver in my attention to him for an instant. It was as if I went into a kind of a trance during our hours together, where nothing could bother me, and there was nothing before or after the pocket of time we were spending together. He always marveled at our special relationship, and how it allowed him to say anything to me. And say everything to me he did. Of course, he had no experience with children and spent his time with cabdrivers, men from the track, rebirthers and new age types, and women he was sleeping with (or trying to sleep with).

He went on at length about his latest health craze, macrobiotics and rebirthing and isolation tanks. About astral projection and reincarnation, how he had been a city planner in Atlantis and a drunken Irishman in Dublin, who disappointed my mom and me with his drunken ways. About affirmations, which he was obsessed with and devoted much of his time to when he was parked in his cab in Boston. About his foster parents, who told him and the other two foster kids that only one of them would be adopted, so they all had to be extra good, but none of them were actually adopted, no matter how good they were. About how when he got into a car crash in a stolen car while AWOL from the navy, the car was worth less than a hundred dollars, which resulted in the lesser charge of "borrowing a car without the owner's permission." About living in a hearse in Haight-Ashbury, where he sold acid. And, always, how I was the only person who really listened to him.

"My next frontier is freedom," he said, talking fast as he caught the wave of his own words. "I read this guru book by this guy, Muktananda. He's just this little cool guy all of the guys I know are hanging out with. He's their guru. Well, their guru is Baba G, but Baba G never comes to America. You have to go to India and go way up on this mountain to see Baba G. But Muka travels around, and his thing is he has a peacock feather, and he touches people with it. He's this cool-looking guy, and he has the red dot on his forehead. There's a chapter in the book on recognition. I've been thinking about that when I'm in the process of recognizing things. And then, another chapter is realization. And when we have those, recognition and realization, we have freedom. That was something I never got until the other day, when I realized I was on the verge of being free. But you can't assume it. You've got to really see it. It's so great when you see it on the horizon, but you can't cheat to get there. You've got to do it yourself. You've got to realize, and then you'll be free. But the freedom I have is that I can see that for the first time, and even before, I think I was seeing something, too, but it was my ego that was seeing it. It wasn't the real thing, and the thing about the ego is it's always fooling you."

"Okay," I said, soaking up every word like a bedtime story.

His words carried us along for hours until we inched our way down a narrow, rutted driveway and arrived at a modern fieldstone house with blue trim around its many windows. It was desolate in the mideighties, even for rural Maine, and easy to imagine it would have been horror-movie remote in 1950 when Reich first settled there. It had a noble beauty, but also a still, haunted quality that made me sad and watchful.

Through a path in the woods we approached a metal contraption that looked like the guns from a tank pointed up into the sky.

"Reich's cloud buster," my dad said, leading me over to its base.

I was instantly transfixed. In school the previous year, I'd been inundated with the drought in Africa, "We Are the World," the sad sight of starving kids my own age. Here it was, deep in the wilderness of Maine, the solution to hunger: a machine that could make rain. I climbed up beneath it, as if to aim the metal tubes. The cloud buster would give us rain. John Lennon would come back. My father would be proven right.

Too awestruck to maintain my usual stream of questions, I followed my dad silently through the tour of Reich's house. Everything was wonderful to me. The fact that he purposely designed the fieldstone steps to be shallow and deep, so that when he was an old man they would be easy for him to navigate; the laboratory where he cut open mice, the violence of which made him seem to me like a very serious scientist; his orgone accumulators, makeshift wooden boxes that he said cured cancer, which were later popular with William Burroughs and William Steig and immortalized in song by the space-rock band Hawkwind.

The house seemed to float amid the mountains. Broad windows looked out onto pretty fields and dense forests, the inspired architecture giving the vista a gold star the very similar woods outside my own house did not merit. Reich was clearly an important man, and yet he chose to live a life much like mine. I knew influential events happened in New York City and Washington, D.C., so I couldn't quite make sense of all this, but seeing that place that afternoon legitimized my existence in Maine in a way. The great world I was so desperate to see and experience was closer than I had thought.

My dad and I were ushered into a small theater, alone. We were the only tourists there that day, a number that probably wasn't unusual. I didn't have to understand Reich's counterculture status to realize this was not like other historic homes I'd toured—Mount Vernon or Monticello, with their school groups and gift shops that sold old-fashioned candy that tasted like molasses and mothballs.

The lights dimmed. I sat next to my father, watching the documentary about Reich's life and exile to Orgonon with his young son, Peter. When he'd run afoul of the FDA, his books and accumulators were destroyed. He was sent to prison, where he died.

My dad leaned down to whisper in my ear, "Reich was poisoned in jail. The government does things like that, you know."

I shivered, the magic of our outing shadowed by something dark. That's what happened to dads who were different, who believed in things no one else did. I hadn't known about such things before. But now I did.

That July, when my mom went into labor, I was in the hospital room. Mom had done a great job of including me in her pregnancy. She was careful to explain what was happening, step-by-step, just as she had with the construction of our house. I think, at age ten, I was probably more distressed by watching Mom give birth than she was by actually delivering the baby. And yet, I was already old enough to understand in some fundamental way that all of these inclusions were how she was trying to make this big change okay for me.

She was one of those moms who was always interested in what I was saying or doing—in almost all of the photos from my early childhood, she is looking at me, as if her happiness depended on mine.

When I became obsessed with ballet, she not only found a way to afford lessons for me, but she and Craig also took me down to Boston to see Rudolf Nureyev dance in *Don Quixote* with the Boston Ballet. She could be counted on to drive me to the library when I'd read all of my books, to help me with Brownie badges, and to encourage my love of baking, even if she modified the recipes to include honey and carob instead of sugar and chocolate. I was important to her, and I knew it. But something was shifting.

Now that she had gotten us to this special sheltered place, she could relax enough to have another family, her "real" family. That's how it felt. They were a unit that fit together—they had the same last name, which I would not take, as if refusing meant I was indifferent to it. They were a part of something that did not entirely involve me, even though I was still Mom's daughter, and Andrew's big sister.

My little brother was a happy child, and exceptionally cute, with a halo of golden blond ringlets and big, blue eyes, the kind of baby strangers stopped to compliment and artists wanted to paint, the antithesis of everything dark about me—my dark eyes, dark hair, freckles, and the dark thing inside of me that had made my father go away, and that kept me yoked to him.

A letter my father sent to Mom that summer starts out: "I just wanted to write and let you know a little of what's going on with me lately, to explain a little of why I've been so out of touch." He went on to make excuses about how he had been giving her privacy around the birth of her new child, had been occupied by an acute back attack, and that his rent had been raised a hundred dollars, so he could not afford the $375 a month and would have to move.

The card he sent me, along with a Madonna tape I'd requested, simply asked: "How's your new brother or sister?"

That fall, Mom and Craig brought home Kate Bush's album *The Hounds of Love* and listened to it nonstop. I, in turn, fell under its spell. There was one particular song, "Cloudbusting," that riveted me: "I still dream of Orgonon. / I wake up crying."

Orgonon really did exist! Those wonderful, brief interludes with my father when he told me things that split open the rest of my childhood like an atom of energy exploded by Reich in his lab. I listened again and again, until I knew every word. I understood its longing for a time that would never come back, its declaration of love in the face of adversity. That was exactly what it had felt like to go to Orgonon with my dad, and to love him from a distance. But no matter how close the song made me feel to him and our time together, during the months I listened to it, he was gone away from me. And I had no idea when I would see him again.

When my father did materialize, just after Christmas of my sixth-grade year, he had a new woman with him. Her name was Eva, she was German, and she had short, dark hair. Having come to America to improve her English, she worked as an au pair in the Boston suburb of Weston, so she was much better with kids. I liked her much more than I did Phyllis.

At nearly eleven, I wasn't the emotionally feral young girl I'd been during Phyllis's reign, which helped me to accept Eva's presence during this rare visit with my dad. I was also just so glad to see him after several years apart, especially during a time I'd felt estranged from Mom and her new family. My dad understood me in a way no one else did—he lived the existence I craved, full of ideas and experiences—and I felt that even one day with him gave me sustenance for my regular life.

I had recently become interested in any clues I could find as to the ways of the grown-up world. The movie that best expressed how I felt, *Pretty in Pink*, reached the theater in our nearby town during the spring of my sixth-grade year. I hated my freckles, and I knew Mom's freckles had also persisted until she was a teenager, so I made a daily vigil to the mirror to see whether mine were lightening. They were not. And then I was gifted with this movie where the opening credits played over close-up shots of Molly Ringwald putting in earrings and applying lipstick, her freckles quite clearly visible, as she's revealed in all of her redheaded glory to be the kind of beautiful, cool girl who was desired by her male classmates. Maybe my freckles weren't so bad after all.

The movie was a revelation. Molly's character had a complex relationship with her father. She was a nerd—she studied diligently, aspired to go to college as a way out of a life she felt stunted by—and yet she knew about fashion and music and culture. She was my hero. I not only saw the movie at the theater on Friday night, dressed in my pink mock-letterman sweatshirt and fake pink pearls, I also went back to see it on Saturday night. I bought the soundtrack, which was my first exposure to so many amazing alternative bands—Echo & the Bunnymen, the Psychedelic Furs, the Smiths—and the whole new world of the urban underground.

If *Pretty in Pink* was how I envisioned my life—even though the characters were a good seven years older than me, drove cars, drank booze, and had sex off camera, the film depicting my aspirations, *About Last Night,* had come out the summer before. When Betty had suggested we go see a movie during her visit, I didn't mention its R rating.

Even Betty realized at some point that perhaps this movie was not intended for a ten-year-old, maybe during the hot sex scenes between Rob Lowe and Demi Moore, or the charged postcoital banter about whether or not an "I love you" spoken at climax counted as the real thing. She leaned over to me in the darkened theater.

"Did you know this movie was going to be like this?" she asked.

"No," I said, not shifting my eyes for fear of missing a single nuance.

I was still too young for the sex, really. I was there for everything else. I wanted to live in a big city where I did interesting work and had cool friends and lovers, and every day shone with the heightened sense of importance that life in small-town Maine lacked.

When Betty visited the summer I was eleven, she decided I was ready for my first manicure, at the beauty school where she went to get her hair and nails done because of their discounted prices. Craig had always cut my hair at home. This was a new and glamorous experience, even if there was really nothing fancy about the fluorescent-lit room with its linoleum tiles. Sitting nervously across from a redneck beauty school student with dramatically feathered hair, I watched as she gently tilted my filthy cast—I'd broken my wrist riding my bike on the first day of summer vacation—to dip my nails into the sudsy water, and so begin the process of grooming me into a lady.

My dad and Eva actually came to visit again that summer, during the same week the Big B and I were together in Portland. Betty took the four of us out to lunch at the most wonderful restaurant in the world—DiMillo's floating restaurant—located in an old boat moored to a dock in Portland's harbor. It floated! There was not a single leaf of kale in sight, except for under the sliced cantaloupe used as a garnish on the plate, and even I knew you didn't eat that (unless you were a glutton like Betty). I was allowed to order whatever I wanted, and I was going to eat fried clams and French fries.

Best of all, my dad was sitting across from me, looking subdued, his face bare of the big beard he'd sported throughout my childhood, his broad shoulders folded into his dress outfit—a newer plaid flannel shirt—his unruly, thinning hair mostly tamed. Next to him, Eva wore the bright, quizzical expression of a foreigner who needs to pay attention to follow the conversation. It was pretty much the perfect day.

Only my dad didn't go in for perfect days in the traditional sense. He reached into his backpack and pulled out plastic bags of prepacked food.

"We're on a macrobiotic diet," he said.

Eva nodded.

"What?" Betty asked sharply, either because she was old and couldn't hear, or because she was old and couldn't believe what she was hearing.

"It's a principle of eating," my father began, instantly launching into a lecture on the ideals of the macrobiotic lifestyle and why it was the best choice, not only for him and Eva but for Betty and me, and the people at the other tables, and even the waiters, and every single other person in the entire rest of the world. He always did his research and was a great talker, so his argument was convincing. Betty was as likely to become macrobiotic as she was to get a face tattoo. I was not having any of it, not today. I'd seen my share of brown rice in my regular life as a hippie kid. My vacations with Betty were all about eating all of the prohibited foods I could, and then eating more.

I was actually relieved by my dad's digression, though, and perked up as I fell into my familiar role as his best listener, ever. Up until that moment, he'd been shut down in his mother's presence. He was always so convinced she was about to publicly humiliate him or try to manipulate him into doing something he didn't want to do—as he felt she'd been doing since he'd gone to live with her out of foster care at age ten—that he'd been pulled up inside of himself almost completely as we sat there. For the long minutes he'd been silent and closed down, I'd anxiously observed him, as on edge as I was whenever I read a tense scene in a book, hating any conflict, even unspoken.

As Betty and I were served our fatty dead qi on a plate, my dad and Eva tucked into their seaweed-wrapped rice balls.

"What is that?" Betty asked, her tone sharp.

And then she lost interest, attacking her meal with the fervor of a once beautiful woman who had long trafficked in the favors of men, and had therefore been on a diet her entire life, and was now going to eat every French fry the universe put in her path.

My father gazed into the middle distance in his usual intense way— he raised spacing out to an art form—before turning to look at me.

"So, Sarah," he said. "We have to tell you something."

I smiled, still innocent enough to be unaware that when the adults "have to tell you something" they are never offering you a trip to Disneyland.

He looked at Eva. She smiled encouragingly. He smiled back at her. Looked at me. "We're going to have a baby," he said.

"Oh," I said, not able to fake happiness, not even for my father.

Here was another baby with two parents, another baby at the center of a family that did not include me. Each of these families contained a finite amount of space, of time, of money, of love, and there would never be enough left over for me. As far as I was concerned, I was the only person who could be relied upon for anything, and it was better if I accepted it up front. Soon after this, I began fantasizing about getting my own apartment, in Portland, or even better, Boston. In my dream life, I was at the center of a vibrant world of new experiences and people, dipping in and out of our interactions without ever needing anything concrete from them.

My sister, Asmara, was born in a birthing tub in the living room of my father's Somerville apartment the following January, just before my twelfth birthday, when my brother was eighteen months old, and his constant need for care seemed to dominate everything at home. My father sent me a card with the news and the explanation that her name meant "love" in Indonesian. I didn't hear much from him after that. Twelve years after my birth, he had not changed at all. It didn't take even a year for Eva to reach the same conclusion Mom had reached in two—that raising a baby with a man who was as much in need of mothering as any child was actually harder than raising a baby without him.

That fall, Eva took Asmara home to the Bavarian town of Garmisch-Partenkirchen, eighty minutes outside of Munich by train, where her own mother lived, and raised her there. My father did not share his reaction to any of this with me at the time. After Eva left, he simply disappeared once again. I still waited for him, but this time, I was also waiting to get out.

By the time I was thirteen, music had become my tether to the big, sparkly world beyond my hometown, which had begun, more than ever, to feel like my bell jar. I had just entered my freshman year of high school. The novelty of a new school and classmates had worn off a few hours into my first day. Bored by my classes, oppressed by the small-minded meanness of my classmates, I was miserable.

Home life also tested my patience. My favorite movie of that time was *Labyrinth,* starring a young Jennifer Connelly as a fifteen-year-old girl named Sarah, who felt her father and stepmother unjustly expected her to care for her baby brother. And so, she wished the goblin king, played by David Bowie, looking gorgeous in blond, bird-of-paradise hair, would take her brother away. One day, my brother drove me past the breaking point. Not by being bad, but by being cute, and being a toddler who needed patience from me. I had never been more of an impatient, impetuous perfectionist than I was at the age of thirteen. I drew on *Labyrinth* as the ideal alternative to our current life.

"If I had the choice between saving you and being David Bowie's goblin queen, I would choose David Bowie, and you would be a goblin forever," I snarled.

Andrew began to cry, more upset by my tone of voice than my words, which were essentially meaningless to a three-year-old.

"I don't know why you'd want to go with David Bowie," Mom said, picking my brother up and soothing him on her hip. "He'd just give you diseases."

That shut me up. Her tone wasn't mean, even though I had certainly warranted at least a minor comeuppance for being a brat to my brother. Clearly, I was in over my head in the adult world, no matter how much I tried to pretend otherwise.

On those nights when I was trapped at home, I felt ready to burst the seams of my skin. After dinner, I went up to my room, threw myself down on my bed, and stared through my skylight at the vast pearlescent dome of the twilight sky. A molten fury rose up. It wasn't anger so much as pure energy, the desire to run and never stop. I sang along to Sinead O'Connor, aching for such power: "I don't know no shame. / I feel no pain."

In the silence after the tape ended, I could hear the wind in the trees and the flat, dry voices of *The MacNeil/Lehrer Report* on the television downstairs. Ripping myself off my bed, I put on my Walkman and turned it up *loud*. I was hungry for anything angry, sexy, wild— the darker and more shredded with feedback and profanity, the better.

As I clomped down the stairs, I shouted in the general direction of Mom, who was playing with Andrew in the living room: "I'm going for a walk."

The music worked its magic, making me feel that much more alive: "If you got some big fucking secret / Then why don't you sing *me* something?"—"Little Angelfuck / I see you going down on a fireplug"—"One day something funny happened / But it scared the shit out of me . . ." The angry lyrics gave me an air of bravado I didn't naturally possess. Blasting the sound of the big wide world into my very being, I paced the quiet country road that ran past the land, walking down to the harbor and back, feeling like I could tear up the asphalt with my desire for everything ferocious and free.

I wanted life to be bigger, louder, deeper, more intense. Punk rock was all of these things, so listening to it leveled me out. It made me feel normal, which was a relief. Not that I wanted to be normal. I wanted to be extraordinary. But while I worked up the guts to try to do something, anything, even though I had no idea what that might be, it helped to hear others release their barbaric yawp; the music let me know the tumult within me was an echo of larger forces, of intelligent life in the universe; I was not alone.

Although I loved punk, the band that inspired my deepest ardor was the Cure. In 1989, they released their eighth album, *Disintegration,* which voiced every dark, romantic longing in my overly dramatic mind and heart. They were touring to promote the album that fall, billing their Massachusetts show as their last ever; their swan song. I had to go.

My father hadn't been up to visit since his last trip with Eva, and his few letters were largely filled with mentions of his new family or questions about mine. Better than the notes, though, were the cassettes he sometimes sent. As my primary access to the counterculture that existed beyond Maine, he was supplying me with the oxygen I needed to survive, as he'd always done.

My desire to see the Cure show trumped my usual discomfort at asking my dad for anything bigger than a cassette. I was still a little nervous about making any demand on him, but I wrote and requested that he drive a friend and me from Boston to the show, about twenty minutes outside of the city. He agreed right away.

It was as if all my waiting by the window had been rewarded. And now that I had the power to go places, if he would not come to me, I would go to him. All he had to do was stay put, and we would be the companions I had wanted us to be for so long. It never occurred to me to be cautious. I was so hungry for my father, and the validation I thought a big life would give me, that I was willing to risk everything in their pursuit. Because I valued time spent with my father—and now, time spent in the lustrous world at large—more highly than anything else, I almost didn't care whether these experiences were bad or good. Yes, good was better, but bad could be okay, too; at least it was something. I was already learning the kind of tricky thinking that would allow me to pursue whatever I wanted, relentlessly, without any concern for the consequences.

chapter four

DISINTEGRATION

Feeling oppressed by the daily routine of my high school life—rising in the bleary early dark, riding the bus to school, enduring the long, tedious hours of entrapment—I focused all of my attention on the gilded adventure glinting in my near future: the Cure concert. The day of the show, my friend Donyelle's parents dropped us off on the stretch of Mass Ave near Berklee College of Music, and we got sucked into the great maw of the city. A black man with long dreadlocks sold incense on the street. The dusky, fruited scent made my stomach dip with anxiety, reminding me I was in my father's city, and I was about to see him for the first time in more than three years. We wrestled our way along the crowded sidewalk to the corner of Newbury Street, where the epic two-story Tower Records held court.

As we rode the escalator up, up, up, as if toward heaven, I was soaring with anticipation, wide open to every new band name I needed to pretend I already knew while filing it away to be researched later. Every T-shirt could identify its wearer as a member of the special tribe

I was eager to act as if I'd already joined, even though I was learning everything on the fly, dizzy with the effort of trying to incorporate so much new information into who I was. I felt opened up in a way it wasn't normally safe to be in my hometown, able to admit how deeply I cared about music and art and the desire to express some of what was deep and raw and real in life, which was just beginning to kick me from within.

Even though I somehow never doubted my father would show up, I was anxious as we waited for him. This concert was important to me, yes, plus I was seeing my dad for the first time in years, which always made me excited in that fizzy, nerved-up way.

My dad pulled up in the white Toyota sedan Eva had gifted him when she left for Germany. It was instantly as it had always been: the smell of incense, the notebook of tightly filled pages of affirmations— none of which had happened, but which he still believed in, as he believed in the track, as I believed in him. He seemed smaller, and his eyes quickly shifted away from mine when I tried to study his face, but he looked the same, and we quickly settled into our old way of being together.

My dad didn't do small talk or ever temper his mood in the slight- est simply because he was in the presence of someone else, which he rarely was anyhow. The advantage to this was that we never wasted time circling each other uneasily, even when we hadn't been together in so long. He just opened the floodgates, and I rode the wave.

"I hope my back holds up at the show," my dad said.

"Yeah?"

"I haven't wanted to upset you, Sarah."

Without moving my head, I tried to see how much Donyelle was picking up from the backseat, and how she was reacting, in order to try to puzzle out what she thought of my dad, and by extension, what she thought of me. We had been friends a long time, since grade school, when I had taken ballet lessons from her mom, and she now shared my passion for finding a way out into the big, wide world beyond Maine.

She was thankfully oblivious to my concerns, a normal teenage girl who was simply happy to be on her way to a concert, her long, brown hair whipping in the wind.

"That's why I haven't been in touch much lately," my dad said. "But it's been real bad. Sometimes I can't sleep. When it's real, real bad, I can't sit down. I can't drive a cab or deliver packages. I can't work anymore. Sometimes all that helps is to walk. I walk for miles and miles around the city until I'm too tired to walk any more."

I watched him nervously, waiting for his hand to grip the flesh of his waist. I felt guilty that I needed a ride to a concert, which was probably going to cause him pain.

We made our way into one of the venue's acres of asphalt lots and parked. My dad planned to wait out by his car during the concert.

"Have fun," he said, not thinking to warn us to be on our guard, or to behave, as other parents might have done.

Everywhere around us were Goths so skinny or rotund they were like characters from a fairy tale, all draped in velvet capes and antique lace that looked as if it might evaporate in the cool night air. Oceans of skin so pale it was nearly translucent were scarred with lipsticked mouths as red as soft, seeping wounds.

I soaked it up, not just the sights and sounds, but also something on the molecular level: a collective exhale, a feeling of having stumbled into a safe haven where we could all be as bold or as dark or as scarred as we were, and it would gain us recognition, not ridicule. I didn't yet have the clothes to dress like them and was simply wearing a baggy black skirt and an army-green sweater, but I'd found my people: the Goths.

We made our way to the sloping lawn at the very back of the venue and waited. It felt as if all of the dials of my experience had been turned up to eleven, and my skin had been peeled off, and I was standing there totally exposed and more sensitive to input than ever before. It was sort of how I felt all the time, just amplified. But whereas in the real world of my droning school daze and quiet family time it was uncomfortable to be an emotional adrenaline junkie, such larger-than-life feeling was celebrated in this space.

The stadium was outside, and it was a drizzly night in late September, everything slightly damp with the threat of rain. Great gusting fog banks rolled in and out of the air around us, making the faded grass look like a moor out of one of the Brontë books. An epic wash of music rolled over us from all directions at once. Robert Smith slouched over his microphone wearily, his pure white high tops glinting amid a sea of black clothes, black hair, black emotions. The drums, bass, and guitars formed a wall of churning sonic sludge, synths like shards of sunlight, as the band opened their concert with "Plainsong," the first song on their new album.

Somewhere in the middle of the second or third song, my father appeared out of the mist, smiling shyly when he saw me amid the other teenagers. He'd found a cheap scalped ticket and decided to see what the Cure was all about. Too unused to him being my dad to react with normal teenage irritation, and having long mimicked his tastes and wanted to share his life, I was thrilled at the possibility of introducing him to a band and an experience he might now value. I basked in the feeling of being interesting to him. And then, as I adjusted to his presence, for once in my life I shook it off. This night was not about him. It was mine, all mine.

Eventually, Donyelle and I left my dad behind and pushed down to the edge of the lawn seats. I looked back over my shoulder, feeling guilty, until the fog swallowed him completely. Then I lost myself in the music, swaying my body freely in the anonymity of the damp darkness, singing along to every single word of every single song, enraptured. The band played forever, three encores in all, before disappearing into the wings in a haze of feedback. I quickly looked over at Donyelle, a little embarrassed at having let myself go so completely, now that I found myself back in my awkward teenage body. We trudged up the hill to where my dad waited.

"Did you like it?" Dad asked.

I nodded my head in the curt, conversation-deadening way of teenagers, reluctant to share the moment even with him. The crowd of elated fans pushed us along to the merch tables. I absolutely had to get a T-shirt, and I pulled us into line.

"Which one are you going to get?" I asked my friend.

"I don't have enough money left," she said.

My dad looked up from where he stood a little ways off, hands in pockets.

"How much are they?" he asked.

"Twenty dollars," she said.

My dad reached for his wallet. As he handed her a twenty-dollar bill, I was filled with gratitude that he was being so cool to my friend. I didn't even get jealous when he didn't pay for my shirt. I'd had a perfect night, and I thanked him as I hugged him good-bye.

That concert changed everything for me. All of my anxiety about being the kind of girl my dad would want to know, and now a desirable girl boys would want to be close to, had built up inside me for so long. Betty had been a model. Mom was beautiful by any standards, and especially well suited to the earth-mother ideal of the seventies. But I hated my freckles, hated how my skin broke out, hated being almost six feet tall, hated my curves, which I hid with baggy clothes. Here was my chance to say, "Fuck it, I don't want to be pretty anyhow."

I bought a black eyeliner pencil and a red lipstick at a drugstore near the hotel where we'd stayed with Donyelle's parents before they drove us back to Maine. When I went to school on Monday (in my Cure concert T-shirt, of course), I'd made my face into the mask that felt safe, even though it drew attention in a way I never would have been comfortable with before. Now I had been given something to aspire to and the permission to be honest: I was in pain. I wanted everyone to know.

From that moment, high school was truly unbearable. I never got beaten up, but the emotional assault from my closed-minded classmates was constant. As much as I'd sometimes found school boring,

I'd always loved to read and learn, but now every second outside of English class was intolerable. One afternoon, I rushed toward an open stall in the bathroom, having said I had cramps to escape gym class. A group of girls were gathered around the mirror, all skintight acid-washed jeans, feathered hair. They turned their hard, heartless eyes of predators on me.

"I don't know why she friggin' looks like that."

"I know, it's fuckin' disgustin'."

My fingers trembling, I slid the lock closed again and again until it latched.

"I heard she's a lesbian."

"I heard she worships Satan."

I stood paralyzed. Somehow, I was going to get out of this school, and when I did, I was never coming back. Finally, the bell rang, and I heard them slam the door. Still shaking slightly, I delayed my exit, grateful for the empty hallways.

As much as I wanted to be a grown-up, I wasn't all that into the specifics of being an adult woman. I didn't want to have my period, which came as infrequently as every three or four months. My skin broke out and my freckles did not go away. There was nothing to do in our little town but eat junk food after school, and I got chubby, which only made me curvier and more awkward. I wanted to live in a rarefied world of ideas—strident punk lyrics, the dark wit of Sylvia Plath, and the old-school romanticism of Charlotte Brontë and Miss Havisham in *Great Expectations*.

Although the Cure concert was pretty much the best thing that had ever happened to me, after the fact, I felt guilty for having left my dad alone to get closer to the stage and I worried he might think I didn't care about seeing him anymore. So I screwed up my courage and wrote him a letter apologizing for acting like a jerk.

My father answered in late October. He wasn't the least bit upset by my behavior: "And Sarah if you acted like a jerk I never noticed, if you acted like a teenager with her friends, you have my permission to act like a teenager for the next 7 or 8 years."

Best of all, my dad had picked up on my mention of another trip to Boston soon, and he actually offered to help make it happen: "This way I can teach you where it's safe + how to get round, + where everything is, of course it depends on parental approval all around + also I'd like to talk with Sue + Craig first." I was ecstatic, so much so that I chose to ignore the rest of the letter, which revealed that my father remained a master of making definite promises that left him all possible outs: "That would be sometime in 1990, or later, or whenever + depending on my still being around these parts."

Suddenly we were having something remarkably like a dad-daughter relationship. He wrote: "Oh yes the weekend would be an exchange, I want to learn how to read music or at least pick out chords in a song. You're still one of my favorite people in the world." I was hungry to be acknowledged and thought it was cool he wanted me to teach him something, even though I could barely read music after having briefly studied flute in elementary school. As an added bonus, he'd signed off, "Love Dad," which was rare for him.

His usual signature was "Love John." This may seem an inconsequential detail, but at age eight or eleven or thirteen, it was fairly devastating to receive a letter from "John," especially when I already had a "Craig," and what I really wanted was a "Dad."

I was high on that letter for weeks. Even though I'd reached an age when most kids had started calling bullshit on their parents, and my dad had certainly given me plenty to call him out on, I believed in him more than ever. The fact that he'd followed through with a ride to the concert, even if it had just been one promise kept in the face of the dozens of times he'd left me at the window, meant that everything had turned around the way I'd always expected. I bragged to my friends at school about how my dad lived in Boston, and I'd probably, you know, be going down to see him all of the time.

Of course, it wasn't going to be quite that easy. I got another letter a few weeks later. This one didn't mention a visit, and his tone made me nervous: "Hi Honey, I'm a little disappointed that you haven't sent me the $20 that I lent your friend. I don't blame you Sarah or even your friend, nobody asked me, I offered the loan + that's what I'm feeling bad about now, that I did, if I gave money to anyone, it would be you. So I hope we can clear this up, at least write + let me know what's going on. I got an idea of something we can do together. But first things first. Love, John"

Mom had sheltered me from my dad's money woes, never letting on he'd given her less than five hundred dollars of child support by the time I was eight, at which point she'd given up. Now I was part of his financial problems. I never would have asked my mom for a loan to repay my dad, and I was too conflict-avoidant to press the issue with my friend, so I just waited and hoped the situation would resolve itself. But I was convinced this was it—this time I'd accidentally done something that would drive my dad away forever—especially when I didn't hear from him again that fall.

I began petitioning Mom to let me go away to boarding school, as a number of my friends, including Donyelle, had done or would do the next year. I had no illusion that I was a prep school girl. But I truly did not believe I would survive three more years in my local high school. I think Mom was beginning to realize that my misery wasn't just going to lift one day, nor were the administrators at Lincoln Academy going to do anything on my behalf. Still, she was careful to temper my expectations. The schools were expensive and exclusive. Even though I was still a perfectionist, and I consumed books as if they were potato chips, I hadn't exactly been inspired to the heights of academic excellence.

My dad resumed contact with me just before my birthday in January. He apologized for having been out of touch, explaining that he'd been preoccupied with trying to get money from the insurance company for a car accident he'd had in April of 1989. His letter included mention of some tapes by the Cure and the Virgin Prunes I'd asked for, which he'd tried to find for me. And plans for a weekend visit soon.

"I want to talk to you, about your life, why you're attracted to punk. What's their philosophy?" And about a woman he knew in Boston whom he'd told me to get in touch with about my hopes to escape to private school. "She said you never got in touch with her, she could be a big help, she knows so much more about getting into schools than you do." Although he'd never taken more than a passing interest in anything having to do with my upbringing or education—preferring, generally, to keep our contact on the astral plane—now that he'd gotten involved, he had strong feelings on the matter.

He had a way of beating me to anything bordering on a negative assessment of the situation and apologizing. So it was hard for me to be upset, even if his contrition never came with any attempts to change his behavior. "I love you very much I know it might not seem that way by the little amount of time I spend with you. Love John."

In many ways, his was the perfect, logical approach. He acknowledged his shortcomings and made sure I knew he loved me in spite of them. But I was a fourteen-year-old girl, and there was nothing measured about my approach to anything. I wanted proof of his love. He missed my birthday, and his belated card began with another apology: "Hi Honey, Happy Birthday, I'm sorry this is late, + my plans haven't worked out about coming up there yet." He explained his back had relapsed, and "Everything depends on me getting something from the insurance co, which I'm not certain of, so I'm really not certain of anything right now. As I find out, I'll let you know."

My father's money trouble suddenly, really, became my problem, too, as he became completely consumed by his insurance settlement, which filled his letters and impacted his plans. He did surprise me by visiting that spring, a trip that was so impromptu he hadn't made a motel reservation and ended up staying at our house like he had when I was little.

My dad and I had not had any one-on-one time together in five years, since before he'd started dating Eva and had my sister, whom he barely mentioned. I did not ask about Asmara; I was still competitive about how much time he spent with her. I found it deeply reassuring that he'd only been to Germany once since Eva had taken her there. Never mind that he hadn't made the three-and-a-half-hour drive to Maine even that often.

I was overjoyed at his presence, but quickly disappointed when the trip didn't have the magical ascendancy of our childhood adventures. He did take me to a record store where he lent me money to buy one of the coveted tapes from the list I constantly updated, prioritizing carefully because I had so little money to spend.

My dad and I had more to talk about than ever before, now that I shared his passion for film, books, and music. But on this visit, my dad wasn't as capable of getting lost in his tangential musings on culture and the cosmic side of life. He was preoccupied with his insurance settlement. On his last day with me, when I was hoping for a final, more special adventure, he took a nap. Although I didn't dare show any displeasure, of course, he addressed the matter in his next letter: "I'm sorry we didn't spend much time together Sunday, my nap set me up good for the ride home, in fact I had this spiritual experience riding back, it was very nice." But then, after expressing gratitude to Mom and Craig, he resumed his by-now-familiar complaint. "I'll have to see how things go. And that brings up something I've wanted to talk to you about, money. I bought that tape for you + you said you were going to give me the difference when you got home + we both forgot, then on the way home I figured Sue + Craig saved me the price of a motel room, so let's call it even, but I just don't like you forgetting, it's a sore point with me right now because I don't have much $. I'd like to be able to give you some or buy things for you like your friend's parents but I can't. And that brings me to the $20.00—I'm a little disappointed, not in you but your friend. If I thought I wasn't getting it back, I never would have lent it to her. You can understand right Sarah? If I give money away, I much rather give it to you, so that $20.00 is yours if you ever get it. Maybe that will make it easier to collect. I love you. You don't have to write to me, or answer this card, don't feel obligated to do so. But if you need someone to write or talk to, please do. John"

I wrote back, ignoring his tone about money, and feeling like I'd been rewarded for the persistence of my devotion. Now that he and I were corresponding directly with each other, our relationship enjoyed a renaissance. I think the safety and distance of the written word allowed us to overcome the fact that we were incredibly close on one level, but in the reality of our daily lives and experiences, we were essentially strangers.

As a teenager, I could also be intimate with my dad in a way I hadn't been able to as a child. I knew from Mom that when they were together, my dad had been obsessed with the Beat writers and insisted they drive the winding back roads of New England in search of first editions and obscure, hard-to-find works by William Burroughs, Allen Ginsberg, and my dad's absolute favorite, Jack Kerouac. When my dad unearthed one of these books, it was a momentary victory for both of them, especially in such isolated rural towns where it felt like the cultural revolution had never happened. Once my father devoured the book, he released it back into the universe. He did not believe it was his to possess. This was frustrating for Mom, given the time and effort that had gone into acquiring the books for him. Not to mention the money.

Because Kerouac was my dad's favorite, I started there, with *On the Road*. He later sent me copies of other Kerouac books, including a second-edition paperback of *The Subterraneans* that remains one of my prized possessions. I made a big show of loving *On the Road*, because it was counterculture and cool, and I felt a bit in the know, not only for having read it, but for being able to say I had been turned onto it by my father, who had hitchhiked the country like its heroes. My dad's irresponsibility was something like social currency, and I cashed in, overjoyed that others might see him with even a fraction of the admiration I had lavished on him. He was a cool guy. He was remarkable. And so maybe I was, too.

I also recommended books to my father that I had read and become enamored of—including *The Mists of Avalon*—to which he responded with a list of the books he was reading along with brief descriptions: "*Fury on Earth*, a Wilhelm Reich biography, remember the place we visited at Rangeley? *Biogenetics*—the guy who wrote this (Lowen) was in therapy with Reich in the 40s. *Primal Scream + Primal Revolution, Rebirthing in the New Age, Rebirthing (The Science of Enjoying All of Your Life)*, these two are about breathing a certain way + it's more of self-therapy, *Occult Conspiracy*. I'm also having some good meditations. Well just to let you know what I'm into right now. If your interested in any of it, we can talk about it when we see each other. And feel free to write anytime. I'm glad your so busy, well I'm glad if your glad. Love Dad"

Outside of the landscape of ideas, our relationship limped along much as it always had: with apologies, and explanations: "Bare with me. I'm also generating income very slowly because of my back."

Meanwhile, every day at Lincoln was like being stretched on the rack. Thankfully, my horizons broadened through older friends, and the drama club, with which I traveled to festivals at other high schools, where I met like-minded students. We drew sustenance from one another to weather the animosity and violence we faced from the majority of our classmates. I started visiting a couple I met at one of these drama outings, Rob and Hanna, who lived an hour away. I'd been drawn to them at first sight, Rob with his dyed black mop, nose ring, and tattoos, and Hanna with her short, spiky hair and bright red lipstick, and had made sure we became friends. I was fourteen when he gave us acid, which I was eager to try as yet another experience, and a way to understand my father better. I had no anxiety as we sat in Hanna's parents' kitchen one weekend when they were away, loving the opportunity to be a part of something bigger than myself, and the ritual, as Rob ceremoniously sliced oranges for us, instructing us on how to rest the tab of acid beneath our tongues and then eat the fruit, the vitamin C from which would supposedly spike our high. The trip itself was lovely, including a hallucination that Hanna's home was a dollhouse, the roof lifted off by a gentle giant. We were in no danger, cozy as we were together, nestled in the safe nest of the universe.

In that one night, I felt as if I'd taken a huge step toward the big life I craved, and I made an active choice to continue pursuing anything that might expand my mind—new people, experiences, drugs, and music. Anything unknown was good, and the illicit was exciting. So much of my time at home seemed like a game of chicken, with me pushing for freedom and Mom and Craig wondering when to push back.

I became remarkably brazen. I smoked cigarettes out the window of my bedroom at night, blowing the smoke through the screen. I came home from hanging out with friends who were old enough to drive, stoned out of my mind, and made the most amazing toasted peanut-butter-and-jelly bagels, which I devoured with tall glasses of milk. In search of an absence from worry and pain, I would take whatever substance I was given and do as much of it as there was to do. Music was like a drug to me, too; it soothed my feelings and evened them out—play it loud enough, and sometimes my thoughts were suppressed. Booze. Cigarettes. Pot. I was still worried about making a good impression, making people happy, and so I didn't get fucked up at school, or do anything that would get me in serious trouble. But now that I knew how to vacate my body, I mimicked it, even when I was sober. I disappeared up inside of myself, where it didn't exactly feel safe, but it wasn't as scary as everywhere else.

Halfway through my freshman year, I sat on the new stairs in the addition to the house and eavesdropped on Mom and Craig in the living room, talking about whether or not I needed therapy. Surprisingly, Craig thought it would be good for me. This gave me pause because I had a new grudging respect for him, helped by an interaction we'd had the summer before I entered eighth grade. A friend and I had started our own business, a bakery, and worked long hours five days a week all summer. In the end, we'd generated a combined profit of three hun-

dred dollars, which her stepmother accepted in payment for the money
we owed for our startup costs. I'd been hoping to buy a Walkman, but
I hadn't earned a cent from the project.

I was sitting at the table one evening at the end of summer when
Craig got home from work. As he walked into the kitchen to put down
his lunch cooler by the sink, he paused near me.

"I think you earned this," he said.

He handed me the Walkman I had been coveting. In fact, it might
have been a little nicer than the Walkman I'd wanted. I sat up from my
perpetual slouch.

"Thanks," I said to his back as he walked into the kitchen.

I was profoundly moved, and not just by the gift itself. He was
paying attention.

In the discussion downstairs, Mom was in favor of me figuring out
whatever was troubling me on my own. In part because I was generally against any interference from Craig—even though I was softening
toward him—I sided with her. More than that, I didn't want therapy. I
wanted to suffer. I wanted the hurt I felt to be visible. Hence the black
clothes, the black eyeliner, the perpetual sulk. It didn't help that my
brother, now almost four, was everything I'd never been or had—a
nice, mellow kid enjoying a stable two-parent childhood—and with
such a big age gap between us, it was almost like we lived two separate
lives. I had no ability to see I might be something of a dark cloud over
his childhood, enjoying as I did the myopia of intense teenage experience.

As my freshman year drew to a close, we began to hear back from
the private schools to which I'd applied. Once again, my happiness
was directly dependent on what came in the day's mail. I got rejected
from all of the schools but Hebron, a small institution in Maine. Even
though it was no elite prep school, it was still expensive.

The wild card was Betty. She had not been up to visit since our
lunch with my dad and Eva, but she sent me weekly letters and continued to be extremely generous with money for clothes and school

expenses. She had long talked about an IRA she'd opened in my name at a bank in Portland, with the idea that the money—around four thousand dollars—would be mine for college. Now I had to talk her into letting me use it for private high school. But the IRA would not mature by fall, and she wouldn't pay the penalty for cashing it in early.

I was convinced there was a factor I had yet to think of, and while daunted, I was still determined, which I expressed to my dad in a postcard in June: "My whole plan for school next year is still up in the air. A new factor limited my options in a major way, but I'll tell you all about that later." In a bright, newsy tone, I informed him I'd gotten an A+ on my Jack Kerouac paper, adding, "Out of the four books I read, I think my favorite was *Dr. Sax*." Mentioning the Gothic-looking female on the postcard: "You always send me really neat cards and when I saw this I thought of you, so I decided to send it. I got your last letter a while ago. It's nice that we've been more in touch this year."

He wrote back a little less than two weeks later, a three-page letter that smelled of his incense and essential oils. It was exactly the kind of glimpse into his daily life and inner workings I had longed for: "My workbook's like a journal I guess that I record my dreams in, do affirmations daily (right now I'm doing a thing called the forgiveness diet that lasts 7 weeks, 70 affirmations a day, x 7 days x 7 weeks . . .) and any other thoughts I feel important enough to write down, or I feel unlazy enough to put in my workbook, I also carry a small notebook around on my travels in case anything important comes up. Long sentence, huh? I really don't know how to write a letter (proper form) as my formal education only went to the 9th grade + I never paid too much attention, my regret now." His response to the news of my postcard included this: "I can safely say I probably could of gotten a good mark on a paper on Kerouac because at one time I loved his writing so . . . It's just that lately, I'm seeing tv, movies, videos, as images that hypnotize people into buying figuratively/and literally ideas + consumer goods of a very limited scope. It just supports my theory of how tough the 90s are going to be unfortunately."

He went on to say he was better, as was his back, in part because he'd given up driving a cab, which meant he was "pretty low on money + must do something pretty soon." He was still hoping for an insurance settlement. If he didn't get one, he was preparing to sue. His plan, once he got the money, was to visit me in Maine, Eva and Asmara in Germany, Betty in New York City, and maybe his "friend" Sarah in Washington before moving to LA for a year of primal therapy. "I've realized from reading a book called *Imprints—the Lifelong Effects of the Birth Experience* by Arthur Janov—author of *Primal Scream*, that I've had lifelong problems that I've never dealt with successfully with all the things I've done, and that Primal sounds like it gets to the bottom/ beginning of things . . . I'm afraid about making such a major change but really feel I don't have much choice esp. if I want to be happy . . . Give my love to everyone. Take care of yourself. And let me know what's up with you when you feel like it."

I didn't really know what primal therapy was, but I liked the idea of going out to LA for a year in pursuit of a specific project, at the end of which it might be possible to be fulfilled. On the other hand, I was incredibly jealous that he had such complete freedom of movement, and that he would use it to go so far away from me.

Mom had to tell me there was no way we could afford Hebron, which meant at least one more year in hell. I was powerless, miserable. My dad wasn't helping. As it turned out, the insurance company had refused to settle, which meant a court case, and he had to start strengthening his back in order to try to get back to work in the meantime. His book of the moment was the *Meditation Practice Manual* by Yogi Shanti Desai, which perhaps influenced his advice: "I'm sorry again about your not going to Hebron. I can understand your disappointment, I only wish Betty did. You said your trying to be happy about going to Lincoln, you can't try to be happy, you either are or your not." Not useful to my fourteen-year-old self.

✦

Every time I felt that we'd made real progress toward getting close, he set me straight soon enough. After our flurry of letters that spring, he didn't call me for the rest of the summer and didn't write again until late August, when he apologized for not having called because he couldn't afford the long distance. It was difficult to be mad at him. In response to my suggestion that he go work at a bookstore, he said it would be too hard on his back, but maybe if he ever got a lot of money he could open a bookstore and I could run it, an idea I of course loved, as I did the fact that he took everything I said so seriously, something that's hard to find as a teenager.

Going into my sophomore year that fall, my prospects were grim. My dad sent me a postcard in late September, acknowledging the obvious: "How's Lincoln? Or should I ask?" And reporting that he'd had a relapse with his back but was recovering more quickly than usual. "I had been doing a lot of walking (everyday) + stretching before it happened + am getting back to that quickly so I'm optomestic—but still a bad speller." And ending with a surprise: "I love you." And the less personal closing: "John."

Even though I got out quite a bit for a fourteen-year-old kid living in rural Maine, it still wasn't enough, never enough. And so I sought ways to make the world come to me. My drama club friend, Rob, had gotten me into the fanzine *Maximum Rocknroll*. I studied it more closely than my schoolbooks, coveting the records that could be ordered from labels like Dischord, watching the mailbox for weeks as diligently as I'd waited for cards from my dad or acceptance letters from prep schools. It was like sending out a message in a bottle and having one come back; the records were able to find me, even as far off the grid as I felt.

My friend told me that if I put an ad in *MRR* looking for pen pals, I would get deluged with replies. So I took the plunge, placing a small ad that simply said I was a female seeking like-minded friends and mentioning my favorite bands: Jane's Addiction, Fugazi, the Cure. I began receiving letters—from California, from Ireland, from prison, and one from Connecticut that stood out among the rest. Oliver wasn't what I'd been looking for at all—he didn't live in an anarchist squat, or give homemade tattoos, or play in a punk band. But. As much as I adored and hungered for the company of wild punks and bohemians, the truth was I didn't do any of those things, either. Basically I just wanted to live in the city and read books and have cool friends.

Oliver was like an ambassador from the world I hoped to enter, and soon. He was twenty-one and in college. He liked music. He was clever and amusing and just dark enough. By his second letter, he was offering up serious musings about life, slightly crass but affectionate flirtations, and casual drug references, which I found highly enticing.

I wrote Oliver back right away, adding him to my diligent correspondence with a half dozen pen pals around the world. It was a necessary distraction, since I hated high school as much as ever. I had not heard from my dad since September, which meant it was difficult to even fantasize about going down to Boston for a visit. Having just enjoyed our bustle of correspondence the past school year, I felt his absence even more.

Even amid the mail's wondrous bounty every week—the tape of my Irish pen pal, Petey, reading me a bedtime story in his lovely brogue, the Canadian zine containing one of my poems—I began looking out for the simple lines of a white business envelope with the address scrawled in all caps. It was like Oliver didn't have to try so hard. And he opened a window into a life that seemed quite a bit like one of the possible paths down which I might go—he didn't really study anything in particular, which I got, since I didn't know what I wanted to be when I grew up. But he did study. And he read books. And listened to music. And he wrote passionately and intelligently on these subjects. He had friends from school, and roommates he lived with in a big house off campus. They drank beers and talked late into the night. Sometimes he went to parties. It all sounded fun to me, like everything I wanted to get out and do, but even more than that, it sounded manageable. I was incredibly relieved to think I could hang in Oliver's world, my future world.

Around the holidays, things started to feel lighter. I was optimistic about my private school prospects—there was a school in Pennsylvania that had expressed interest in my application. Now, faced with the possibility of having my dreams come true and actually leaving Mom and the particular way we did things on the land, I was freaking out a little bit. But every day that I was forced to drag myself onto the school bus and endure the mundane torture of high school only reinforced my certainty I couldn't stay. And so, I dared myself toward the one thing that terrified me most, reassuring myself that I'd figure it out once I got there.

I was still corresponding a few times a week, almost constantly, with Oliver. A few months in, our letters became affectionate. He told me I seemed mature for my age (complete teenage-girl bait) and wished he could say good night in person. He called me in mid-January. I liked his runaway cackle, which made me feel like a genius when I set it off. I liked that he knew about cool bands like Operation Ivy and had been to way more shows than I had. I liked that he was opinionated and strong-willed and not afraid to disagree with me.

A week before my fifteenth birthday, he sent me a note wishing me a "Bappy Pirthday," and saying he enjoyed talking to me very much. It was rendered in a pig-Latin-type language; deciphering it only added to the intrigue. He also mentioned that he'd pled guilty to possession with intent to deliver psilocybin, stemming from an incident in which he'd received hallucinogenic mushrooms in the mail. I took this in stride, the daughter of the father who often referenced his 120 acid trips.

Amazingly, I got into the private school of my choice in Pennsylvania. Mom spent several weeks looking through the papers. I was in an agony of anticipation, my whole life hanging in the balance. My dad had still mostly disappeared from the picture, but I sent him a note with an update. I received a newsy postcard from him in mid-February. "Pleasantly surprised to get your card. Glad to hear about George School + that you're happy. And thanks for the warning that they might contact me. Did you get the CD's I was concerned I didn't pack them well enough. Let me know please. Love, Dad."

Another card from him on March 1 began, "Just wondered if you got my card, figured this would be a good way to find out." I had not answered his card in the ensuing two weeks. He wanted an answer immediately and had included a postcard with a box for "yes" and a box for "no," so I could check one and send it back to him. I took the rest of the card's content at face value. "I am doing well, I started physical therapy 3x a week for 3 weeks today. I have been doing psycho-therapy twice a week for a couple months. I feel better. How are you? And school doing? Have you decided where your going yet? My court case is finally coming up this month, 4 years since the fact. I have my fingers crossed. Hope to see you soon. Love to Sue + the family. John."

I checked the box for "yes" and sent the card back, happy he was suddenly keen to be in touch with me. I eagerly awaited his next letter. And waited, and waited.

Meanwhile, my relationship with Oliver grew more intense. As his letters inched toward romance, they also included musings on whether other people wished they could start over, and how he hoped I never felt as crumbly as he did. Even when he confessed to having made a "lame-ass" suicide attempt, it only drew me toward him. I often felt pretty crumbly myself, and I valued that he trusted me enough to confide in me. This was exactly the kind of *big* emotion I reveled in—the kind of help I would have offered my father if I'd been old enough to understand his struggles—not the trite bullshit of high school. It felt as if I were experiencing the grown-up life I was so hungry for, like Oliver's interest in me was a sign that I did have value, even if most of my classmates couldn't see it. Plus, Oliver could still be silly and tender and obliquely flirtatious in a way I liked and could just barely handle, saying it was too bad I lived so far away—or he'd probably ask me out, although I might hate him if I met him or not like the way he looked—and encouraging me to find something, anything, of value. Walking the halls with his voice in my head, I was linked by his stories to this bigger, smarter, more grown-up reality. Once there, no one would call me a dyke, or stab me with hateful looks, or distrust me because I read books for fun or liked music that sounded like noise to them. Once there, I would be the perfect, fantasy version of myself. Maybe I would even be happy. At least I'd be living.

chapter five

THE BREAK

Mom had no choice but to tell me that we couldn't afford the private school's tuition. I ran upstairs, slammed the door, threw myself down on my bed, and sobbed. I was exhausted and heartbroken after two years of applications and soaring hopes and dashed dreams and dragging myself through long days at a place that hated me as much as I hated it.

A smattering of college brochures had trickled in, but I hadn't paid attention, as I was so fixated on my prep school dreams. Mom happened to see one that looked promising: a brochure for an early college in the Berkshires called Simon's Rock. I read it. If I got accepted, I would be allowed to *drop out of high school* after my sophomore year and begin taking college courses the next fall. Mom told me that she'd always planned to help me attend college, and while we couldn't afford private high school with its more limited financial aid, if I got accepted to Simon's Rock with a scholarship, she would find a way for me to go. I had never wanted anything so much in my entire life, and I don't think I will ever want anything that much again.

Even the application was magical. They asked us to write an essay on Plato's "Allegory of the Cave." Plato! Here was something extraordinary. I sent off my paperwork and waited for Simon's Rock to set me free and let my real life begin.

It wasn't long before I got a letter inviting me to an interview and introductory day at the school. Mom agreed to drive me down. I was ecstatic, and she was excited on my behalf. Finally, here was a perfect solution. Not only would it free me from the confines of Lincoln, it would challenge me intellectually, which Mom was determined to see happen if she could.

On the appointed day, we drove down to the campus in Western Massachusetts, almost into New York state. We turned down Alford Road, drove a few miles, crested a hill, and descended into a slight valley. On the left was a big red barn, which was the school's art center. On the right a little gravel road with a small, tasteful sign that read SIMON'S ROCK COLLEGE OF BARD. As we drove onto campus, we passed a guard shack on the left and came upon a cluster of low buildings with clean modern lines and breezeways. I was nervous, worried about making the right impression, not just with the administrators, whom I wanted to think I was intelligent, but also with the other students, whom I wanted to think I was cool.

As I stepped out of the car, I saw a thin, pale boy with bright green dreadlocks. Both of us were too shy to smile, but we exchanged the kind of small nod that acknowledged our kinship. There wasn't a redneck or a jock or a bully in sight. I loved it all. At the end of the day, Mom and I were both high on the place, its pretty peacefulness, its broad-minded community and high-minded academic ideals. But first I had to get in.

If I had checked the mail with reverence before, now it was the only moment in my day that actually mattered. As soon as I walked in the door from school, I threw down my book bag and raced to the dining room table.

"How was your day?" Mom said from the kitchen.

"Fine," I said, sorting through the mail. Nothing.

If no one was home, I ran the grassy path to the mailbox, picturing the letter with the school's seal waiting for me in the wooden mailbox. Nothing.

One day when I walked in, Mom watched me carefully from behind the counter.

"What?" I said.

"You got a letter from Simon's Rock," she said.

"Really?" I said. "What did it say?"

"I didn't open it," she said. "It's addressed to you."

I held the envelope in my hand, my finger under the flap, and paused. She cradled the tomato she was slicing and smiled at me. I opened the envelope, took out the paper, and read:

"Dear Sarah, we are pleased to offer you . . ."

I looked at Mom, stunned, overjoyed, terrified, everything all at once.

"I got in," I said.

"You did?" she said. "That's great, Sarah. Congratulations."

I could hear everything in her voice that I, too, felt—the relief at having survived these two awful years, the joy at this wonderful place we had found that seemed just perfect for me, and the uncertainty at exactly what that would mean.

My dad had continued to be silent that spring, but he sent me a letter in early June that opened: "I had a dream about you last nite + when I woke up it was as if I had been with you. It was nice. It made me wonder how you were doing? Did you receive my books? What if anything you think of them? Enclosed is a card to let me know. I always wanted to get a James Dean card in the mail." For the first time in a year, he talked about coming to visit, in his usual specific but elusive way: "I have a round trip to Brunswick ticket good until June 19th, I've been waiting til I accumulate some money but that might not happen, I'm going to see if they'll extend the time on it . . . Whot da ya think?" He also mentioned that Morrissey was playing at Great Woods that summer. "Does that still hold any interest for you? Let me know. Love, John. Hello to everybody."

I dutifully sent off the James Dean postcard the next week, my text written in the neurotically neat all caps I had adopted after briefly mimicking my dad's script, written in a spiral, to be arty. I didn't mention Simon's Rock, but told him school was out June 13 and, yes, I was going to see Morrissey. "I'll call if I'm around in Boston. Maybe we could see each other."

That June, Oliver's letters yo-yoed between affectionate declarations of how much he liked me and increasing blackness—but always accompanied by intelligence and humor. His letters were missives from somewhere important. And he continued to talk to me in an adult way I craved about love and sex, mentioning his own experiences, and wondering if I had experienced either, and if I could understand how much they changed things. I hadn't and couldn't, but I wanted to know.

I never questioned why a twenty-two-year-old man would want to take time out of the fabulous, busy experience I so aspired to in order to talk to a fifteen-year-old girl. But the scenario was perfect for my dramatic, dreamy sensibilities. Since we were separated by age and distance, I didn't have to worry about the details of fooling around or losing my virginity. It was much easier to be thrilled when he confessed secrets about his troubled romantic life, which he'd never told anyone else, or joked about us moving to the woods and living there, and how I'd hire him as my maid—or marry him—when I was rich.

I received a letter in which he declared his love with all of his usual silliness and charm. I was ecstatic, swept up in what felt like my first love. Almost every day that week he sent me a letter, some hinting that he might have violent tendencies—or at least fantasies—because of inadequacies he felt, but mostly lovely insinuations of the feelings we didn't dare speak. We talked on the phone for hours, me going on excitedly about my plans for school that fall. He was no longer taking classes and had yet to earn his degree, but I still thought of him as a college student and was excited to join his world. Even though I was only fifteen, I had leapt ahead and was going to meet him where he was.

I was happier than I'd been in years, maybe ever. And then, I began to hear less from Oliver that July. It was a familiar feeling, as if the tide of his attention and affection was suddenly going out without any warning or explanation. I could only assume what I always did with my dad: if there was no specific reason, the fault must be mine.

At least I had Simon's Rock. I'd gotten a summer job at the one restaurant in our village, Anchor Inn, which opened for the season on Memorial Day and was packed with tourists through Columbus Day. I was obsessed with earning enough money to ensure nothing would prevent me from going to Simon's Rock and worked as many shifts as I could. As my mom had explained to me from the start, while boarding school was not financially viable for high school, they were committed to helping me attend college. As long as I took on the maximum loans, and a work-study job, and Mom took on a loan, too, it was going to be possible. Even as entitled and emotionally farsighted as I could be at fifteen, I knew enough to be extremely grateful.

As I counted down my final shifts at the Anchor Inn in late August and began packing up my belongings in preparation for my attendance at Simon's Rock's "Writing and Thinking Workshop" for all incoming freshmen, I received a two-line letter from Oliver: He was a lost cause. I should forget about him.

I shook. I cried. I sent him impassioned pleas, telling him that he was no loser, that he was special, that I loved him, and so there was hope; there was hope as long as we had each other. He didn't write back. That was it. He was gone. I was devastated. The problem must be me, just like I'd always known it to be.

Suddenly, after I had waited and waited for what felt like forever, the summer was over, and it was time for me to leave home. I dyed my hair purple, determined to make an impression from the first moment I arrived. I woke up at six in the morning on the day of my departure, covered my freckles as best as I could, carefully painted on my black eye makeup, and loaded the last of my possessions into Mom and Craig's Toyota Tercel hatchback. Mom had to work that day, and while Andrew was a cheerful, obedient kid who never caused trouble, he was only six and couldn't be left home alone, which meant Craig was driving me the six and a half hours down to school.

I stood in the living room as Craig took the last of my bags out to the car, giving Mom and me a final moment of farewell. I looked at Mom. My eyes filled up.

"Let me get a picture," she said.

She'd always taken a picture of me on the first day of school, and here it was, the last time she would ever do so. My eyes brimmed over. I managed a cloudy smile, my arms crossed over my chest. I hugged Mom good-bye, feeling the grief of rootlessness, as if I no longer had a home, wanting to run back up to my childhood room and never leave. But I knew I had to go, and that I was incredibly lucky Mom was letting me do so under such extraordinary circumstances at such a young age. It was as if she'd seen how stuck I was and, instead of forcing me to stay small out of fear, or showing the kind of love that diminishes a person just to keep her close, she'd handed me the reins to my life along with a challenge: if I thought I was so smart, which she fully believed I was, then I should prove it, read some books, wrestle over their meaning with people who were smarter than I was, put something of real value on the line in my life.

"I love you," she said.

"I love you, too," I choked out through my tears.

We had been in something profound together, from the moment I had been conceived, all of those brave choices she had made in order to get herself free and get us to the land. Even though I had felt betrayed when she had her second family, and part of that urged me out on my own, I also felt that we were still in it together and always would be. As her oldest child, her only girl, who had the exact replicas of her hands and feet, the same pale freckled skin, the cleft of the Tomlinson chin, and the name Tomlinson, too, I was about to take all of that and go out into the world to make my fortune, but we would always be joined together.

Simon's Rock was as good as I had expected it to be, even better. I had gotten everything I'd wanted. I was still sometimes sad for no reason and deeply insecure, but I thrilled at my new life, and for once, I had the good sense to value it in the moment.

I'd landed on the smoking hall, even though I had checked the box that I didn't smoke on the housing form, for fear Mom would see. I lit a cigarette on day one and didn't put it out—simply hiding it during holidays at home—for the next fifteen years.

I fell for the most glamorous boy I'd ever seen. Nok was half-Thai, a product of the melting pot of New York City. He was handsome and worldly, even though he was only one month older than I was, which put us at the far end of the spectrum of the youngest kids in our class. I was far too shy to approach him directly, but I made plenty of eyes at him from across the dining hall. And the next day, I was happy to discover we were in the same writing and thinking workshop, a week-long intensive program designed to get us accustomed to the school's educational principles. It was based on a great books curriculum, so we read everything, starting with Sophocles and Plato. We were expected to discuss the ideas behind the work and make connections to other writers and thinkers and our own ideas and lives, both in the class-room and in response journals, where we wrestled with the material in a more personal way, as well as papers, where we formed our theories into more developed arguments.

It was all so good. Getting up, rushing down the hallway to get ready in a long line of sinks, smiling to the new friends I was already making—my boisterous, hilarious, always-in-motion RA, Lucy, with her badass mama-bear vibe, and a petite dark-eyed hippie, Beth, who I forgave for liking the Grateful Dead because she'd actually gone on tour with them over the summer, living on saltines and Captain Morgan with orange Crush, earning my admiration for her independent spirit.

Hurrying up the path to the dining hall for coffee and Cracklin' Oat Bran, then down the path to the classroom buildings, new notebooks and pens stuffed into the black velvet backpack Mom had sewn me, I found everything unexpected and wonderful.

At my classroom building, I nervously slipped into a nondescript room dominated by a big round table. I ducked my head, excited and happy and scared to be there. I had gotten my wish, and I had no idea what it would be like, or if I would be able to pull it off. I glanced nervously at Nok. He smiled at me. A great, wise smile I would find out was the perfect expression of his dark, dry wit. I smiled back, dropped my eyes.

At the end of the first day of class, we all made our way to the dining hall, where after we ate, we could sit on a balcony overlooking campus and smoke cigarettes and gossip. We had homework, but most of us had been waiting forever for a moment like this, and we weren't about to go back to our dorms and crack books just yet.

We hardly slept that first week, staying up late talking and flirting, dragging ourselves out of bed for class in the morning, cramming as much experience as we could into every moment. Classes were helmed by brilliant, turned-on professors and peopled by equally brilliant, turned-on students. It was as if I'd had my brain cracked open and fried in a pan like that antidrug commercial, except for one crucial difference: I'd always wanted to fry my brains with opinions and feelings, just like this. Such intense thoughts and experiences were where the good stuff happened.

By the end of the first week, it felt like Simon's Rock was ours. We loved it, and it loved us back. We knew our way around campus, through the airy atrium with its central pond filled with rocks and greens and frogs, into the library, where we picked up our reserved reading for class and flirted among the stacks of books; across the flat courtyard that led up to the student center, where we smoked cigarettes and caught up, before going to the wall of cubbies, where we might find a note from a teacher or a friend, or a slip letting us know we had a care package; and then, down into the bookstore, where we could buy Pepperidge Farm cookies and the books we needed for class, which I loved feeling all stacked up in my arms; and the wilderness we escaped to just beyond the edges of campus, across Alford Road, past the big red barn, to Green River and the Labyrinth, through cornfields and out into the woods; or up the gravel road behind the dining hall, where Nok and I walked on the first Friday night.

We had dropped acid, and everything was heightened, not so much from the drug itself as from the intensity of paying attention to see whether the drug had affected anything yet, and also from looking for signs as to what was happening between us.

I almost couldn't believe it could be this easy. I had stepped into a perfect version of my life—the cutest boy in our class, whom I'd liked from the moment I saw him, was walking into the night with me, just me, and we were laughing and talking about the books we'd read that week and about writing, which we both liked. The air smelled so cool it was almost damp from the dense groves of pines and hardwoods that surrounded the road on each side. We crested the top of the hill, and the world opened up to reveal a fat, silvery moon hanging just above a perfect little chapel in a vast green lawn.

Next to the chapel was a building with a low porch roof. We climbed up, as if ascending into the sky to touch the moon, the acid coming on in a way that felt warm and dreamy, as if I were one with the world. He leaned me up against the building, and we were kissing under the effect of the drug and the moon and the happiness of this first perfect week of heaven. We wandered back toward our dorms around curfew, although I already knew that the door to my dorm was always propped open, or if it wasn't, I could climb in through the window of the student lounge. There was no need to worry.

Until the next day. I was nervous about seeing Nok. I thought he was everything I wanted, and he had to be my boyfriend. My happiness depended on my ability to make him like me, but I doubted myself, deeply. I didn't know what to say, how to be cool around him, or anything. Nok told me that he didn't want to be tied down. We'd never gotten to the point of being anything, really. But I was distraught, and I hung on.

The following week, we slipped into his dorm room one afternoon when his roommate was at class and fooled around in the dim late-afternoon light that wafted in from beneath the blinds, full of the heightened excitement of hearing people moving to and fro in the corridor outside. We didn't have sex, but it was more than I'd ever done before. I knew he wasn't a virgin, and I was sure everything was happening as it should with a beautiful boy who was gentle with me and knew how to smooth over an awkward moment with a dry, self-deprecating joke. Even when he again told me that he really thought we should just be friends, I held out hope for our future.

When Nok quickly began seeing a beautiful older student, I did not handle it well. As always, it was proof that I was nothing and no one cared. I had been a fool to expect my new life to be any different than my old. What I wanted was perpetually beyond my reach.

I was enamored of the upperclassmen, because they seemed so much cooler and more in the know, and I made friends with as many of them as I could—like Natalia, a pretty redhead who smelled of cigarettes and Obsession and always had a complex romantic life unfolding around her, and her roommate, Stephanie, who had grown up in Boston. Stephanie's friend's band was opening for one of my favorite punk acts, 7 Seconds, at the Channel in Boston during one of our first weekends at school. I rode to the show with them, overjoyed at how far I'd come. I was only fifteen, but I could now legitimately say I was a college student hanging out in the city. My real life had begun.

Cocky with my newfound independence and a sense of my own maturity and worldliness, I reached out to my dad to let him know I'd be in Boston with some friends for a concert. I had only seen him once since the Cure concert two years earlier, but I still felt close to him because of our letters.

Even though I was intent on seeming cool in front of my new friends, I was sure my dad could hang. And, as always, I really just wanted to see him. Actually, I wanted to impress him: if I hadn't been able to woo him with the sweet girl I'd been, I would woo him with the wild child I'd become. Because Stephanie was friends with the opening act, we pulled up behind the venue where the bands loaded in their gear. My dad approached, sussed out the situation, and immediately had to get on top of it. He saw a skinhead with braces, bomber jacket, and shaved head, his neatly rolled blue jeans above oxblood Doc Martens.

"I didn't know you hung out with skinheads, Sarah," he said. "There's a lot of ignorance and hatred in that culture. You have to be careful."

"Not all skinheads are racist," I snapped back. "I'm friends with S.H.A.R.P. skinheads, and they fight for equality and tolerance."

"That's still fighting."

"Someone's gotta fight for what's right," I said.

He stepped back a little, surveyed me and the pack of drinking, smoking kids.

"You know what, if you don't want me here, I should go," he said.

Just like that, I did not want him there. I wanted to be fifteen. I wanted to drink beer and kiss the cute guy I'd been eyeing from the opening band. I wanted to go up front for 7 Seconds. I stared back at him, not begging him to stay, for the first time in my entire life, not making everything okay for him.

"Fine, Sarah, I'm gonna go," he said.

"Okay," I said. "Bye."

He walked off toward the street. I stood there, stunned. Maybe I hadn't been particularly welcoming, but I hadn't been actively trying to reject him or push him away. I didn't have it in me to want to hurt my dad. I'd just needed him to acknowledge the sophisticated girl in the big city I'd become, after years of striving, largely out of my desire to be close to him. I hadn't even stood up for myself. I had simply side-stepped my usual role. And by doing so I had betrayed him. He wasn't walking away, like a parent would, to give me space. He was reacting out of his own chronic insecurities and issues, and I would not be for-given. He would not see me again for the next ten years.

chapter six

THE SHOOTING

After my dad left, I threw myself into the pit by the stage. I went to where the heat and the noise and the boys were. I wanted to get slammed around and feel something on the outside that hurt more, or at least felt different, than how I hurt on the inside.

At the show's end, I was sweaty and wrung out, my body high on the adrenaline of the music and contact. I wanted the feeling to go on and on. I asked for another beer. I went to the after-party. The dingy apartment with stacks of empty beer bottles in the kitchen, the crappy stereo playing lo-fi punk loud, the crowd of people laughing, talking shit, and drinking just the right amount of too much; I needed all of this to shut out everything I felt.

At the end of the weekend, we drove back to Simon's Rock. I was hungover and sad. Instead of wanting to take a long, hot shower and climb into bed with a tall glass of water and my journal, I wanted more of everything, for the distraction to never stop. I didn't ever want to pause and feel what had just happened. And so, for a long time, I didn't.

A few weeks later, I got a card from my dad that read: "I'm terribly sorry about last weekend, I hope it didn't upset you. I have been a compulsive gambler for on + off, mostly on, almost 20 yrs. I've completely ruined my life over it. For the last two or three months I've been trying to get myself together enough to come together with you. My final realization was that I couldn't unless I quit gambling, because the only two things I was sure about was that I loved you + that I wanted to be honest with you. There was no way I could do that + still gamble. But quitting is not a cure-all. I just see how self-centered + really insecure I am, I don't know what else to say, but I wanted to say something. Thank you, just being around you has a positive effect on me. Love Dad"

The adult I longed to be thrilled at the grown-up way he'd leveled with me. But it was both too much and not enough. I'd had friends whose parents were alcoholics. But I didn't understand what an addiction to gambling meant. I didn't understand why he couldn't just stop. That part didn't really matter, though. What mattered was the confession itself. This was his first truly honest letter to me, and I saw it as the beginning of something new between us, a deeper, stronger relationship. I didn't want to jeopardize this by admitting how much he'd hurt me, so I wrote him back a gentle, conciliatory letter.

While I dug into my college adventure, a part of me continued to watch the mailbox. I kept expecting a letter, any day now; and then, any week. The fact that I sometimes doubted him now only increased my desire for our new closeness. I knew what he was capable of, and I wanted the good stuff all of the time. Instead, I got nothing. When he called me a month later and promised to visit me at school in a few weeks, I decided I'd believe it when it happened. Of course, it never did. He was once again gone, and his absence was his only consistent presence in my life.

I was older now, though, and really, I was more interested in boys than in my father. In mid-October, I gathered my courage and called Oliver. It was clear even to naive, fifteen-year-old me that his mental state had worsened, and it was hard for me to feel much more optimistic about his future prospects than he was. But I swooned when he told me that I was the most beautiful person he knew, and he'd fallen in love with me that summer. We talked about meeting up, and I held on to this dream, even amid my new life, more comfortable waiting on the promises made by a man who'd given me little to believe in than I was in my day-to-day reality.

My feelings for Nok had, for the time, mellowed to the point where we could be friends. He had a hard relationship with his dad, too, and we could talk for hours about our disappointments and anger, and our fear that these men had planted the seeds of their failings within us. We also talked about writing and love and life. I was fired up and wanted everything to happen all at once. Even though Nok had so many more advantages than I did—money and looks and natural talent and cool—he didn't seem to want anything. This made me jealous, because he was cocooned in his not caring, a lot like my dad was, and it also made me crazy because a part of me was still in love with him, and I wanted so much more for him than he wanted for himself. It was easy to cling to my crush; wanting from afar was how I was used to feeling. At one point that year, Nok said to me: "Your depression is a badge you wear." He was right, it was.

But now that I had the means to create the adventures I craved, I found I was a good instigator. We were seriously underage, and technically, there was a rule against us drinking or consuming drugs, but there was always a way, and I was drunk almost every night of my first semester, and sometimes high or tripping, too. Especially for a perfectionist, it was a welcome escape, the one time when I didn't have to try to be good.

In early December, the band I had gone to see in Boston with Stephanie came to play at Simon's Rock. I loved the feeling of being in the know when they rolled up and nodded their heads at me in acknowledgment. I loved knowing the words to the songs, knowing I had a place at the after-party. Drunk on cheap beer, I fooled around with a boy in the band, one I picked because he picked me. He was special because he had been up onstage, which meant he was better than the rest of us in some way and had a more direct link to the music I loved so much it often felt like the only thing keeping me sane.

He and I made out in his sleeping bag at the top of the stairs in a little nook where no one would bother us, and then fell asleep in an empty bed. For years, my friend Natalia and I referred to sex as "unzipping the sleeping bag," even though I hadn't had sex with him. Of course, she'd also fooled around with a guy in the band, but they really had unzipped the sleeping bag, and now he was obsessed with her. As was her boyfriend back home.

Natalia was also dating a cute skinhead boy from my grade. He hung out with a group of tough guys who had a mean edge that didn't seem anything like the S.H.A.R.P. skinheads I knew. I was friendly with one of the boys because we had a class together and liked the same punk bands. But I always steered clear of him when he was with his friends, which included a big boneheaded body builder, and a small, tightly wound Taiwanese-American kid, Wayne Lo, who had begun making statements in class about how people with AIDS should be quarantined in Canada and bombed.

My classmates and I were not having any of this kind of talk. We had fought hard to get to a place where it was safe to be ourselves, gay or straight or sexually ambiguous, liberal in politics as well as attitudes toward culture and love, and we weren't allowing any hate into our paradise. So we ostracized the whole group, and they pulled tighter into themselves.

But Natalia liked having sex with her guy, and she wouldn't give it up. I became like her lady in waiting, fascinated by every detail of her romantic life. No one ever got obsessed with me. I didn't expect them to stay in contact after we'd made out. I didn't even expect them to want to make out with me. What had happened with Nok had been an anomaly. The prompt ending had been what I should have expected all along.

Before it seemed possible, my first semester roared to an end on a frantic wave of all-night paper-writing marathons fueled by buckets of General Foods International Coffees and hot cocoa mix. I was supposed to see Oliver in New York City when I visited a school friend during break, but he never contacted me. When I confronted him, he broke off our relationship again. Back home on vacation, I was exhausted and moody, balking at any rules Craig tried to establish after my new-found freedom. He felt my attitude was bad, my lifestyle unhealthy for someone my age, and that I didn't appreciate my mom's hard work enough. I wasn't exactly crazy about my own behavior, either, but I also felt ignored and misunderstood, and wanted out. I slept for hours, wrote bad poetry, fell in love with the director Hal Hartley's films, and smoked in secret, nursing my heartbreak and recovering from the mad adventure of my first months away. My dad sent me his usual Christmas card but any real conversation between us had ceased. I wrote in my journal: "Just like him, I'm constantly having self-realizations and learning from my mistakes and flaws, but I never apply my valuable knowledge. We both continue blindly, making no real accomplishments in our struggle for some form of success or peace of mind. We're both pathetic dreamers. This makes me believe I'm doomed by my genes, which is the same excuse my father makes for his failures. It's really quite pathetic. I have to wonder if I'll ever reach a place in my life where I'll spend my time living instead of dreaming of living." Happy sweet sixteen.

I celebrated my sixteenth birthday not long into our second semester. The girls on my hall got me a cake, which Beth decorated with a paper cutout of a cheerleader because she remembered me joking about my days as a junior high cheerleading squad captain. My friends went in on a carton of my cigarette of choice—Marlboro Reds—a gesture I found totally awesome. We partied up in Natalia's mod, an on-campus apartment reserved for upperclassmen, and everyone came, which meant the world to me. I got drunk and had fun, happy to have hit a legitimate milestone, and to celebrate with real friends. But being close with kids who were as intense and sometimes as troubled as I was had a darker side. One of my best friends left my party, slit her wrists in her room, and was found just in time. She was expelled the following week.

Alcohol took the edge off my feelings. It allowed me to let go of my perfectionism and fear of failure; it made things messy, and that was okay. We all got drunk together. Having the best time and being silly was a good thing. When we were drinking, I felt closer to the way other people seemed to feel all of the time. It was a huge relief.

Sometimes when I was drinking, I'd even feel pretty and make out with a boy at a party. I never thought these boys would be my boyfriend or even like me. I was desperate for love, but all of the small intimate moments and admissions of vulnerability it would take to get there were just too much for me. At least I could be glad that these isolated incidents were proof that my life was blossoming.

That March I went home with my friend, Lucy, for break. A few days into the trip, we borrowed her mom's car and drove out to see Lucy's friend who lived in Sandwich on Cape Cod. The girl's mom was out of town, and we thrilled at having the house to ourselves, to party, yes, but also just to have a brief, lovely respite from adults.

I liked Lucy's friend, but it was instantly clear how much we'd moved away from normal teenage life during our time at Simon's Rock. Yes, we had curfews and more vacations than regular college kids, but we were in college. At sixteen, I had already taken on thousands of dollars in student loans and was making decisions that would affect my future. But this was vacation, and I didn't want to think about anything for a few days, and so we turned to the great levelers: music and booze.

Some of the girl's friends showed up that evening—including a trio of cute skateboarders who looked at Lucy and me shyly until we'd all drank enough to turn the big sprawling home into our playhouse. I was always on the lookout for boys, always wanting something to happen, and I drifted toward a thin boy with chin-length hair as fine as corn silk. I can't remember his name or even a time when I could. We made out and slept on the couch. He was very sweet, and I was grateful to him for it.

In the morning, his friends came tearing into the room. We sprang apart. Suddenly he was up and already moving away from me. I kept looking at my boy, wanting something from him, willing him to come to me, but he didn't. The three boys laughed and joked about how drunk they'd been the night before, about other parties with people I didn't know. I couldn't bear it anymore and went outside to smoke. Lucy and I were sitting on the front steps when the boys whooped out of the house.

"Come back tonight," Lucy's friend called after them. "Bring more beer."

They piled into their car and sped off. My heart sank. Sometimes it felt like every new experience only left me filled with longing.

"He didn't even say good-bye," I said.

"Oh, Pooter Bear," Lucy said, using her nickname for me. "Boys like that have never met anyone like you."

"Like what?" I asked, my tone indignant, even though I was also pleased.

"Like that," she said, pointing at me.

I looked down. I was wearing big chunky silver rings, the black velvet miniskirt Mom had sewn for me, my Docs, and a green cardigan with ripped-out elbows.

"I'm not that weird," I said.

"It's not just that," she said. "It's everything. You go to college. You have opinions about things. They're from a small town. They don't know what to do."

We sat inside all afternoon, drinking Diet Coke and girl talking. That evening, the boys returned. When they came in, though, it wasn't the same. We were trying to recapture something spontaneous and fun from the previous night that now felt forced. We held our cans of cheap beer awkwardly, staring at one another from far away, until one of the guys suggested we shotgun them. It was like the night before, but not. I was drunk again, but in a different way, and whereas before I'd been happy with whatever happened the previous night, now I felt pressure, like if something didn't happen with the boy, it meant he didn't like me.

I got trashed and ended up puking, and then sobbing for an hour in the bathroom with the boy and his friends trying to take care of me. The boy I liked was patient and kind, but I was a mess, and finally Lucy took over. She got me calmed down and sobered up, at least a little. We all watched TV, and my boy and I started fooling around again. He pulled me up onto my feet, taking my hand, and that alone was enough to make me happy.

At the top of the stairs, the door to the girl's mother's bedroom was open, the bed neatly made, welcoming. This was a lot compared to a night crammed together on the couch downstairs. I paused, and then, as I knew I would, I went forward, as I always did. We climbed onto the bed together and the kissing soon became heavy.

I was a sixteen-year-old freshman in college. The closest I'd ever come to a boyfriend was my pen pal, Oliver. Nok was the only boy I'd ever kissed more than once. But I wanted this. His hands went under my top, and then he pulled it over my head. I didn't tell him I'd never done this before. I didn't tell him I wasn't on the pill. I didn't ask him about condoms or anything else. The details were fuzzy—except for the pain—even as they were happening. Luckily for both of us, we were accidentally well matched, both shy and mostly trying to be good.

In the morning, I drifted out of a hard sleep: first, my pounding head, then my ashtray mouth, then my queasy stomach, then my soreness where he had been. I couldn't remember the details, but I was glad I had done it. I wanted to talk about how I felt about what had happened, but not with him. With Lucy, as soon as he left.

He had rolled away in the night, but his arm was still around my shoulders. Somehow, I knew he was a nice guy, and I was glad. I had already heard too many stories about how often that wasn't the case.

I snuggled closer to him, let his silky hair fall across my face as the room lightened around us. When he stirred, I was suddenly embarrassed. Was there blood? I hadn't thought to look. What did he think of me?

I burrowed my face into the back of his neck. I could feel him smiling, and it made me smile, too. Then I pulled away. We both kept our eyes down as we got dressed, me searching the bedspread we had slept on, grateful there was no blood or any other sign of what we had done. I sat on the edge of the bed, not quite ready for it to be over. I wanted a kiss, but I wouldn't ask for it. He sat down next to me, our bodies touching.

"So," I said.

"Yeah," he said.

I turned and dared to really look at him, his fine blond hair falling across his pretty face, so that he felt able to look at me, too.

"Nice to meet you," I said.

He laughed, and I laughed, too.

"Nice to meet you," he said.

We both leaned forward and kissed one last time. He stood, and I let him go. I didn't go downstairs until I heard the door slam and the boys' car drive away.

Lucy and I were alone together in her car. I knew, and was glad, that I was never going back there. The boys had said they would visit us at school, but I doubted they ever would, and I thought it better that way. We lit cigarettes and pulled onto the road.

"So what happened last night?" she asked.

"It happened," I said.

Everyone in our dorm was well aware of which girls were virgins and which were not, and who the girls who were not had lost it with, and how and where, and whom, if anyone, they had slept with or had their sights on sleeping with on campus.

"It did?!" she asked. "How was it?"

"Fine, good," I said. "But I could be pregnant."

"Pooter Bear," she said sternly.

"I'm probably not," I said.

"Whatever happens, it'll be okay," she said.

"Yeah," I said.

She looked at me and we both laughed. We had wanted life to happen to us, and it was.

For the next month, sitting in class, I would remember the boy's feathery hair brushing my face, the shy smile that was more intimate than the sex we'd shared, and the memory was thrilling, and then I remembered to wonder what, if anything, was happening inside of me, and I felt a trickle of worry. Then, it went away. Between response journals and papers, it came back. And again, while drinking forties with Beth and the girls on our hall, and again, while smoking and playing Spit with Lucy.

I went to health services. I was not pregnant. I had not contracted any STDs. I had intuitively picked someone as innocent as I was. Or I had been lucky. Or a combination of both. I would never know. During my exam, I didn't mention that I still got my period only occasionally. It seemed like a fortunate health irregularity to have.

As much as I liked my purple hair and my red lipstick, and I desperately wanted my first boyfriend, I still wasn't good at being a girl. I wanted to spend my energy on books. I wanted to run around as hard and loud as the boys, drinking as much and knowing the words to the same songs, and showing I could hold my own with them, as I had tried to prove I could with my dad. Feeling like I was honoring my father—with the acid I was taking and the books I was reading and the free spirit I was cultivating—was important to me. I had not heard from him since his Christmas card, now several months in the past. It was not uncommon for my dad to disappear for six months at a time, but his absence at just the moment I was becoming my own person, and everyone else in my family was supporting me, felt like the worst rejection yet. I didn't know until years later that he'd gotten his settlement, and when he'd lost all of the money at the track, he'd become suicidal. All I knew was I had taken the risk in order to be a person he would respect, who had ideas and lived with consciousness, and he wasn't interested in talking with me about any of it.

Even though Mom did a good job of not letting me worry, I knew it was touch-and-go, month-to-month, to keep me at Simon's Rock. I also knew she wouldn't let this rare and special opportunity pass out of my grasp. Everyone was invested, except my dad. But his was not the only absence I felt that year.

Oliver also remained absent, until late May, just as my first year of school ended, when he let me back into his life again. I never thought about the timing of his disappearance or his return. He was no longer in school, instead working full-time at a store, but for the summer at least, I wasn't a student, either. I was a prep cook and busser at the Anchor Inn. Conversations with him were once again a lifeline to the big world.

There was a small window of time, a week maybe, during which it was a relief to be home, catching up on sleep, eating without being ruled by the dining hall's schedule, and unwinding from the pressures of school. After that, I fell into an emotional gutter, convinced each tomorrow would be the one in which I was finally happy and perfect.

There was still no word from my dad. I went back over our last interaction. It was hard to be clear on what had happened. In my joy at my new freedom, I had eased up on my vigilance. It seemed impossible our relationship had ended over a disagreement about skinhead culture, which neither of us truly cared about. But sometimes it's only possible to fight about the things that don't matter, not the things that are slowly and silently tearing you apart. He was gone, and I could feel it was a different absence than it used to be.

At least Oliver wrote to me nearly every day in June, a familiar mix of on-point, charmingly idiosyncratic love letters and dark confessions about how he and his life were shit and he wanted to die. And again, I wasn't scared of his love or his depression. I had missed him, and I was glad he'd come back to me. My forays into real dating and sex hadn't left me feeling any more connected than I had felt as a lonely girl dreaming about them. It felt safe to have him far away, to be back in my familiar role of patient listener. But his darkness had deepened. By mid-June, he was wishing he'd stayed away.

I got through the summer by working as many shifts as I could at the Anchor Inn to save money for school the next year, while getting nowhere with a new crush, and going to visit friends in Portland whenever I could. I still hadn't heard from my dad, and when I finally did in mid-July, I learned he was in the hospital. It was unclear why, but I assumed a nervous breakdown. "I suppose I should care, but I don't," I wrote in my journal. "I certainly don't hate him, but it's hard for me to worry about someone who is meaningless in my life." Oliver was going MIA for weeks at a time, too. I was eager to get back to school.

I had applied to be a resident assistant because the job paid well and came with a single dorm room. I was nervous, though, as it required a commitment to not drink or do drugs, and I had drank nearly every night of my freshman year, usually to the point of being messy. I didn't want to be a hypocrite by breaking the rules I was meant to enforce, but I didn't know what it would be like to be at school without my alcohol escape hatch.

I had barely passed my driving test, and Mom and Craig had given me their old Toyota Tercel hatchback so they wouldn't have to shuttle me the six-plus hours back and forth to school. Craig pulled it up onto the lawn and made me show him I could jack up the car, take the tire off, and put on the spare, so I'd be prepared for whatever happened.

On the morning I left for school I backed my car off the lawn, where I had loaded it up the night before, through the opening in the stone wall, and smack into a tree. Afraid I was going to get in trouble, I taped up the light and decided to get it fixed myself once I got down to school without telling Mom and Craig anything about it.

On the drive, I'd had some anxiety about what the new year would bring, but it was wonderful to be back. I loved my new dorm, Kendrick. After I unpacked enough to feel settled, I attended RA orientation. The school was actively trying to subdue the rampant party culture, which I had mixed feelings about. I loved to drink, and many of my best experiences during freshman year had occurred at the free-wheeling parties that happened every weekend and most weeknights, too. I felt like the new class of students should have the right to the same growth—from engaging in *all* that school had to offer: ideas, friendship, books, music, politics, inspiration, and, yes, partying. I let it be known in the least confrontational way possible that I intended to be the kind of RA who helped my kids learn how to handle their drugs, rather than narcing on them.

Then it was time to go down to the student center. I smiled at the newbies in what I hoped was a reassuring way, filled up with love for this place and excited to share it with them. A tall, thin boy with the bluest eyes and a shaved head stopped in the middle of the student center, his gaze fixed on me. Without thinking about it, I smiled at him, as I had smiled at the others. As he watched my smile take shape, his face erupted into the biggest grin. When I met him later that day, he smiled at me with the same intensity.

"Hi, my name is Matthew," he said with a Tennessee twang, practically batting his eyelashes at me.

He was one of my charges. I immediately liked all of my kids, but at sixteen, I was younger than most of them, and it was a little unnerving being responsible. At the same time, I knew I didn't entirely belong in the cliques and romances they were forming as workshop week unfolded, just as my classmates and I had done the previous year.

I missed the upperclassmen, but one of my old drinking buddies was back and living in my dorm. And his roommate, Galen, was the kind of friend who could cheer me up just by giving me a hug, an occurrence I noted with appreciation and wonder. With a compact physicality and full beard that made him seem like a grown man, Galen stood out among us teenagers. He normally wore his long, curly hair pulled back into a careless ponytail, which I fashioned into high valley girl dos after dinner as I sat on his lap on the balcony, smoking Parliament Lights and singing, "Sixteen clumsy and shy, I went to

London and I . . ." He called me "Sarah Pop," and I called him "Gale Boppers," and we often kissed hello, not in a romantic way, but with a comfort and ease that was special and rare for me.

I wasn't normally physically comfortable with anyone, especially not boys. My idea of intimacy was chain-smoking on a friend's bed while she chain-smoked on the other end. So I don't know why I felt safe sitting on Galen's lap, leaning back against his broad chest, or letting his beard tickle my face as he kissed me. Maybe because he was so easy to be around, and because he'd been obsessed with my friend Natalia the previous semester. I'd commiserated with him about his longing, because it was a feeling I knew well.

Nok was back, too. I still adored him, but even I had limits to how long I could keep a flame burning with no fuel. It seemed like everyone was having relationships but me. I just couldn't leap into the fray and commit to a person. It all seemed too messy and scary, not just what happened behind closed doors, but the idea of being linked to that person publicly, the pressure to choose the right person and have the right relationship.

For the first time, I didn't want to get older. I wanted my freshman year back. I wanted to be experiencing everything for the first time, but I couldn't, and so I sat and smoked and tried to enjoy myself as the freshmen had their fun. Nothing thrilled me more than when one of them came to me with a problem, trained as I'd been by my dad to adore the intensity of a good tête-à-tête, and reveling in feeling needed.

Beth was an RA in my old dorm, Crosby, but I didn't go over there much, except to sit in my best friend Claire's second-floor single and stare at the students who passed by. Most of my friends the previous year had either been girls from the smoking hall or upperclassmen, but my second semester at school I'd become aware of Claire. She was beautiful, but in a spirited, old-fashioned way. She didn't wear makeup or dress sexy. She had obvious intelligence and a nervous intensity like a hummingbird.

Claire wasn't a smoker or a party girl, and we often marveled that we'd found each other, since our two worlds could have easily kept us separate, even though we lived in the same dorm. Claire and I spent hours together, talking about books and music and art and culture. She loved Hal Hartley, too, and Blondie and Sylvia Plath. We might just as easily dance around her room to "The Tide Is High" or talk about the wit and wonder of *The Bell Jar*. Like me, she dreamed of having a big life but felt anxious about if and when everything would happen for her. I envied her because her attitude and smarts were so undeniable. In the frenzy of an all-nighter, she once wrote a paper in which she said "Karl Marx can go suck an egg," and it was still good enough to earn her a B.

With her powerful persona, Claire was quick to get mad or disappear into her room if she felt slighted. But the intensity of her love and loyalty when she was pleased was as ferocious as her displeasure when she was not. I was devoted to her happiness. I suppose she felt the same way about me, although I still had the feeling that I was an absence of presence, and so it was hard for me to imagine inspiring love in anyone.

We were instantly inseparable again our sophomore year and spent long hours in her room, talking endlessly about the subject that obsessed us: love. Under Claire's direction, we were reading Marguerite Duras, especially *The Lover*. We were determined to create an independent study for ourselves on the subject of love, as though, if we could read the right books and have enough inspired insights, we would somehow master the experience.

We were such well-matched friends that we were both equally sincere in our intentions, and totally naive about the fact that the only way to begin to understand love was to put down our books and join the messy world. Plenty of boys were in love with Claire. She was always storming out of rooms and having asthma attacks and otherwise making a scene. When she cut you, no one went deeper, and when she loved you, no one made you feel more seen. I was her perfect foil; giving my constant, unending devotion without ever laying down any consequences for anything she did, no matter if she hurt my feelings, which she inevitably did, given her intensity and my sensitivity.

Claire was also with me in the most important class of my life: my first fiction workshop. Immediately, I was completely, irrevocably hooked. I loved the feeling of honing in on the description of an obscure feeling—both on the page and in a round-table discussion of a story's themes. I knew this was how I wanted to spend the rest of my life.

The guy with the smile, Matthew, began hanging around me more and more. I thought he was cute and liked the attention. His ardor was almost as intense as the depths of my insecurity and self-loathing, which obscured the many ways we were a poor romantic match.

One night, he "fell asleep" with his shoes still on, curled up in my little twin bed. Eventually, there was nothing for me to do but get into bed with him. That was more than the invitation he needed. He "woke up," turning his face toward mine, already straining toward the kiss. In the instant our lips met, he was fully in it.

"I remember you were the first person I saw at school," he said. "And when you smiled at me, I thought you were the most beautiful girl I'd ever seen. I fell in love with you right then and there."

"I was just doing my job," I riffed back.

"You were so pretty, and you had such a great smile."

"Still got all my teeth," I said, wanting the attention, needing the affection, but unable to handle it without going into my default mode: sarcasm.

In the morning, Matt was the one smiling. He had decided: he was my first boyfriend. Still, I held back, uncomfortable with the relationship. I realized that we had different ways of being and wanted different lives. But he was so sweet, and he liked me so much, and it felt so wonderful to let go, just like when I'd started getting drunk.

It came time for the sex. Even in the dark with the door locked and in the presence of a person who literally could not have seen a single thing wrong with me, I was nervous about what would happen and how. But I didn't feel comfortable talking about it, either. There was also the matter of condoms, which I'd never seen in action before, and which stressed me out to no end.

At the same time, we were teenagers and all hormones, and it didn't take long for us to end up naked. Matt pulled out a condom and put it on like it was no big deal. He began to move, and the bed began to squeak, and squeak, and squeak. I froze.

"Are you okay?" he asked gently.

"The bed's squeaking," I said.

He rocked harder and squeaked it louder, laughing.

"Everyone can hear," I said.

"So what?" he said.

I made him stop, get up, and put the mattress on the floor, so we could do it silently. Luckily he was totally unfazed by anything I did. As we lay together afterward, Matt kissing me before falling into blissed-out slumber, I lay awake, paranoid everyone on my hall had heard, uncomfortable in my body, unsure in my skin, wanting everything but terrified I was doing it all wrong.

We never even came close to having sex without a condom. And yet, that fall, I missed my period, for weeks and weeks. Matt was over-joyed. He wanted us to move to Tennessee and raise the baby together. When I went home for break, I knew I had to do something. Mom remained calm and took me to the doctor who had given me my first pelvic exam. I wasn't pregnant. But I still hadn't had my period. I told her this wasn't uncommon for me. She couldn't find anything wrong. I was incredibly relieved not to be pregnant. So everything was fine, until I had sex with Matt again but still didn't get my period. I hadn't gotten pregnant before, but I could be pregnant now. I started keep-ing pregnancy tests on hand, which didn't exactly make me any more relaxed about sex.

Matt was a devoted boyfriend. He dressed up in an oversize pink tuxedo shirt and took me out to dinner at the town's Mexican restau-rant. He literally sold blood to get money to spend on dates. When I mentioned this fact to my mom—like many teenage girls, I was not a humble despot—she laughed. "Your father used to sell blood," she said.

The boys in my dorm could be hard on Matt, and I could be short-tempered with him. But he had several female devotees in his class, including a pretty girl named Maxine, who did not try to hide her crush. It was a small school, so our paths crossed often, but we didn't have more than a nod-and-smile relationship. One night, there was a knock on my door. I expected a friend, or one of my kids. I was surprised to see Maxine.

"Matt isn't here," I said.

"I'm not here to see Matt," she said.

I didn't say anything, just waited to see what she wanted.

"Why don't you like me?" she asked.

I was too horrified to speak. This was my worst nightmare: (A) being confronted in any capacity by anyone, and (B) having to lie to avoid hurting the feelings of someone I didn't particularly like when I was already fed up with the situation.

"I don't dislike you, Maxine," I said. "I just think that my relationship with Matt isn't any of your business, so you should stay out of it."

She nodded. There wasn't anything else to say. I watched her round the corner before shutting my door. When I mentioned her visit to Matt, he seemed nonplussed.

As the end of the first semester of my sophomore year approached, I began thinking about transferring to a school with a good writing program, maybe Sarah Lawrence, Wesleyan, or Bard—which students of Simon's Rock could automatically attend. I didn't know what to do. I couldn't stay, but I couldn't go. Finals loomed. Break was in a week.

That weekend Galen found me in the Kendrick atrium. He was a terrible mooch of cigarettes, which were always in high demand on campus, since most of us were broke. But I was always happy to give him a smoke in exchange for one of his great, witty philosophies on anything, profound or mundane. I automatically began to shake one out of my pack for him, but he surprised me by holding out two unopened packs of Parliaments.

"I got you back for all of the cigarettes you've bummed me," he said.

I stopped short, stunned, always sure people weren't really paying attention to me, or what I brought to their lives, whether it was friendship or a smoke.

"Well, that might not be *all* of the cigarettes I've bummed you," I said.

He laughed, leaning into me as he lit a cigarette for me. I slumped against his body, happy and comfortable around him, as always.

That Monday night, I was studying for my environmental science exam in my room when I heard a strange noise from the direction of the road that led onto campus. It sounded like fireworks, but I didn't see how that was possible. It was December in the Berkshires. I figured I'd just imagined it. Then I became aware of a flurry of activity in the halls outside my dorm room. I ran into another student's room and waited there with her. The sound came again. Louder. Closer. What was that? More fireworks? It couldn't be. I heard yelling outside. More running. I poked my head into the hallway and then stepped out. None of the adults were anywhere to be seen. Someone said it was Wayne Lo. He had a semiautomatic rifle, and people were injured. Another RA, my friend Jay, had told our kids to stay in their rooms. Stunned, I went back into the room, and the girl looked up.

"They're saying Galen's been shot," she said to me, cradling her phone.

"What?"

More frantic movement outside. We looked out her window toward the empty dining hall and saw activity through the glass walls of the student lounge, which also housed the snack bar. I'd begun crying, and I couldn't stop. It was impossible. Galen was the best of the best.

"It's just a rumor," I said. "We don't know anything."

We looked out the window. A handful of police officers were advancing up the snowy hill, in classic television poses, guns drawn. As I braced myself for more gunshots, the police officers burst through the door and disappeared into the student lounge. I watched them arrest Wayne. The rumors were true.

chapter seven

ANYWHERE BUT HERE

People called between the dorms, sharing bits of information. Someone had talked to someone in the library, where Galen had died. The person on the other end of the gun was definitely Wayne Lo. Our classmate. Based on his overly aggressive behavior on the basketball court and his stupidly hateful opinions in the classroom, we had thought him an asshole and a homophobe, and we had felt justified in our dislike of him. He had hated us enough to want us dead, and he had done his best to make it so.

Both Galen and Wayne lived in Kendrick, and Wayne had shot into the dorm's atrium as he'd run by. The bullet holes were clearly visible. After the police took Wayne into custody, they fanned out over campus, dealing with the carnage. We waited, crying, talking, hugging, accounting for friends who were not immediately visible.

Finally, we were given some instructions. We RAs were expected to round up our kids and keep the peace until we were summoned to the dining hall for an informational assembly. As we walked out of

Kendrick, police tape already crisscrossed the front of the dorm, hot yellow against the pristine snow. I peered down through the naked trees and the darkness toward the library, spinning red and blue lights flashing frantic through the cold, clear night. I looked over my shoulder, feeling like a gun was trained on me as I crossed the suddenly unfamiliar quad Wayne had sprayed with bullets, my body responding with pure panic and the instinct to flee, my mind unable to weld any logic onto the situation.

I found Matt in the crush of students moving toward the dining hall. He'd been with Maxine, and she'd given him some kind of a muscle relaxant. He was pretty fucked up. I was annoyed with him and with her. I didn't think it was an appropriate response. I didn't want him to be out of it; I wanted him to be in it with the rest of us—in the pain of this fucked-up situation that meant life would never be the same.

We all slunk into chairs around the same tables where we'd eaten dinner a few hours earlier. I looked through the glass doors to the balcony where Galen and I had sat on dozens of nights, smoking. I could feel myself still on his lap, the smell of his hair, which usually needed a wash, the bristle of his beard as he kissed me. All gone, all gone. The tears had never completely stopped, but now they came on hard again. I clung to one last hope. The announcement hadn't been made yet. Maybe there was still some way out of it. I looked at the dean, the provost, his wife, the resident directors. Our Kendrick RDs, Floyd and Trinka, were still nowhere to be seen, which was odd. It was rumored they'd been evacuated earlier in the night.

There was a flurry of movement at the front of the room. The cops and administrators in charge began to speak. It was all facts now, nothing but the coldest, hardest facts. Wayne Lo had gotten a gun, an SKS-47. He had started at the guard shack, where he had shot our security guard Mary. She was alive, but badly wounded. Then he had shot our professor Nacunan Saez as he was driving off campus. Dead. Then he had shot Galen as he exited the library to investigate the disturbance and help out if he could. Dead. Then he had run up the path toward the dorms, shooting three students along the way. His gun had jammed. He had gone to the student lounge and told a student he found there to call the cops. He had surrendered. He was in police custody.

"You are safe now."

Only, this was our home, and now we would never feel safe again. They were closing Kendrick so they could begin their investigation. Those of us who lived in Kendrick would stay in other dorms. Finals were canceled. Campus was closed. We could leave in the morning if we wanted. We could stay if we chose.

We cried and hugged one another and held on, hysterical or in shock. We talked and talked, but there was nothing to say. It was already past midnight. We were wired. We were exhausted. I was still sixteen but felt a million years old. Finally, after three hellish hours, they dismissed us, and I walked with Claire and Matt to her room. I used Claire's phone to call my mom. I pictured the phone ringing above the counter in the kitchen, letting it ring and ring to give her time to wake up, get downstairs, and answer.

"Hello?" she said.

Hearing her voice, I started to cry hard again.

"Mom," I said.

"What is it, Sarah? What's wrong? Are you okay?"

"There was a shooting, Mom. Wayne Lo got a gun, and Galen is dead. He killed Galen. And our teacher, Nacunan. His gun jammed, so he couldn't kill the rest of us. And the police have him now. But, Mom, he killed Galen."

I heard hard plastic hit the wood of the counter, then silence.

"Mom? Mom?" I said, looking from Claire to Matt, panicked.

"Mom? Mom?" I said, desperate.

"I'm sorry," she said, her voice slurred and weird. "I fainted." She paused. "Galen, really?"

I had introduced Galen to Mom and Craig when they'd been at school for parents' weekend in the fall. He had the kind of sly sparkle people remembered.

"Yeah, Galen," I said, crying harder.

"But you're okay?"

How to even begin to answer that question.

"Yeah," I said, the word more of an exhalation than anything else.

"What's going to happen now?" she asked.

"I don't know," I said. "They wouldn't let us go back to Kendrick. Matt and I are in Claire's room. They're closing campus. Finals are canceled. I don't know."

"Okay, try to get some sleep. We'll talk in the morning. I love you."

"I love you, too."

I hung up. Claire and Matt and I looked at one another, the glassed-over, hollowed-out glaze of survivors, hanging on to the in-out of our breath, nothing more. Around dawn, my system thankfully shut down. I slept in Matt's arms, on the industrial carpet.

The next day, the phone began ringing. Mom and Craig had gotten in the car and started driving, their urge to bring me home stronger than any other thought. They were parked at the arts building across from campus, but the police weren't letting any of the parents through. I didn't want to leave my friends, the only people who understood exactly what I was feeling, but campus was a horrible, bloody place.

A small group of us walked down to the library, the sunshine impossibly bright and normal. Police tape covered the entrance to the library, bullet holes visible in the cement walls, broken glass in the snow. A shrine had already gone up featuring notes, photos, CDs, flowers, candles, and Galen's favorite things: cigarettes, Moxie soda, Taco Bell hot sauce, the tools he used in his beloved job doing lighting and tech for the school's theater, a plastic chicken in reference to his favorite non sequitur: chicken enchilada. As we watched, hunched together in a small, sad pack, a stretcher topped with a gray body bag was wheeled out of the library. A group of adults stood a respectful distance away, keeping a watchful eye on us, as if they didn't think it was a good idea but realized everything had gotten so fucked up it wasn't really their place to say. It was terrible but necessary. Seeing Galen's covered body made it real.

I went back to Kendrick to pack. When I walked into my room, the red light on my answering machine was flashing. I listened to the messages, hopeful: Mom calling to tell me she and Craig were on the way. Friends from home who had seen the news report. If the story was already in Maine, it had to have reached Boston, which was in the same state as Simon's Rock, and only three hours away. And yet, my dad hadn't called.

I climbed into a van that drove us by the place where Nacunan had been shot, and the guard shack. It stopped at Alford Road. Across the street, a throng of parents braved the December weather, eager to catch sight of their children. Fighting them for space was a pack of news reporters and photographers, their TV cameras and telephoto lenses already pointed at us. The sight of the reporters reopened the gash. They didn't know Galen. They didn't care about Simon's Rock. They could never understand what had been lost.

I climbed out of the van and pushed past the microphones and cameras, head down, looking for Mom, wanting that hug. When she hugged me, I felt that intrinsic comfort of *Mom*. I was able to breathe finally, for what felt like the first time since the shooting. We were jostled in the pandemonium of the parking lot, where students and parents were crying, and journalists were mostly getting snubbed. Nobody seemed to know what was supposed to happen next.

We were allowed back onto campus. Craig backed my car up outside of Kendrick. He took a crate out of my hands to load it for me.

"You got in an accident, huh?" he said, his voice gentler than normal.

I looked at him blankly, having totally forgotten that I'd knocked out my headlight and gotten a shoddy repair job at the cheapest place in town.

"I'm sorry," I said, panicked I was in trouble. "I got it fixed."

"It's okay, Sarah. Don't worry about it. We're just glad you're okay."

I stood frozen, relieved and stunned. It was probably the nicest thing he'd ever said out loud to me. He had always been there in my life, but I had never felt close to him or had any sense that he saw me as his daughter. Now it hit me: he loved me and would have been sad if I had died. The thought had never occurred to me before. I needed love just then, and I was grateful for his kindness. But I was still so loyal to my dad that I couldn't really let Craig's caring touch me. And it didn't change the fact that my father hadn't called.

As soon as we got home, I wanted to be back at school. I was obsessed with the news coverage and made Mom buy the *Boston Globe* every day. I spread it on the floor in front of the wood stove, craving the fire's comfort, and looked at the picture of Wayne Lo in a Sick of It All T-shirt and handcuffs. In that moment, I wanted him to die. I read partway through the first headline, and then my tears became too thick for me to read anymore.

The story that was unfolding was damning and terrible. Wayne had received ammunition in the mail the day of the shooting. The package had been noticed in the mailroom because the return address belonged to a gun dealer. Wayne had a reputation on campus for being intolerant and hostile. This was clearly troubling, and the dean was called. Apparently, after some administrative discussions and concerns that it would be illegal to tamper with the mail, Wayne was allowed to pick up his package. An RD went to his dorm room, but Wayne wouldn't open the package in front of her. Quoting the school procedures catalog and claiming they needed two RDs to search his room, he wouldn't let her proceed further. Wayne apparently also spoke to the dean about the package; he showed him an empty ammo case and some gun parts, and he claimed it was a Christmas present for his dad. Then Wayne took a cab to a nearby town, used his Montana ID to prove he was eighteen, and walked out of the store with an SKS assault rifle. He brought the gun back to his room and modified it to take more of the hundreds of rounds of ammunition he'd received in the mail that day. During this time, one of Wayne's friends called in an anonymous tip saying Wayne had a gun and had said he was going to shoot the Kendrick RDs. Instead of intervening with Wayne immediately, the school let him attend a dorm meeting I'd been at, as had Galen. Wayne was then allowed to go back to his room, unsupervised. Meanwhile, the other adults in charge helped the Kendrick RDs evacuate with their small children, which was why, when Wayne started shooting, there were no adults in our dorm.

Galen's funeral was impossible, but at least it was comforting to be around his family and my Simon's Rock friends, who I was certain were the only ones who would ever understand. Then, it was back home to Maine and the real grief descended.

My dad and I spoke around the holidays, but he didn't get it: what had happened or what it meant. He hadn't been paying attention to how much I'd loved Simon's Rock. I wanted him to do something to make me feel safe. He did not. He didn't ask about the shooting, and when I brought it up, he barely seemed to register what I was saying. I felt the opposite of what I had with Craig, as if my dad would not have cared if I'd been shot and killed, as if he didn't love me. He said he would visit me during my vacation, but I didn't really believe him, and—true to form—he didn't follow through.

I was desperate to get back to school and be with my friends. But I was afraid to be back on campus. I couldn't imagine driving past the guard shack, going into the library where Galen's body had fallen, seeing bullet holes inside Kendrick.

The RAs returned early to attend a two-day crisis management training led by a woman who was brought in when airplanes crashed. We were given a fat manual written by the National Organization for

Victim Assistance with the title "Managing the Trauma of Crisis." As far as we were concerned, it was total bullshit.

It felt spooky to be on campus, and being one of the only people in Kendrick that night felt like sleeping on a ghost ship. I locked my door but knew that wouldn't deter phantoms. I had dreamed about Galen right after he died, and I wanted him to come back, but I was also afraid. My new room looked out over the dining hall. I lay awake, feeling like the scene of Wayne surrendering was playing on an endless loop outside the window.

Wayne's trial lasted a month. His lawyers claimed several different psychological explanations, including that he'd been suffering from paranoid schizophrenia, pointing to passages from Revelations he'd copied out and hung on his wall. It was hard to picture this happening in my dorm, impossible to imagine a scenario in which one of my fellow students behaved like this. I wondered for a moment whether he was, in fact, crazy. But none of us could really believe it. The court-appointed psychiatrist who diagnosed him with narcissistic personality disorder seemed to have it right.

My dark secret was that as much as I hated Wayne, I also felt guilty. I knew we hadn't been nice to him. I couldn't help but feel we should have known better after we'd all absorbed so much meanness in our previous lives. We'd helped to create the monster in our midst. But we didn't deserve to die for this. I'd been raised by liberal parents and was vocal about my liberal beliefs, but they ended with Wayne. When he was sentenced to life in prison with no possibility of parole, I was deeply relieved. I didn't care if he could be rehabilitated; I didn't want him to have the opportunity to enjoy his life.

In the wake of the shooting, things got dark. The boys in the freshman class turned to cough syrup. These weren't the happy hallucinations of our freshman-year cavorts in the Labyrinth. One of my guy friends bumped against a corner in the student union, again and again, like a windup toy that had lost its way. We tried to round him up before he got busted. My kids needed me more than ever, but I had less and less to give.

I started drinking again. My favorite destination was an upper-classman's off-campus house, where Beth and Claire and our friends snuck away to get drunk. When I had tried to be good, it had all gone bad, so why even try?

As spring dawned, Matt shaved his eyebrows, an outward signal that he was having a hard time coping. He went home at spring break, and it was unclear whether or not he would return. He'd repeatedly asked me to move to Tennessee and marry him, even though I'd just laughed and said I couldn't get married at seventeen. I felt incredibly guilty that I couldn't give him even a little bit of everything he wanted from me.

None of us had words for what we needed, or the pain we felt, and so we drank, and we rubbed one another raw with our frustrations, our crushes, our competitions, our need to always, always, always be together, and our irritation that none of it was helping.

Graduation day arrived. Due to the enormity of our loss that year, Senator Ted Kennedy had agreed to speak. The Secret Service men scattered throughout campus gave everything a strange, dark vibe that didn't seem entirely at odds with the mood that lurked beneath the festive graduation ceremony. Grammy came, with Mom and Craig and Andrew. My dad didn't even send a card.

Craig once again backed my car up to the bridge that led to Kendrick. It was all over. The best place I'd ever experienced was also the place where the worst thing I'd ever experienced had happened. I couldn't imagine how anyplace else could compare. But I'd decided to transfer to Bard for my final two years and was eager for a new start.

A summer at home in Maine certainly wasn't going to be the answer. Nothing had any flavor or color. I worked as many shifts as

I could pick up at the Anchor Inn and got myself down to Portland as much as I could, but even that seemed flat and dull now. I didn't just want something to happen. I wanted the same thrill I'd found at Simon's Rock: the inflamed conversations and hours of perpetual motion jokes it was possible to have with truly brilliant, weird, damaged people, my people.

I was at least grateful for the relative lack of tension around the house, especially compared to the previous summer. Mom and Craig had both been supportive and kind in the aftermath of the shooting, which I appreciated. Even more than that, my mom especially got all that had been lost, not just the lives but also the miracle of this oasis we had found. I was still fiercely independent and always eager to run off to the next adventure, and with Andrew still only seven, I continued to feel that the three of them formed a complete family without me. But after the year I'd had, a part of me just wanted to stay at home forever, where it was safe. And so I was glad for these few months when I didn't have any choice but to be there, during which the impending unknown was momentarily delayed.

By the time I drove down to Bard at the end of the summer, I was cautiously optimistic. Through a paperwork snafu, Bard had assigned me a Simon's Rock friend, Beth, as a roommate. Maybe I actually could have broader creative horizons in a new place that wasn't shadowed by the shooting, but with friends who understood what I'd been through. I felt good about this new stage of my life. That lasted for about a day.

I was entering my junior year of college as a seventeen-year-old kid who had survived a school shooting nine months earlier and had received only the most cursory counseling for that trauma. I mostly dealt by smoking as many cigarettes as I could in a day and drinking as much as possible at night. The school was populated with brilliant, artistic kids, many of whom would have been a lot cooler if they hadn't been obsessed with acting like we were living in the East Village.

Leaving my room always felt fraught. I was shy. My skin was bad. I didn't feel like my clothes or my comebacks were right. I didn't want to care, but I did. When I crossed the quad, I felt self-conscious, and I hurried with my head down, smoking, trying to act hard even though I felt anything but. I still adored conversation as much as ever, the joy of landing the perfect zinging remark, and I sometimes rallied and stormed the talk at a meal or party, loving how everyone laughed and got stirred up by an idea I threw out. But, like the revelry of a perfect buzz, I could only keep it up for so long.

My real savior at Bard was my classes. My fall semester writing class was with a New Yorker named Peter Sourian. He took a shine to my writing and me, and this small kindness was a lifeline. He always started each workshop by reading the day's story because he believed it was helpful for us to hear our work read aloud by someone else. The first time I was critiqued, he was a few lines into my story when he paused.

"You were read to a lot as a child, weren't you?" he said.

"Yeah," I said, smiling. "Why?"

"I can tell by your love of language."

It was one of the first times I'd encountered the idea of "being a writer" as an inherent talent made up of qualities I might naturally possess or be able to cultivate.

Sitting at one of the round polished tables in the arts building, the autumn leaves shaking free of the trees outside as we discussed fiction and literature, I was happy.

When we returned to school after the Christmas holidays, Beth and I moved into an insanely great room in Manor House. It had a small antechamber in which we kept our desks, and a short door that led out to a turreted balcony overlooking a vast field, the river somewhere down below. It felt full of possibility, and I loved the room deeply.

Not long into the semester, Claire showed up. She and her boyfriend had just split. She was already breakup skinny, and she seemed to get smaller even though we smuggled her peanut-butter-and-jelly sandwiches out of the dining hall several times a day. For the next few weeks, she slept on the narrow space of floor in between our twin beds. Eventually, she got a job near campus and moved in with a Simon's Rock friend.

Despite her troubles, Claire was still my source for much that was cool. She made me mix tapes featuring riot grrrl bands like Bikini Kill and Bratmobile. She was the person who made me a tape of Liz Phair's *Exile in Guyville*, which was like my journal but witty and badass. That year she gave me another gray Memorex tape, marked with a band's name and album title, but no song listings; another installment in our ongoing attempt to understand love. It was the tale of a relationship coming apart, confessional and dark and sexy. The male singer's tone was deep and knowing and said as much as his lyrics. I was smitten and listened to the tape again and again, his voice leaking into my bloodstream, his words admitting to dark secrets of the male psyche I'd first gotten a glimpse of through my dad. It was a relief to hear them spoken out loud.

I had become deeply obsessed with Courtney Love and her husband, Kurt Cobain, and the music of Hole and Nirvana, as well as their whole aesthetic and philosophy and love story. I collected every article, photo, musical recording. I dreamed about them, loved them. I was in our room in Manor in early April when I heard Kurt Cobain's body had been found with a shotgun nearby. Kurt was one of the matchless ones. He was just like us, but he was also so much better than us. He was that rare doting dad, that courageous artist who'd made something beautiful from darkness. He was exceptional, too exceptional in the end. And now he'd left me, too.

My own dad had started writing to me again. But for once, his letters fell flat. He still didn't ever really acknowledge the shooting. His incessant desire to make plans with me without any specific follow-through was beginning to wear thin. In the past, there had been moments when he had paused long enough, in his letters, or on the phone, to ask me how I was. Those moments were fewer and farther between now. After everything that had happened since our fight in the parking lot, it was hard to imagine catching up.

For my senior year, Beth and another Simon's Rock friend, Sarjan, and I moved off campus, into an old farmhouse. Oliver resurfaced, and we had long calls on the house phone, which I cradled against my neck while I sat at the kitchen table, drinking and chain-smoking. I lived on cigarettes and gin, resolute in my avoidance of all fat and most food. All I wanted was to be skinny and in control, and as my hip bones jutted through the fabric of my favorite striped dress, I had a clean, strong feeling.

One night when I was tipsy on the phone with a very drunk Oliver, he surprised me. "You should come see me," he said.

"Okay," I said.

I was eighteen. I had my own car. He was only a few hours away. We had been declaring our love to each other, and then not talking, and then talking again, for three years at that point. Beth did not want me to go.

"I have to go," I told her. "I have to see what happens."

She was, reasonably, afraid that he was going to hurt me, literally or figuratively. He had told me about once pushing a girlfriend in front of a car. It was unclear whether this was true or not, but either way, he had said it. He was also the man who had gotten me through my last horrible year of high school, who had listened to me for hours when I felt like no one else would, who had given me hope that there was life beyond my limited horizons. As I got into my car, Beth stood in the driveway with me.

"I can be there in four hours," she said. "Call me. Call me."

"I'll be fine, Beth."

I smoked and smoked and smoked on the drive down. The slightly run-down house I pulled up in front of looked like as if it had been ground down by generation after generation of careless students drunk on cheap beer.

My meeting with Oliver was instantly weird; not bad, but not familiar the way I had expected it to be. He seemed smaller than I'd anticipated, not shorter exactly, but regular size after my immense imaginings. In my letters I'd been able to ask him to come down to my level, to reassure me about his intentions, to make me feel valued and not at all like the silly stupid girl I always feared I was. In person, I was too scared to ask. I wanted to draw close, but I didn't dare. He stared at me, not giving anything away. We didn't know where to look, what to say, where to sit.

"Let me give you a tour," he said. "We can stop at the liquor store."

He drove me around his town in his car, pointing out the places that felt tender and familiar to me because they had been featured in so many letters and phone calls. The tour was a good idea, something for us to do, somewhere for us to look. He stopped at the liquor store and emerged with a bottle of his favorite whiskey, Canadian Club. We went back to his house and got drunk. Fast. The more I drank, the more I wanted to be close to him, and the more frustrated and hurt I became when nothing physical happened. I knew it was something disappointing about me. He'd told me how he'd longed for this, but here I was, and he didn't want me. Finally, he came for me on the couch. We kissed. And kissed. He pulled at my dress.

"How'd you get so skinny?" he asked.

After years of worrying he wouldn't think I was pretty enough if we ever met, I took this as a compliment. I was happy. Until I woke up in the morning—my head, and the sun, and the air crashing down on me—and I realized we hadn't had sex. We hadn't made any tender declarations of love. He had rejected me, after all. He wasn't touching me or even looking at me. He was totally closed down. "Oliver?" I said, unsure what to ask.

"You should go."

I sat up as if he had slapped me, and was already moving away. It felt as if spikes were being driven into my head, and my heart hurt just as badly. He was sending me away almost as quickly as I'd arrived.

I staggered up, trying to get out of there before I started to cry. No matter what, I thought, I couldn't let him see me cry. Oliver sat on the steps of his porch and watched me drive away, a not particularly friendly look on his face.

I was sick with hangover and disappointment and shame on my four-hour drive back to Tivoli. I chain-smoked, listened to Hole, and held on to my steering wheel as if it could hold me together. Beth was at the house waiting for me, as she was there for me every day that year, a life raft of comfort in a world I found increasingly inclement. Oliver and I never really spoke about what had happened. I was too embarrassed to admit I'd wanted more, and even though I still loved him, it no longer felt safe to do so.

That fall we started our senior year. On the one hand Beth, Sarjan, and I couldn't have asked for more. We were three close friends living in our first apartment, and we spent hours sitting in the kitchen, talking, smoking, drinking coffee, weaving a web of comfort around ourselves after hard days on campus and as we questioned what to do next. On the other hand, we never really found a way to fit in at Bard, which wasn't giving us much confidence about life postgraduation. In the spring, I'd be a nineteen-year-old college graduate. The great big world I'd been in such a rush to go out and meet suddenly bore down on me.

But I had one sure thing onto which I could pin all of my hopes and dreams, and which felt like a lance against my deepest fears and insecurities. Every year the school, which was known for its writing program, chose the most promising writing student entering the senior class. The award was named for the school's most famous former teacher: Mary McCarthy. The previous year, I'd been chosen. At first I hadn't believed it. But then I'd felt as if a sunbeam were lighting me up from inside. My time at Bard had not been easy for me. My drinking and bad romantic judgment had crested one night at a party, when I'd climbed into bed with my latest obsession and he'd purposely burned me with a cigarette. Afterward, Beth gave me some tough love: "You're lucky you're a girl. If you were a guy, the shit you do would be scary."

I knew what she meant. And she was right: I was not feeling in any way strong or clear. But I had poured everything into my writing, and my teachers had recognized this. I was on the right path.

chapter eight

ANYWHERE BUT THERE

My dad began sending me a flurry of letters, always setting the groundwork for an upcoming visit that never came. He continued to move forward, no thought spared for his past behavior or the possibility it could have affected me. I was fed up as I read his latest card.

"Fuck him," I said, lying on Sarjan's bed. "I'm so tired of all of his bullshit about his gambling and his back and all of his problems. It's all he ever talks about." I felt myself moving into a stage of my life where I knew for sure that I existed without my dad. It was unsettling, but also a relief.

Although the power dynamic had shifted slightly, it wasn't enough to change the pattern of our relationship. I still diligently wrote him back, earnestly responding to every plan he suggested, telling him which bus station was near my apartment, and when I would be on break. Everything seemed without consequence anyhow. Nothing that I wrote or said made him get on a bus and come see me.

Oliver drifted in and out of my life. Now that I'd met him, and our connection hadn't bloomed into whatever I'd thought it might be, the yo-yoing felt like a definite rejection and caused me more pain than ever. When Beth was home, she kept an eye on me, sometimes checking on me from her window, which because of the way the house was gabled looked into my room. She took the paring knife out of my hand the night I carved Oliver's initials in my ankle, trying to release a little of the impossible pain within me with a manageable physical pain. When she saw that I had passed out with candles burning in my room, she came in and blew them out so I didn't burn the house down.

Claire had settled in New Orleans and was living alone in a studio apartment in the French Quarter, and Beth and I decided to visit her for Mardi Gras. Lulled by an enjoyable reunion I'd had with Matt over New Year's, I'd agreed to let him come meet us in New Orleans, even though he and Claire maintained an uneasy friction in the best of times, and were bound to get on each other's nerves with all of us crammed into her apartment.

On the first night, he and I snuck out of Claire's apartment, went down to the enclosed courtyard of her building, and had sweet, familiar sex against a wall. After the social stress of Bard, it was so nice to be around his constant good-natured affection. And then, without reason, he confessed that he'd been fucking that girl Maxine while we were dating, and many of our classmates had known and assumed I had, too. I'd believed him when he'd said he loved me, when he'd asked me to move to Tennessee and marry him. I pushed away from him, sick with disgust and shame at letting myself get played like that. He'd made a fool out of me, despite how loving he'd always been toward me. No one could be trusted.

"Go," I said, backing across the courtyard. "I don't want to see you right now."

"But, Sarah," he pleaded.

I could excuse so much, forgive nearly to infinity, let a man storm my castle even when it was clear I shouldn't, but once I pulled up the drawbridge, it was done. I understood why he'd slept with Maxine. I had been aloof and sometimes mean, and she'd doted on him and made him feel valued and seen. I could forgive him for that. I couldn't forgive him for betraying me so publicly while privately—and relentlessly—declaring his love and devotion to me.

When he was gone, I sat stunned, smoking on the balcony overlooking the glittery Mardi Gras parade floating down the street outside Claire's apartment. I started drinking. It became one of those drunk nights where everything felt sparkly and possible. The Rebirth Brass Band was playing their usual Preservation Hall show. The music was fierce and good and free. We danced, and it was everything we'd wanted the adventure to be. Partway through the sweaty set, Claire and I ducked outside and sat down on the sidewalk. There was a way we could talk together, our minds meeting with a feral hunger for information and experience. We both understood each other intrinsically, and it felt good to have a moment alone together even as everything was changing.

"I can't believe I'm graduating," I said. "I have no idea what I'm going to do." In less than three months I would graduate from college with a creative writing degree, and it was beginning to dawn on me that the world at large didn't give a fuck about my Mary McCarthy Prize.

"We should move somewhere," Claire said.

"Where?"

"I don't know. Maybe Portland, Oregon."

"Okay," I said before I had time to get scared or doubt that we could do it.

We shook hands, and it was decided. When I graduated in May, we were going to move to the other side of the country, to a place I had never been, and build a life that I couldn't imagine yet. But that didn't matter. I had a plan. With my best friend. I felt a huge weight shift, not off me entirely, but it wasn't so heavy anymore.

Much of my extended family came to graduation. We had a big dinner. It was wonderful, being acknowledged for how hard I'd worked.

More than that, the madcap dream Mom and I had embarked on in the name of my sanity had actually paid off, even with the shooting, even with the darker moments my family didn't know about.

My father, again, did not attend, and he did not send a card. His letters always promised our reunion would happen, always in some future that was constantly being pushed back. I had too much pride, and enough of Mom's natural Protestant reserve, to keep me from just showing up on his doorstep, no matter how much I wanted him. Now, though, I wanted him less than ever before. Having everyone fuss over my graduation threw into stark contrast how incapable he was of even the most basic manners, let alone real affection or genuine closeness. It hurt. But I was also beginning to see him as the Boy Who Cried Wolf—the Dad Who Promised to Visit—and like those villagers, I no longer believed.

I went home to Maine to finalize what I would bring with me cross-country, and to say good-bye to my family. On the morning I prepared to leave, Craig came out to the driveway and stared into my car. "Where's Claire going to put her stuff?" he asked.

"In there," I said, pointing, even though there wasn't much visible space.

Craig started pulling shoes out. "Do you really need so many shoes?"

I shrugged, glad for his attention and assistance, but trying to act like I didn't need either on the eve of the big adventure I'd longed for, always.

Finally, it was time to say good-bye to Mom. I was nineteen years old, I had saved just shy of three thousand dollars, and I was setting out on a cross-country drive in the time before cell phones. She was remarkably Zen about the whole thing. I'd recently begun to appreciate all of the values Mom and I shared: how she'd ridden a bus down to join me freshman year when I'd marched on Washington in support of reproductive rights, how she took me to see movies that mattered to me—*Howards End* and *The Crying Game*—and read the same books—

The Secret History—which we loved to talk about. I knew I'd miss her, as much I also knew I needed to go.

She always really shone when it came to special-occasion gifts and cards, and she had given me a beautiful ring when I graduated from Bard, along with a letter. It said that while she sometimes wished I had slowed down and enjoyed myself more instead of always rushing to grow up, I had turned out so well that it had obviously been for the best. She said she didn't worry about me because she could tell I had a good head on my shoulders, but if she could give me one piece of advice it was this: "Beware of needy men. They will only bring you down." I loved receiving the letter, loved being spoken to like the adult I was desperate to be, and valued the feeling of closeness between us.

Now I was going far away, and I didn't know when I'd see her again, probably not until Christmas. I had to go, but I felt the same way as I had when I'd left for Simon's Rock; a part of me wanted to stay small and live there with her forever. She hugged me. I started to cry. "I love you, Mom," I said.

"I love you, too, Sarah," she said. "Be careful out there. Call us."

"I will."

She walked me to the door, and as I got into my car, she waved to me from the doorway of my childhood home, the home we had built with our own hands, the home we were going to live in forever.

Claire and I were driving, driving, driving. We had decided we would stop in all of the cities that interested us on the northern route to the West Coast and move to whichever city we liked the most. It was amazing to me that all of this had always been out there, waiting to be seen, and I had never even known to want it. Now I was going to go everywhere, meet everyone, try everything. First up: Toronto. We could have easily stayed in Toronto forever, but we didn't think we'd be allowed to just move to Canada. So we kept on to Chicago, where things got real.

Claire and I had developed a method for traveling in which we took turns being the one in charge. It was exhausting and demoralizing to have to ask for directions, and to always feel like the loser who didn't know how anything worked. In Chicago, it was thankfully my day off. She got us to the Art Institute of Chicago. Sitting in the coffee shop after perusing the exhibits, she said something about art that miffed me because, as usual, it felt like she was implying she knew more than I did. Even though she was probably right, and I almost never talked back to her, this time it was too much. I accused her and her family of being snobs. She, understandably, didn't take this well. We sat staring at each other in silence. Thousands of miles from home. Thousands of miles from where we were going, not that we even knew where that was. With a person whom, in that moment, I didn't like, and who didn't like me. We both had very strong personalities, but because I was so good at being the loyal listener, we normally fit together well. Now, suddenly, we didn't seem to fit together at all. I had never felt so alone. There was no choice but to keep going. We got up, not looking at each other, and resumed our trip.

By the time Chicago was safely in our rearview mirror, our rift was repaired, but emotional turmoil always simmered below the surface of our friendship. Although my mom usually stayed out of such things, she once—after reading an article on the subject—told me she thought Claire and I had a toxic friendship. Sometimes Claire seemed impossible to please, and I'm sure she felt some version of this about me, too. We were like each other's best worst boyfriends, ever.

We pulled into Seattle, which loomed large for me because of Kurt and Courtney, but we weren't quite sure. We drove down to Olympia, which Claire was big on because of Kathleen Hanna, but still, we weren't sure. We drove further to Portland, which seemed a little more manageable but had a few drawbacks. It was small, and we quickly dubbed our new lodging the hostile hostel. We skulked across the street to the Safeway and bought cigarettes and the Gummi Savers Claire ate the way I smoked. In a nearby park, we wrote a list with the headings "Portland" and "Seattle" and the pros and cons of each city. The main distinction was that Portland had more all-ages venues and hangouts, which would impact our social life, since I was only nineteen and Claire twenty.

"I guess we're moving to Portland," Claire said.

"I guess so."

We found an apartment in a West Coast–style structure, the kind of low-slung two-story apartment building that resembled a cheap motel, which was all new for a couple of East Coast girls like us. New was good. We were into new. After we paid our security deposit, broker's fee, and first and last months' rent, neither of us had the money to pay the next month's rent. The building manager took a shine to me and gave us pans, dish soap, and paper towels, but we needed jobs, soon. I walked the neighborhood, applying for restaurant work, and Claire hit up the city's many coffee shops. We pooled our money for groceries. For breakfast and lunch, we had peanut-butter-and-jelly sandwiches. For dinner we had store-brand pasta with jarred tomato sauce. To drink, we had either milk because it was nutritious, or Kool-Aid because it was cheap. We sat in our apartment for hours, Claire painting her nails bright pink, me sitting on the linoleum kitchen floor smoking, blowing my smoke out through the screen door. I could tell that she was sometimes frustrated with my morose, melodramatic jags. Scouring the city's alternative paper, the *Willamette Week*, she found possible adventures. She got us out to a screening of *Repulsion*, an art performance by Miranda July, and a gig by the band whose singer, Judah, I'd had a crush on since Claire had gifted me his definitive album at Bard. I was scared about money and my writing and wanted to stay home and get drunk, which just made me withdrawn and sad. But Claire was prone to her own jagged mood swings, so she never called me out.

Upon arriving on the West Coast, I had become obsessed with the Modern Lovers Greatest Hits album. When I felt overwhelmed, I drove over the Hawthorne Bridge, into downtown Portland, and back over the Burnside Bridge, again and again and again, my windows down, smoking, listening to the song that perfectly captured that moment: "I go to bakeries all day long, there's a lack of sweetness in my life."

The longing in Jonathan Richman's voice felt like a magnet that gathered up all of the metal filings in my heart: the homesickness, and free-floating nostalgia and grief over what I had chosen to leave behind, and the longing for something new and better, and the worry that maybe I didn't really belong on the East Coast anymore, and maybe I didn't belong out West either, which meant I didn't belong anywhere I'd found.

I got called in for an interview at a Caribbean restaurant, Sweetwater's Jam House, which had opened in an old hamburger joint in Northeast Portland. They assigned me shifts on the spot and sent me home with a container of delicious red beans and rice, simmered with cinnamon sticks and coconut milk, which Claire and I devoured as a welcome diversion from our usual fare. Claire was simultaneously hired at a local coffee chain, Kobos, and she was soon bringing home day-old pastries, which seemed incredibly decadent after our stripped-down diet, and fresh juices, which probably kept us from getting scurvy.

In my journal I looped back again and again to anything that might give me an excuse to return to the East Coast. Meanwhile, there was no way I was going back because that would have meant failure, and failure was absolutely not an option.

When I went home at Christmas that year, I visited friends in New York City and made plans to see Betty. She was still the same madcap city girl she'd always been—her hair just as dark and sleek, her lips just as bright red, wearing a jaunty velvet hat and leopard-print blouse. And yet time was creeping onward. She'd had her lids lifted a few years back, but her eyes seemed less bright, sometimes confused. She walked slowly and had difficulty catching her breath after decades of smoking. It was hard to watch her stop in the midst of a busy sidewalk in Manhattan and let the crowds break around her, whereas before she would have had a rude quip for anyone who jostled her. But she still loved New York City, the city she had come to sixty years earlier as an eighteen-year-old orphan with dreams of turning her beauty into a glamorous, posh life. Even with all of the difficulties she had faced, she didn't resent the city for the more difficult path it had unfolded for her and showed the remarkable adaptability that marks a true urban dweller.

Since retiring, she'd gotten her exclusive address on West End Avenue by moving into a city-run social services program that paired senior women with unwed mothers. She had regular meals, scheduled events and outings, and a social worker. And she was only a few blocks from her daughter, Mimi, who had managed to hold on to her rent-stabilized prewar apartment on West End Avenue for twenty years. I had never met Mimi before, but Betty had arranged for us to have lunch.

I picked Betty up and we shuffled slowly down to Mimi's block. As we reached the building, the doorman stepped forward to let us in, recognizing Betty. She acknowledged him, not so much with friendly familiarity but as if he were her regular porter at the Ritz, where she'd been living en suite for decades.

We took the elevator up to the eighth floor. It was small and slow and rickety, and I felt nervous as it rose, mostly because I was well aware of the colossal force of nature that was Auntie Mimi. She had always sent me affectionate cards and small gifts, but I knew she and my father had been estranged for years. He called her a gold digger and claimed he kept his distance to avoid her manipulation. Betty was extremely proud of Mimi's beauty, sending me pictures: Mimi had a fine, striking bone structure and the fabulous blond hair of a Prell model. And yet one of the highest compliments Betty gave Mimi was: "She has a lot of nice antiques. You should get on her good side."

I let Betty lead the way, very slowly, down the hall to Mimi's apartment, where we were to rendezvous for lunch. When we reached the door, Betty knocked. There was no answer, no movement behind the door. Betty knocked again. Still no answer.

"Mimi, open the door. It's Betty. Sarah is with me. And we want lunch."

Betty's voice was loud and nonmelodious. It carried. I slunk into myself, teenage style, glancing around me at the other doors in the narrow hallway of what had clearly become a very affluent building. Betty knocked again and again. Then, to my horror, she turned and knocked on one of the other doors in the hallway. The woman who answered was well put together even in her house clothes. Her smile was strained.

"Hello, Elizabeth," she said. "Are you here to see Millicent?"

"Yes, we're supposed to have lunch. This is my granddaughter, Sarah. Isn't she tall? She's visiting me from Portland. She went to Bard, and she's a writer. We were supposed to meet Mimi here at one, but now she isn't answering her door."

"I'm sorry, but I haven't seen her today," the woman said.

"Can we use your phone?" Betty asked.

"Of course, Elizabeth," the woman said, stepping back to let us enter.

We moved through her tasteful, impeccably decorated apartment with its end tables and accent mirrors and walls and walls of books and entered the living room. Betty sat down in a chair near the telephone, and the woman and I sat on the couch.

"She's a psychologist," Betty said, pointing to the woman. "She went to Columbia. Her husband's a lawyer."

I nodded politely, feeling like I was objectifying the woman, because I knew Betty's observations were really pointing out how well Mimi had done for herself to end up with such upscale neighbors. I appreciated the woman's kindness now, and in the many moments when she had clearly been drawn into helping Betty and Mimi with their domestic dramas, reluctantly I was sure. But I was embarrassed. Eventually, Betty gave up on Mimi, and she and I went to lunch alone.

"Mimi must have forgotten," Betty said.

"Yes, she must have," I said.

I didn't know why Mimi hadn't been able to handle a simple lunch with her mother and niece, any more than I knew why my dad hadn't been able to handle so many moments with his daughter over the years. But if that's how Betty wanted to play it, that's how I would let it be played. Mimi had forgotten about our lunch, the end.

Betty smiled at me.

"After lunch, we'll go to Macy's. You should wear more makeup. And comb your hair. Do you have a comb in your purse? You should always keep a comb in your purse."

"Yes, Betty."

That afternoon, Betty rammed her way through Macy's, literally pushing men and telling them to get out of her way as I slunk along behind her, and mortifying me by talking at great length about my bad skin with a woman at the cosmetic counter. I did the trick I'd mastered of pulling up inside myself. As much as I thrilled at the department-store glamour and her extreme generosity, being there with her didn't feel good. But it was the closest thing I had to being with my dad, and that still meant more to me than I would have cared to admit.

That March, Claire came into the kitchen one night. She had an expressive body and face that magnified every emotion to the nth degree and radiated it with intensity. Right now, she looked unhappy and resigned, as if she had to take out the trash.

"I can't do this anymore," she said.

"Do what?" I asked, looking up from my journal.

"This," she said, nodding her head around our apartment. "I can't live like this anymore," she continued. "You're so unhappy. And I can't be around it anymore."

I was too embarrassed to look at her. But I also knew how hard that must have been, so I forced myself to meet her gaze and nodded. "What do you want to do?"

"I found a place," she said. "I move out at the end of the month."

"Okay," I said.

I was totally freaked out, but simultaneously relieved. As long as I lived with Claire, I was bound to the promise we'd made each other on that long-ago night in New Orleans. But now that she was moving out, I was free. I just had to figure out what that meant.

chapter nine

MY FAVORITE PART OF THE DAY

I asked around at the health food store where I worked and found an open room. The spacious three-bedroom apartment had a big sunny kitchen and a giant claw-foot tub, and was decorated with vintage furniture and art: everything in late-sixties bright green and orange, accented with house plants, and prints of those freaky kids with the big eyes. I could feel that something was happening here, a life full of energy and creativity and humor, but all expressed in a way that was totally foreign to me, and I wanted to join.

My new house mom, Shelly, was an older badass bass player from Seattle who drove a banged-up late-sixties Chevy Nova with a baseball bat under the seat for when guys disrespected her. She became like my mentor from some kind of punk-rock Big Sisters program. Her boyfriend, Bryan, was a young, angel-faced drummer who had just moved to the city from the suburbs. Needless to say, within a few months I owned my first pair of black vinyl pants. I did lights at their shows, which I got into with a fake ID

I'd acquired from a friend. My world was being opened up inch by inch, and I couldn't get enough.

Shelly worked at the coffee shop in the little slice of heaven known as Powell's Books. She trawled the Asian markets and cooked up big pans of vegetarian curry, which she was kind enough to feed me when we happened to be home together.

Shelly and Bryan took me out the first night I used my fake ID at a club called EJ's to see the Weaklings and BlackJack, a band known for playing a blistering twenty-one songs in twenty-one minutes. And they were there for my first minor romantic disappointments in my new city—the few dates and kisses that went nowhere.

No matter that I hadn't really connected with any of these men; their departure made me feel abandoned and at fault. I felt worthless and low. Although I had gotten myself out of my small town, found my life's work as a writer, graduated college, and gone to meet the great wide world, none of my accomplishments touched the deep lack my dad had created within me, or altered the way it played out with men. It was almost as if I craved these rejections as proof of the failings I knew to be true of myself.

The other bedroom in our apartment was vacant, and a coworker, Raina, expressed interest. We decided that she would come see the room one night, and then we'd go out for drinks. When she knocked, I was still getting ready, and I threw a ballet sweater on and ran downstairs. When the door swung open, I was surprised to see that above Raina's fire-engine-red hair, dramatically penciled-in eyebrows, and bright red lipstick was a tall, lanky guy with a shaved head wearing a Bill the Cat muscle shirt. I showed Raina and Scott the room. Then we had beers on the front porch, and I noticed that Scott had the kind of understated confidence that made me want to lean in closer to hear what he would say next, which usually proved to be something sarcastic and clever. I came out to find them talking close, but I couldn't exactly tell whether they were together or not. I let it go. We drank a bunch and went to the club Satyricon for more, and at night's end, Scott and Raina folded me, very drunk, into a cab.

I was often scared, and down, and out of sorts. But I felt more committed than ever to my new life in Portland. I got a tattoo as a testament to this moment in my life when I could feel the decisions I'd made shaping the path I was on, even if I had no idea where it would take me. I didn't mind the needle as it inked my bicep, feeling in its burn a promise to myself that I would stay the course, figure out how to live and write, and when I did go home, I would be changed and new.

My tattoo was just beginning to scab and flake in thin, black strips when Raina and I went to EJ's after work to see Scott's band. Raina fit right in, with her black stretch jeans and bondage belt, and when the guys in the band saw her, they called out to her with affectionate jibes. Scott looked elegant, his long spider legs splayed in his black stretch jeans as he rang out guitar solos and shouted backing vocals while the band snarled through a taut set of old-school punk. He was cuter than I'd remembered, but I was Raina's friend, and she was there to see him. I lurked by the bar, drinking Bud. When it was time to go, Raina was suddenly nowhere in sight, and I somehow found myself standing on the sidewalk alone with Scott. Once again, I felt drawn toward him, not so much as the result of a specific physical attraction, which was there, too, but as if our frequencies matched.

"It was good to see you again," I said, sticking my hand out dumbly.

"Likewise," he said, taking my hand, not releasing it.

We stood there for a long minute, just looking at each other, our hands joined, not holding hands exactly, but not letting go, either.

"There's a party next door tomorrow night," he said. "You should come."

"Okay," I said. "I'll ask Raina."

But I knew the invitation was for me in particular, and I felt happy and smiled at him with new significance. We looked at our hands and laughed, stepping back.

"All right, I gotta load out," he said. "See you tomorrow?"

I nodded, and he smiled at me. His eyes were very blue. I smiled back.

The next night I finished my shift at the café where Raina and I worked, feeling like I was covered in a sheen of oil, and I carefully powdered my nose and reapplied my bright red MAC lipstick. Raina led the way on her bike over the Burnside Bridge and into downtown Portland. This was the farthest I'd ridden on my bike, a heavy vintage fixed gear Shelly and Bryan had helped me find, and I was terrified. I hated bikes after breaking my wrist on one in junior high, but I'd had to sell my car, and everyone in my new life rode bikes, so I wanted to do the same. The bus malls were nearly deserted, and it felt as if the city was all ours as we headed up the faintly inclined streets toward the Portland State University campus, where sprinklers misted the air. We turned onto a single block of houses marooned between a parking garage, the highway, and the school. Punks spilled out of a duplex and shouted in greeting when they saw Raina.

I kept my eyes to the pavement in front of me, feeling shy, and wanting desperately to avoid crashing in front of these cool kids. I couldn't get off my bike soon enough. Raina quickly got absorbed into the party on the stoop, but I lingered at its edge, looking for Scott but not admitting to myself that I was. I heard a noise from the porch next door.

"Hey, we're hanging out over here, if you wanna come over."

I looked up. Scott was sitting on the steps of a single-family house next to a cute boy with pretty doe eyes, also in stretch jeans and black creepers. They were both smoking cigarettes and drinking cans of PBR. Suddenly I didn't feel so nervous. I drifted over to his house and sat on the steps below him.

"Don't feed the animals," he said, nodding toward the party next door.

I laughed. It was a relief to see that while these were his friends, he wasn't completely ruled by punk. He could think for himself. He and Chris, who was also a musician, had the slightly grumpy rapport of the two old guys from the Muppets, and it felt comfortable to sit there with them, drinking beer and smoking.

Their friend Tony drifted over, carrying a box of cheap wine, forever earning himself the nickname Tony Box Wine. He hooked a dead plant that had been orphaned on the porch into his belt loop and did a silly dance.

"That's my cue," Chris said. "I can tell it's only gonna go downhill from here."

As Chris drove away, Scott nodded toward his front door.

"Shall we get away from the peanut gallery?" he said.

I laughed and stood to follow him inside.

Scott led me upstairs to his room, where Johnny Cash gave the finger from above his bed, and empty PBR cans littered the floor amid a casual clutter of guitar strings, paperbacks, and orphaned black Chuck Taylors. It took less than a minute for us to kiss. There was nothing cautious or awkward between us, and we kissed passionately for a long time. I was feeling absolutely dreamy when he pulled back. We both laughed. My red lipstick was smeared across his lips and chin. I wiped at the smudge of color.

"I think I might like you," he said.

"I think I might like you, too."

"I should go tell Raina. We've been hanging out, and it's nothing serious, but I want to make sure she's cool."

"Okay," I said, nervous at the thought, but liking his directness and the confidence it gave me that he could handle the situation and handle it well. He seemed to have a subtle ease in a world that had perplexed and overwhelmed me since graduation, and it made me feel both safe and curious to see what he would show me next.

We leaned close together in the bathroom mirror, Scott wiping my lipstick from his face, while I tried to clean up the lines where my bright red mouth had smudged. When we were both mostly presentable, he went next door to find Raina while I waited on his porch. A few minutes later, Scott returned and nodded me back inside.

"What did she say?" I asked.

"She said she kind of figured."

I knew what she had meant; it felt inevitable, like he and I had been moving toward each other from the first, even if I hadn't entirely been aware of it until now. We lay down on his bed, stretched out end to end, and kissed until the sun came up.

"I have my period," I said. "And I don't want to have sex anyhow."

"That's okay. We'll wait."

I liked that; we would wait, as if we were already working toward something more than a drunken fumble or a one-night stand.

When we lay still in the cool early-morning air, we stared at each other, barely able to stay awake but not wanting the night to end. I felt something new, a mix of excitement and comfort that I liked and wanted to experience again. As his eyes fluttered closed, and I could feel myself losing him to sleep, I leaned forward and kissed him again. He smiled, his eyes still closed, and kissed me back.

We had drifted off to sleep for an hour or two when I woke up suddenly. Something was falling onto my head. It happened again. Handfuls of change—dimes and nickels and pennies—were sprinkling down on us from above, thrown from one of the next-door apartment's open windows directly through Scott's open bedroom window.

"What the fuck?" Scott said, already sitting up and leaning out his window, not caring that he was naked. As his head and shoulders disappeared behind the curtains, I heard laughter coming from somewhere nearby.

"What are you guys doing?" Raina said. "Come have breakfast."

"Fuck off," Scott said, laughing. "We're sleeping."

He came back inside and brushed the change onto the floor. As he pulled me close to him, I felt again that something had already been decided, that he and I had already become a "we" in our own eyes and the minds of our friends.

"What was that?" I asked.

"Raina stayed with Chris last night. They wanted us to go have breakfast."

"Oh," I said, glad to feel less guilty about where I'd ended up, if that's how these things went. "Do they hang out?"

"They have," Scott said. "He says her tits are too small."

"Right," I said, thinking how cool Raina was, and how stupid boys were, feeling glad that maybe, just maybe, that wasn't my problem anymore, at least for a while.

Late that afternoon, Scott and I got up. He made me coffee, and I drank it black because he didn't keep milk in the house, just the staples: coffee and beer. It was nice sitting there, talking in his sunny room, where the books scattered amid the detritus of the rock lifestyle—*A Confederacy of Dunces* and *Faust*—pointed to his humor and intellect. Scott looked at his sheets and laughed. I followed his gaze and felt myself blush. My tattoo had shed. There were black flakes of skin, along with loose strands of my reddish brown hair, which was always shedding, and a red spot of menstrual blood on the sheets. He picked up a single strand of my hair. "I could make a voodoo doll," he said.

And just like that I wasn't embarrassed anymore. He was only two years older than I was—twenty-two to my twenty—but he was assured and easy around me in a way that made me feel less on guard than I normally was with guys. I liked him. I really did. More than that, I was feeling something I'd never been inspired to feel before—I was already falling in love.

We put my bike in the backseat of his car, and he drove me to my house and pulled up outside. Suddenly, I was nervous again. He kissed me and kissed me.

"I've got practice," he said. "But I'll call you later."

"Please do."

Just like that, I wasn't nervous anymore.

"How was your night?" Raina asked when I got upstairs, her tone suggestive.

"Good. Scott's cool."

"He's a pain in the ass," she said, laughing.

"Maybe," I said, not letting her kill my happy butterflies.

Scott did call that night. I wanted to see him as soon as possible, immediately even. I was sure he'd find some reason not to like me, and I felt that if I could just be with him, constantly, maybe I could distract him enough to keep this from happening.

"I'm beat," he said. "I think I'm in for the night. What about you?"

"Oh, yeah. Me, too."

I hid my disappointment, lowering my head as if against a strike, as I prepared for him to blow me off.

"Are you working tomorrow?" he asked.

"No, I'm not."

"Maybe I could come by before practice in the afternoon?"

I was overjoyed until the next afternoon arrived, when I was so nerved up I couldn't sit still. I fluttered around my room, cleaning this and tidying that, and primping long past the point where it actually made any difference in my appearance. A guy I really liked seemed to really like me, too. And he was very much in my new world, which was making me happy enough to think that, maybe, I wouldn't move back east just yet, as I'd been planning to do if things didn't look up.

I led him upstairs without making eye contact, trying to acclimate myself to his presence. I sat down on my bed, and as he sat down near me, I couldn't quite look at him. I felt as if I were being pressed under a magnifying glass, and I was sure I'd come up short. There was no way I was pretty enough, smart enough, cool enough, not to disappoint him.

"Hey, don't get all weird on me," he said.

"I'm sorry. I'm just nervous, that's all."

"Don't be nervous. It's just me."

He leaned over and kissed me. He smelled familiar, like shaving cream, and Old Gold cigarettes, and his own smell, masculine and kind. He didn't back down, but he wasn't rough. Gently, with just enough smart-ass humor, he coaxed me open, petal by petal. By the time he had to leave, we were laughing and talking like old friends.

"All right, I've got to go to practice," he said.

Instantly, it was as if the afternoon of closeness hadn't happened. My heart cracked a little. I was sure that once he was gone, he was never coming back. I wanted to keep him close, and I knew that to tell him any of this would make me seem needy and lame.

"Okay, have a good practice," I managed to squeak out.

Don't ask him to come over later. Don't ask him to come over later.

"What are you up to later?" he asked.

"I don't know. I have the night off. I might do some writing."

"I'll call you later. Maybe I can come over after practice."

And just like that, I was glad again. By the time I walked him out, I was exhausted from the constant abacus of adjusting my emotions, trying to stay one step ahead of my insecurities, but I was also ready to be happy, almost.

Scott and I started dating, and suddenly, the whole city became my family. He was a central figure in the city's small, tightly knit punk-rock scene and took me everywhere, introducing me as his girlfriend to all of his bandmates and friends. Dozens of bartenders and bouncers and strippers and musicians, and the guys and girls who hung around the scene, looked out for me, and I loved the instant feeling of belonging.

My relationship with Scott unfurled almost effortlessly. After we'd been hanging out almost every night for nearly two months, I went to see Scott play at EJ's. I'd already grown accustomed to the routines of band life. I was used to hanging around after he played until all of the bands were done, and he'd helped load out the gear into the band van before we could leave. Given my high level of anxiety, it was a relief for me that we had quickly gotten to the point where I could assume we were going home together. So, on this night, I ordered a beer as his set ended. As Scott finished loading gear, I followed him onto the sidewalk in front of the club, already looking for his car.

"Hey, Sarah, I need to talk to you for a sec," he said.

My adrenaline spiked. *This is it. He's breaking up with me. I knew it was too good to be true. I knew I'd do something stupid and scare him off.*

"That's cool," I said. "I totally get it."

I started to walk away. I knew better than to get upset or fight him on his decision. Any display of emotion on my part would only turn him off more. He grabbed my hand and pulled me into a little cubbyhole in the side of the building, leaning in close to me.

"What's up, crazy?" he said, looking down at me with a tender smile.

"You're breaking up with me, so I figured I'd find my own way home."

"What are you talking about?" he said, laughing, but not meanly.

"You said you wanted to talk to me."

"I just wanted to stay alone at my place tonight. I'm totally beat. I've been at your house every night this week, and I need to catch up on my sleep."

"Oh," I said. I was relieved, but not completely. I still had that fear that any time apart would be enough for him to realize he'd made a mistake and end it.

"Are you cool with that?"

"Of course," I said, forcing myself to rally.

"I don't have practice tomorrow night, so we can hang out after work."

Adjusting to the emotional intimacy of a relationship wasn't easy for me, and the more I liked Scott, the harder it got. I didn't know how to be, or who to be. It never occurred to me to be myself. Not that I was ever faking it exactly. It was sort of like how makeup didn't hide my freckles but made them more manageable. I was just trying to be my more manageable self.

Weirdly, Scott seemed to like everything about me. He even loved my freckles. He claimed he'd inherited this from his mom, who had a thing for his dad's freckles.

Having weathered some trauma as a kid, Scott was the kind of self-reliant person who assumed most people were jackasses, and he was better off taking care of himself. (My eleven-year-old self had finally found her kindred spirit.) But when people gave him a reason to trust them, he was incredibly loyal and fun loving.

He'd had more of everything than I'd had: more sex, more relationships—including two girlfriends he'd lived with—and more of the basic kind of life experience I was trying to catch up on fast. He had a modest job but always had enough money and made me feel that he was happy to treat me to breakfast or a beer. While I worried about whether or not I'd be a good, published writer someday, he was already a really good guitar player. Everyone in the city's punk scene seemed to know him and want him in their bands and at their parties. But he never took himself too seriously, and he'd be the first one to throw on a fluorescent green wig and ham for the camera with a face that joked: "Aren't I pretty?"

The only thing I seemed to have that he didn't was a college diploma, as he'd dropped out of Evergreen after his first year. I was actually embarrassed for having gone to college, convinced that my new punk friends would think I was a snob, and I edited it out of my brief life history. Scott told me I was nuts, and that he was proud of me for being intelligent. All of his love and healthy self-esteem couldn't help but have a good effect on me, and he started to wear me down with the idea that he wasn't leaving anytime soon. I started to feel the same way and began to think about putting down real roots in Portland.

One night, after Scott and I had been dating for a little more than two months, I was at EJ's, waiting for his band's set to begin. I was at the back of the club, drinking a longneck Bud and playing Guns N' Roses pinball. As it blared "Welcome to the Jungle," I dug in hard, my arm muscles tensed, straining to keep the ball from the gutter. Scott came up behind me and stood close, nuzzling against my neck.

"Hey, what's up? Are you guys playing soon?"

"I love you," he said.

I turned to him, one big smile. "I love you, too."

The ball zipped down between the flippers and was lost. We looked and looked at each other, and he kissed me and stood close for a long breath before walking away.

I pulled the trigger of the gun to launch a new ball. As it sailed up into play and the machine wailed at me, I started to cry. I was so happy and relieved and grateful. Tears streamed down my face as I effortlessly arced the ball through the game, again and again and again, playing the best round of pinball I'd ever played. I was in love.

Not that life didn't keep on happening. I'd had my period on the first night I spent with Scott, and then I didn't have it again for months and months. We went out and bought a bottle of Jim Beam and a pregnancy test, drinking Jim and gingers until we felt fortified enough to take it. As we waited for the results, I was afraid to look at Scott, afraid of scaring him off. But he didn't look away. He looked right at me. "Whatever happens, it'll be all right," he said.

I wasn't pregnant. So I went to Planned Parenthood and completed that crucial step in any midnineties relationship: I got tested for HIV. I was clean and went on the pill. We began our life together, a reassuring source of stability when so much else felt beyond my control.

Sweetwater's Jam House remained shuttered while they prepared to open in a new location. When the café I'd been working at went out of business, I began collecting unemployment. My check was $78 a week and my rent was $268 a month. This meant I could just barely afford to buy myself packs of the Old Golds I'd started smoking, and occasionally, a tallboy of PBR from the Korean market across the street. But things were still tight. One morning after Scott had stayed over, he came back from the bathroom and found me picking up change that had fallen out of his jeans.

"What are you doing?" He laughed.

"Nothing," I said, too embarrassed to fess up.

"Do you not have any money?" he asked gently.

"My check comes on Friday."

"I don't like the thought of you walking around with no money. What if something happens?"

I shrugged. It wasn't like I had a lot of other options. He handed me five dollars.

"If nothing else, buy yourself a coffee or something."

I was deeply moved by his act of generosity, and the fact that he had really seen me.

Scott and I had been dating for four months going into the holidays. Even though I did my best approximation of cynical and Goth, and faced down the anniversary of the shooting eleven days before Christmas each year, I still loved the occasion as much as I had when I was a little girl. When Scott invited me to Christmas with his family, I was nervous just thinking about it, but also giddy with joy. This was a big deal, a step I'd never taken with a boyfriend before.

I didn't think much about spending my first Christmas away from home. I was twenty, after all, finally an adult. I would be fine. A week before Christmas, a box arrived in the mail from Mom. A few nights before we were scheduled to drive up to Scott's parents' house in Port Townsend, I had him over and said I was going to do my little Christmas. As usual, we were drinking bourbon. The first thing I pulled out of the box was my childhood Christmas stocking—red felt with goofy googly eyes and a hat. I loved that stocking. I loved Christmas. I loved my mom. My eyes started to mist up.

"Are you okay?" Scott asked.

"Yeah, sure, great."

I reached for a narrow wrapped package from the top of the stocking and held it in my hand, my heart crumbling with homesickness, tears flowing freely.

"This is my toothbrush. I get a toothbrush every year in my stocking."

I was crying too hard to unwrap my new toothbrush.

"That's it," Scott said. "I can't stand to see you this sad. I'm putting you on a plane home for Christmas. I don't care how much it costs."

"No, no, I want to stay with you," I said through tears.

"Are you sure?" he asked, looking genuinely worried.

I nodded my head and started tearing through the Christmas packages as quickly as possible, as if I were ripping off Band-Aids.

"I know what will cheer you up," Scott said.

"What?"

"Christmas specials. Let's go to the video store."

"Really?" I said. I knew Scott, like most grown men, was not quite so into Christmas, or Christmas decorations, and definitely not into Christmas specials.

He was already putting on his leather jacket. We were soon curled up in bed at his house watching the special he had known would make me happier than any other: *The Nanny Saves Christmas*. I was very happy. And he, well, he was happy that I was happy.

I made a batch of Grammy's holiday nougats—like Mexican wedding cookies with a powdered-sugar coating—and the hippy cookies I'd loved from the land—made with whole wheat flour and honey— wanting to share my own history with Scott's family. We arrived at a big comfortable house where Scott's parents, three younger siblings, and the family dog all greeted me warmly. It was a lot compared to the quiet Christmases at my house growing up, and I instantly felt timid. But they were lovely. Scott's mom drew me out in conversation, and his dad made the kind of bad jokes dads are supposed to make. We had crepes on Christmas morning and watched *A Christmas Story*. At night, Scott and I quietly had sex on the pullout couch in the spare room.

That January, Sweetwater's opened its new location, a ten-minute walk from my apartment. I was tired of being broke and bored and couldn't wait to get back to work. On the first day of training, a tall, stylish woman with close-cropped hair said something offhand that threw me back to midcoast Maine.

"Where are you from?" I asked.

"Portland," she said.

I stared at her in confusion. We all lived in Portland.

"Portland, Maine," she clarified, laughing.

Her name was Marya, and she was two years older than I was, but we had hung out in Portland during the same years, and we knew many of the same people. Talking about home with her, it was okay to be a little homesick, and okay to be where I was now, living a life that was actually starting to make me happy. Like me, Marya was fiercely competitive, even when it didn't really matter, and we alternated who had the most sales and who sold the most specials. After a busy night, we both liked a shot of Gosling 151 rum with a Maker's Mark and soda back and a cigarette. We were fast friends.

Waitressing was good for me. I could be very shy, and while I wanted to look and be perfect at all times, my skin still broke out and made me self-conscious, and so it was good to have a job where I had to deal with it and go interact with people anyway.

Between waitressing and my first real love, I began to settle into my life in Portland.

I was spending quite a bit of time with Scott's family, and his dad was a welcome antidote to mine. He was handsome like Clint Eastwood, and had a gentle ease about him. Although he'd wanted to be a musician, he'd become a pharmacist to support his family. When Scott's parents visited us in Portland, they always took us out for a sushi dinner, during which his dad never failed to eat a mouthful of the spicy green horseradish, slap the table, and exclaim: "Wasabi!" It was comforting.

That July, my lease ran out. I wanted to move in with Scott. As always, I was focused on pressing forward, growing up, and I knew this was the next important step. Scott was more wary about the decision. He'd lived with girlfriends before and knew it was a serious undertaking. His reluctance hurt my feelings, and for the month the subject was up for debate, our interactions were fraught. I weighed each of his words as if they were measurements of how Scott felt for me and how committed he was to our relationship. He raised the subject one night in June.

"I've been thinking about it a lot, and I'm ready for you to move in," he said.

Of course, as soon as he gave me what I wanted, I was petrified.

"Are you sure?" I said.

"Yeah, that's what you want, right?"

It was what I had asked for, yes, but what I really wanted was a little more complex. I wanted Scott to promise he'd love me forever and never leave me, and I wanted him to mean it. Anything less than his complete devotion was scary for me. At the same time, I was twenty-one years old. I was in love for the first time. I knew there was a whole world out there, and that Portland, Oregon, might not be my ideal hometown. As I moved in, a vague unease grew within me. We went down to the basement for the beautiful antique bed frame he'd inherited from his grandmother and assembled it in our room. As I lay down next to Scott that night, he curled himself around me, winding his legs through mine, pulling me close to his chest, entwining his arms around me, as if trying to touch every inch of my skin with his. I felt deeply, purely happy.

"This is my favorite part of the day," I said every night I fell asleep beside him.

chapter Ten

DON'T WAIT UNTIL YOU'RE PERFECT

I was still baffled as to how to be a writer, but I was trying. I signed up for a creative nonfiction class at the local community college. I attended readings and befriended writers. I began to write. Short stories. Essays. I sent them to literary journals, collecting my rejection slips as the successful writers I admired had once done. Mostly my day-to-day life revolved around Scott, and for a time, I was comfortable with that.

On the other hand, I was getting frustrated with waitressing. I wanted to learn more about writing and publishing, but there were few jobs in those fields in Portland. I got a job temping at a cool real estate office. Upon learning I was an aspiring writer, one of the Realtors said, "Oh, you should meet my client, Win. I just sold him the Tin House from Ursula Le Guin's story, and he's going to start a literary journal there."

This was big news. Despite my love for Scott, I was really starting to feel stuck. Marya had gotten accepted to law school and departed for her new life. Claire had moved back east and got an apartment in

Brooklyn with one of our old Simon's Rock friends. They had been two of my primary outlets for talking about books and culture and had shaped my tastes in important ways. Marya had gotten me into cutting-edge fiction like *Infinite Jest*, and although I'd had trouble with it, I read every word out of respect for her. It was this accomplishment that landed me a job as the first copy editor at Portland's new literary journal, *Tin House*, where my first task was to edit a story by none other than David Foster Wallace. Not long after that, I got a paid internship at the *Oregonian*'s website, Oregonlive.com, and I learned how to write HTML code and post articles about entertainment-related topics. My favorite part of the job was that they let me write articles about local readings and interview authors such as Kevin Canty and David Sedaris, who sent me the most charming thank-you letter after our meeting. I'd found a larger community of writers and thinkers, and I wanted to join them. I began to feel isolated and left behind in Portland, that familiar dread of being unable to stay and afraid to go.

Scott respected my friendship with Claire, but he was not crazy about her. She had the kind of erratic, high-maintenance personality that made many men uneasy, especially him, because he considered that kind of behavior bullshit. And he had seen the havoc she could wreak on my emotional state. She regularly called from the East Coast and questioned my life in Portland on every level: Was I writing? What was I writing? Was I getting the stimulus I needed? The support? Where could I possibly go in such a small city? What could I achieve? Even though Scott was supportive, wasn't his band, his music, his desire to stay in Portland coming before my need to grow? She was asking from a place of love, but she had an intensity that could feel judgmental.

By the end of our calls, my responses grew monosyllabic, and I was often crying. Scott gave me my privacy, but as my sobs grew audible, he was unable to resist checking in on me. When I hung up, I threw myself down on the bed.

"Why are you friends with her when she makes you feel so bad?" he asked.

"Because she's my best friend."

I couldn't tell him that part of the reason I was crying was I knew Claire was right. A rift was growing, and I would have to deal with it eventually. I think Scott sensed that she urged me to want more than I could have in my life with him.

That Christmas, when I was twenty-two, I traveled east and was again due to have lunch with Betty and Mimi. Arriving outside Mimi's apartment building a bit early, this time I called in advance to make sure she was receiving company. And even having been welcomed by her on the phone, I was nervous as I rode the elevator up and rang the bell. Although she was sixty, her face was hardly touched by time, her skin smooth and bronzed. She had brassy blond hair and precisely lined lips and eyebrows. It seemed that maybe she had not left her apartment in several days. As she welcomed me, I slid sideways past a chrome clothes rack parked in the narrow hallway, through a wispy curtain, into her living room.

"Let me get a look at you," she said.

Meanwhile, I wanted to get a look at her apartment. The antiques Betty had encouraged me to covet were crushed against one another, arranged for space rather than effect: cluttered with stacked baskets and clusters of picture frames, many featuring photographs of Mimi. Small decorative tables had been called into active labor, loaded with a half dozen lamps. "I forage the neighborhood for discards," she explained.

I followed Mimi through the tunnel of cleared floor to her bedroom, which opened from the living room. Under glass atop her dresser were pictures of me as a child, some photographs I'd never seen before. There I was as a baby with my father and mother, later in a black gown, graduating from college. I felt an eerie sensation, like I'd been living in a snow globe my aunt could have reached out and shook anytime but didn't. She pointed a manicured nail to a photo of my father with a dark, bushy beard. "That was taken when John traveled to San Francisco in the sixties," she said. "He went from being an acid freak to a Jesus freak in six months."

I had not seen my father in seven years. Facts had always been hard to come by in this family, so I basked in the relative normalcy of Mimi's candid stories.

Through the bathroom, and into the kitchen, I met her cat, Lovey. Mimi prepared to style her hair, plugging in her hair dryer over the sink. I sat in a chair, one of the few empty surfaces in the room, and my aunt offered me something to drink: water, juice, or beer. I admitted I was "out late with my friends" the night before and opted for water.

"Oh, if you had too much to drink last night, you need a beer."

"No, really, water would be great."

"A beer will make you feel better."

Laughing inside, I agreed. Mimi opened her refrigerator and pulled out a can of Schlitz. I laughed outside, too, when I saw that women on the Upper West Side, or at least this woman, drank the same cheap beer I'd overindulged in during college.

"Do you want ice in that?"

"No, thank you."

"I always put ice in my beer so I get rehydrated while I'm drinking."

She poured us each a glass of beer, hers with ice. As she styled her hair, she leaned over and looked at my feet.

"Let me see your shoes," she said.

I held up one of my Beatle boots, mystified.

"Betty never likes the shoes you wear," she said. "Those look better."

Her comment reminded me to be nervous of Betty, who had criticized more than my clothes to my face, telling me to lose weight, put on more makeup, comb my hair.

The building bucked a little, as the elevator rose toward our floor.

"Hurry, finish your beer so your grandmother won't see us drinking," Mimi said.

"I'm over twenty-one. I can drink."

The look she gave me just made me drink faster, even though the elevator was a false alarm. A few minutes later, the elevator again lumbered toward us. Mimi turned off the light in her kitchen, so Betty wouldn't see what we were drinking.

When Betty arrived, I sat on the couch with her while Mimi finished primping.

"You look nice," Betty said. "Your makeup is perfect."

Does she need to have her cataracts removed again? I wondered, but with relief.

"Bring us some juice, Mimi," Betty called out. "Sarah and I want juice."

With obvious patience—in stark contrast to the snide remarks my father and Betty had made about her—Mimi came into the living room, a smile on her face.

"I have apple juice," she said, smiling at me.

Turning to Betty, she asked, "Did you take your medicine this morning?"

Betty waved away her inquiry. "Bring us some apple juice."

Mimi returned with two short glasses filled with ice and juice. She set one glass down on the coffee table in front of Betty and handed me the other.

"Drink your apple juice, Sarah," she said, beaming at me.

I took a sip and tasted Schlitz over ice.

So that was my auntie Mimi.

Back home after the holidays, I was increasingly eager to leave Portland, exhausted by waitressing and frustrated by my attempts to find a rewarding job related to writing. Scott really, truly did not want to live anywhere else. But we were deeply in love, and I couldn't imagine my life without him, as I told him—and myself—again and again. I decided that if I went away to graduate school for journalism, it would be a temporary fix. Once I had my degree, I'd be better set up to get a rewarding job in Portland or a city Scott might be ready to check out by then. Long distance would be really hard, but it seemed doable.

Of course a plan that makes sense intellectually can still hurt your heart. When it came time to fly to school in Boston in the fall of 1999, I arranged for a ride from a friend. I was afraid if Scott took me to the airport, I wouldn't be able to make myself get out of the car.

The night before my flight, I had more packing left than I'd thought, and I was frantic. Scott stayed in our extra bedroom, growing morose as it became clear we weren't going to get any good time with each other, and then I would be gone, and we wouldn't see each other for at least six weeks. Finally, exhausted, I went to make the bed, but I couldn't find any sheets.

"I'm done," I said, leaning into the office. "Have you seen the sheets, so I can make the bed?"

"I don't know. You must have packed them all."

"I didn't. I'm sure of it."

We were both tired and sad, and the tension ratcheted up between us. I turned and went back into the bedroom, feeling icky and awful. I hated to make anyone upset, especially Scott, and I was incredibly sensitive to anything that felt like a rebuke, particularly on the night before we were going to be apart for so long. I dug up a sheet in the closet we had shared, but it was covered in the strange blue mold that sometimes grew in the house. I brought the sheet to my nose. It smelled earthy, not entirely clean. But it was fine, and I was too tired to care. I made up the bed and lay down alone, feeling like I was being punished for my ambition and my hunger to see the world, like it was costing me the love that felt like a home of my own. I was wide awake when Scott lay down. He didn't touch me. I started to cry, needing my favorite part of the day, but knowing I'd been the one to give up this ritual, even just temporarily.

I knew if I went away without us having sex, it would feel like a wedge had come between us, especially because in the past, Scott and I hadn't been able to get enough of each other: in his car, and my car; on the couch and in the stairway of our house, even though our roommates were home; in the stairwell under the Morrison Bridge on our way back from a party; once in the middle of the Hawthorne Bridge when it was closed for construction. And now, we weren't even letting one centimeter of our skin brush up against each other.

Too soon, it was time to get up. The friend who was taking me to the airport waited downstairs, with a bottle of orange juice and a bottle of vodka. I held the vodka in my hand, too sick with sleeplessness, and too hungry for success, to take a drink. I sobbed as she pulled away from my home. As I had told Scott again and again as my departure date approached, I still loved him and wanted my future with him as much as ever, but I also needed more than Portland could give me. I knew there was no turning back. I had outgrown that time in my life, as good as it had been, just as I'd outgrown paradises before: Simon's Rock, and before that, the land. There was nothing to be done but to move forward and hope the deep, true love I felt for Scott would help him to come with me somehow.

At school, I missed Scott terribly. I missed his bratty sense of humor and the nonchalant care he took of me. I missed the routines of our life together. I threw myself into school. At least I liked the challenge of conquering a new way to write. Seven years into my decision to become a writer, I remained obsessed. But sometimes journalism felt like working in a factory. Luckily my inner perfectionist was always eager for the A, and so I forced down my unhappiness and worked as hard as I possibly could.

I was very aware that I was once more in my father's city. It had been eight years since I'd seen him, and we had long ago given up the pretext of planning visits. I had no expectations left for him to disappoint. I had certainly never anticipated any financial help when I'd taken up my plan for graduate school, and I wasn't expecting him to treat me to cups of coffee. Still, I was drawn to him as with almost no one else. After I'd been living in Boston for a few weeks, I sent him a postcard telling him I was there. It was impossible not to want him to surprise me, but I didn't let myself hope. I wasn't even sure I'd get an answer. He did eventually write me back, and we began a sporadic correspondence, but any mention of visiting was vague. By Christmas, we had lived nine miles apart for four months. He hadn't made any effort to see me, and was clearly not going to see me for the holidays. It was the closest we'd been to each other, geographically, since I was two. Clearly, this didn't mean as much to him as it did to me.

During our time apart, Scott relented. He would be willing to come to Boston and try it out for one year, after which I would agree to move somewhere else if he really didn't like it. I was so happy I was high. I was getting everything I wanted. I had that deep feeling of peace that comes at the end of a very hard time. After the past twelve months of scrimping and studying and counting the days, I was ready to be happy, my career and my love both moving forward.

I flew to Portland to spend Scott's last days there with him before we drove cross-country together. I had loved driving the northern route with Claire five years earlier, and I was ready for the cute his-and-her scenes pictured in so many romantic comedies. But Scott didn't seem to be enjoying himself, and I had no idea why. We were together. This was our adventure. This was our new life.

We made it to Cambridge, where we rendezvoused with Beth at our apartment. I saw it through Scott's eyes. It was small. It was rough around the edges. We bought a cheap futon and frame and put it on the floor, which was a far cry from the beautiful, comfortable, antique bed we'd had in Portland. I got defensive, but as usual, I hid anything other than a completely positive reaction, except for when my insecurity flared up in the form of a cutting remark; beware of the passive-aggressive perfectionist.

I threw myself into my work. Instead of lingering in bed with Scott in the mornings, as I'd fantasized about doing during grad school, I sprung up to make calls, tackle my assignments, and take long runs through the streets of our neighborhood, always propelled forward, always on the move.

But he was unable to pretend he was anything other than miserable. We went into the holidays on edge. I still loved Christmas like crazy. The one thing he had plenty of was the one thing he didn't really care about: money. His job paid very well, and he had no chance to spend what he earned. He handed me a small wrapped package. I didn't dare look at him, focused very intently on unwrapping the paper. Inside was a small black box. I was fluttery with excitement as I flipped back the lid.

Inside were two beautiful diamond studs. My heart sank, even as I was talking myself up. My love of glam rock–style bling was well documented; every outfit I wore was topped with a vintage rhinestone necklace. I'd never owned diamonds before. I knew Scott well enough to be sure he'd done his research and bought me the best and biggest diamonds he could afford. I loved them. I was touched. But I had thought it was a ring. Although I never told him this out of a fear of hurting his feelings or making him feel bad, there had been a moment when I had said yes in my mind, but he had not asked me. I smiled at him and threw my arms around his neck, making up for my regret.

"They're beautiful, Scott," I said. "Thank you so much."

"I thought about it, and I'm going to say something right up front," he said.

"What?" I asked, still convinced there might be a proposal in there somewhere.

He paused. "It's okay if you lose one," he said. "I won't be mad."

I laughed, knowing this was a huge part of the gift. We'd never been able to afford anything nice, and I already didn't trust myself with my new earrings. He knew just what to say.

I had now lived in Boston for more than a year, and my father had still not made any effort to see me. I was, however, having more regular contact with Betty again. In many ways, she was still the same as she'd always been: a ferocious correspondent who sent three or four cards each holiday and didn't need to have any particular news as an excuse

Scott had gotten trained in IT and basic computer tech and w
trying to make a career leap in conjunction with his move. But it bega
to seem like he might not find a job. He was worried about money. H
missed his band. He missed his friends. I was full of good ideas for
how he could apply for more jobs, put an ad in the local punk magazine for people to play with, and when he didn't immediately jump to
make things better, I was convinced he wasn't trying hard enough. But
I believed if we weren't fighting, there was no problem, and if we loved
each other, everything would work itself out.

Scott got an IT job. He had been desperate enough to feel he had no
choice but to overlook this position's downsides, which were consider-
able: it was in a suburb outside the city, and it was graveyard shift. Still,
Scott gamely put on a pair of black slacks and an ironed gray shirt and
went into work. It took him a while to adjust to his new sleep schedule,
and he was tired and drawn. But he found the sweet spots, bringing me
stuffed French toast in bed when he got home from work at seven in the
morning and convincing me not to get up for a few hours.

When Scott left for work at night, I was alone in the apartment, as
Beth was working at a high-end restaurant, Number 9 Park. I dared to
admit I was ready to begin writing my first novel. It started as a May-
December love story between an older female writing professor and a
young male student, inspired in part by one of my favorite movies at
the time, the Tennessee Williams–penned *Sweet Bird of Youth*.

On Saturdays, I let Scott sleep late, sometimes until nearly eight
o'clock at night, because he could be cranky when he first woke up.
And because he always looked tired, with deep circles under his pretty
blue eyes. And because, secretly, I relished my time alone. I could
always write for another hour or two when given the chance.

As the fall progressed, our apartment became chilly, and then
frigid. I sat at my desk all day long and shivered, wrapped in blankets. Wordlessly, Scott came home with a space heater he'd bought and
plugged it in by my desk. It still made him happy to make me happy,
and he did so in these small, lovely ways all the time.

to write a letter. She remained incredibly generous, even though the picture frames and costume jewelry she sent as presents often appeared worn, as if they had been regifted.

She'd also begun calling me that fall. She was sometimes confused. But in a moment of clarity, she made a request.

"I want you to be the executor of my will," she said. "I don't trust Mimi or John to do it. I want you to be the one in charge."

My instinct was to say: "No, that's too much, I'm only twenty-four, and I can barely afford a bus ticket down to New York, let alone what else I might have to do if it comes down to it. You don't trust your own children. I'm weak enough to be an easy mark for them and whatever they decide it's their right to do with whatever little money and possessions you leave behind." But I never said no.

"I don't really know what that means, but I'll do my best," I said instead.

Of course, whenever Betty called, it was impossible for me not to think of my dad. I had pretended that not having him in my life was a nonissue, a simple, passive absence that prevented him from disappointing me or causing me pain. But it was an active, constant hurt. Every day that I lived nine miles from my father and he chose not to see me was a day that he rejected my presence in his life. And his rejection would always be more powerful, and tell me more about how much value I did or didn't have, than all of the positive feedback from Scott and Beth, or my new friends, or the increasing number of editors who were giving me assignments.

Now there was also the matter of the nonengagement earrings. Scott hadn't proposed that night, but we had talked about marriage and kids. As we looked forward to our five-year anniversary that August, I couldn't imagine being with anyone else. I was beginning to feel I'd found the foundation for my own family, but to start that family, I needed to make peace with my family of origin.

During the spring of 2001, at age twenty-five, I hadn't seen my father in nearly ten years, but I found myself thinking about him more than ever. I was often distracted from my work as I sat at my desk on deadline. But now I didn't just approach him with the narrow focus of the child's constant, unrelenting want. I had gained the smallest amount of perspective, enough for me to recognize the damage he was doing to me. I realized that the fact that he was not physically present in my life did not lessen the profound presence he had, and would always have. I didn't see how I could be a parent until I made peace with the absent parent he had been, whether he was a part of that process or not. I began writing letters to him in my mind while I was out running. We could reconcile, and we could have a relationship, whatever that might look like. Or if he did not respond to my efforts, I would be the one to put our relationship aside. In my father's letters of the past nine years, he'd said he would see me when he quit gambling, his back healed, his court case settled. Having discovered what I truly wanted to say, I wrote him a letter inviting him back into my life. "Don't wait until you're perfect," I wrote, "or it will be too late."

As soon as I mailed my letter, I felt serene. Whatever happened, I had made my stand. I had done my absolute best to have a relationship with my father, and if he was absent from my life, it was not because I was the bad, unlovable girl I had always seen myself to be, but because he could not be the dad he was supposed to be.

chapter eleven

DECIDE WHO YOU LOVE

I tried not to have any expectations about how my dad would respond to my letter, or more accurately, how "John" would respond. As part of protecting myself, I'd begun calling him John instead of Dad. Even when I heard back from him in mid-March, and he suggested we meet for lunch on his fifty-fifth birthday, April 3, I didn't let myself get too excited. I waited for him to write or call to cancel. When he didn't, I still couldn't quite believe I was going to see him that day. I sat at my desk, obsessing over an article I was writing, until I was about to be late to meet my dad. Now that was a turn of events.

As I rode the red line to South Station and walked to No Name Restaurant, his choice, I was queasy with nerves. I had seen my dad fewer than a dozen times between when my mom left him when I was two and when we had our falling-out when I was fifteen, and then I had not seen him at all for nine and a half years.

He was seated at a table by the window. I was surprised I recognized him so quickly. Of course I did. He was still my dad, even after nearly a decade. A plain cap framed his broad face, with its carved-wood cheekbones, and his dark eyes, which reminded me of Betty, and our family legacy of absent parents.

His skin was smooth and unlined, but when he smiled, he was no longer familiar. The intervening decade had been hard on him. His front teeth were stained and broken. When he stood and hugged me, he smelled familiar. But when he sat down again and removed his hat, he was nearly bald.

"Hi, Sarah," he said, laughing nervously. It was all still there in the way he said my name, the sound of his voice.

"I think I need a beer to settle my stomach," he said.

"I could drink a beer," I said, trying to sound as if this were a novel concept.

"I don't usually drink, but the bubbles help," he said.

Grateful for the excuse, I ordered one, too. We both had the swordfish. When it was brought to the table, sizzling on metal plates, it was slick with hot grease. My father looked down, obviously disappointed. "It's not as good as it used to be," he said.

"Mine's good," I said, overbrightly. I wasn't going to let him ruin this for me.

I felt something during that lunch I'd never experienced before in regard to John: doubt. It was obvious how much care he'd put into preparing to meet me: his new white sneakers, his flannel shirt under his carefully matched sweater. This showed nervousness on his part, which made me feel powerful. Also, he was clearly poor. This had never occurred to me. He had always promised me some wonderful future when he would have it together, and we would be reunited and happy. Suddenly I understood that he was old. Other dads were beginning to think about retirement, preparing for endings, not beginnings. His window for creating change was closing fast.

I still felt like a little girl around him, but I was trying to be a grown-up. There was so much between us, and yet we were strangers, which made it awkward and fraught. It also felt weirdly normal, and nice, a dad and his daughter having lunch on his birthday.

After we ate, we walked around the waterfront.

"That's where Whitey Bulger and the mobsters used to bury their bodies," he said, nodding toward a parking lot. "It used to be a totally different world down here, back when I was driving a cab. Across the water there, where Downtown Crossing is all department stores now, was the Combat Zone. That was what they used to call the city's adult entertainment district, you know, the red-light district, where the strip clubs and triple-X movie theaters were. Out in Jamaica Plain, where you lived last year, we never wanted to take any fares out there. I had someone pull a gun on me in JP once and take all of the money I'd earned for an entire shift. I went home with nothing."

His stories about his years as a Boston cabbie fascinated me. They evoked a time I'd missed out on because of his choices. We came to the oversize milk bottle outside the Children's Museum. Only, now I was big, and it was no longer giant.

"Do you remember when we came here when you were little?" he asked.

I nodded my head. I could remember being there, but I couldn't distinctly remember that he'd been the adult there with me.

My dad insisted on walking me to my train, and I bristled. Maybe he just didn't want the visit to end, but I was too insecure to think like that then, and all I could think was how nice it would have been if he'd been half as attentive when I was fifteen, or nine, or three. As he hugged me good-bye, I was unbelievably exhausted. He was intense, and something else—the phrase that came to mind was "emotionally crippled"—and now his intensity was turned on me. As much as I craved his attention, I was suddenly struck by how much responsibility it could be. Luckily, I had no expectations. I had no idea whether I would ever even see him again. I had sent him a letter, he'd responded, and we'd spent time together. After so many years of so little contact between us, that was enough to make me feel grateful.

My reunion with my father was a relief, but it didn't solve everything. Scott's unhappiness in Boston made me uncomfortable and resentful. I had no idea if Boston was my home, but I was defensive about having moved us there. And in many ways, I was thriving. My journalism career was taking off, and I was enjoying real mentorship from my editors at the *Boston Globe*. For the moment, it was good. Scott was making more money than he could spend, more than we'd ever had in our years together. For my birthday, he'd offered to buy us plane tickets to the country of my choice. I picked Italy.

Neither of us had ever been to Europe before, and much of the trip was lovely, but we had totally different definitions of how much was the right amount of everything—walking, sightseeing, sex—and returned to Boston feeling further apart than ever. We tried to go back to normal. I didn't let myself think about the moments we weren't in sync, and just kept looking forward to the moment when we connected again.

Scott and I had begun seriously talking about moving in the fall. Our two best choices seemed to be Portland, which would make him very happy, and New York City, which would be good for my career. But we couldn't decide.

Scott and I were in real trouble, and I knew it. In all of those years, we'd only had two fights. Now, as both our fifth anniversary and the end of our lease loomed, I made out with another guy. It didn't change the fact that Scott and I still wanted to be together, but we began to fight all the time. Scott told me how he'd always been sure I was going to move back east, how he'd never been able to trust in my commitment to Portland or him, how cold and passive-aggressive I could be, how he'd needed my love and kindness so badly when he'd moved and had felt utterly bereft and alone when I'd withheld it.

"Fine, I'm a terrible person," I said. "I'm terrible. I'm awful."

It was what I had always known to be true, and now I had proven myself right. He was going to abandon me, as I'd feared from the start. But Scott didn't want to leave. Horribly, he found that, as unhappy as he was with me now, he couldn't imagine being happy without me. We panned through the rubble—the ineffable, impossible differences in our personalities and goals and lifestyle preferences—until we found the gold: we both still loved each other so fucking much. But. We kept coming back to this: I wanted to live anywhere but Portland, where Scott felt most at home, and where I felt most stagnant and stuck. If he wouldn't move somewhere new with me, I would stay in Boston, even if he left for Portland.

"Please come with me," he said.

"I can't," I said, feeling like I'd lose everything if I went backward, my writing, my self, my future.

"Then let me stay," he said.

"You can't," I said, my heart breaking. "You hate it here."

John surprised me by sending me a note and following up with a call to make plans. If he was going to be back in my life, I knew there was something important I had to tell him. But as always, I was nervous about anything that might seem like a demand.

"I know it's probably not my place to say, but you might want to think about going down to New York to see Betty," I said. "The last time I had lunch with her, it was clear she's not doing well. She asked me to be the executor of her will, which I'm not sure I feel comfortable doing. I mean, I'll do it. But it's a lot, and I'm not sure if it should be me. So . . . I don't know. I guess I don't know how much longer she has."

"Wow," John said. "Okay."

There was a long pause. I waited for the hammer to come down. I knew John would never lash out at me, but he was deft at the more serious power move: absence. I hated to think my concern for Betty might cost me my budding relationship with him. But she had done so much for me, and even though she was hard to love, I respected her like a force of nature—an Estée Lauder tornado—and I couldn't stand to think of her coming to a lonely, unpleasant end because of my cowardice.

"Okay, I'll call her," he said. "I'll figure out a way to get down there. Maybe we could even go down to visit Betty together. It'll mean dealing with Mimi, but that's okay. I didn't want to face her, so I've been avoiding them for years, but maybe it's time."

I realized with relief that his silence hadn't been the result of anger. Sometimes it just took his brain a little while to process things, as if all of the acid and the many years he'd spent alone had gummed up the works a bit.

John and I made plans for our next visit. He was very curious about me, as he'd always been intrigued by my life during the brief moments he'd been in it. He wanted to know what I was writing about, and what Scott and I liked to do in Cambridge. We agreed to meet up at an Indian place Scott and I frequented in Central Square. When I first walked in, the sheer force of my dad's presence again stopped me short. This man, whose absence had torn such a hole through my life, had a physical form, too.

As soon as I sat down, he started talking.

"I had an amazing meditation today," he said, his voice booming through the quiet restaurant where businesspeople and MIT professors were savoring a quick hot lunch. Heads turned. He didn't notice. I did, but I'd spent much of the past ten years with punks, and I was sanguine about being stared at. "I've been doing deep breathing with a snorkel. And this morning, I did it for two, three hours, and I had this breakthrough."

I smiled at him and sipped my water. So here it was, the reality, not the fantasy: This was my dad. He was still a great talker. I began to relax and feel easy in his presence . . . until it was time for me to leave.

"I'll walk you home," John said.

Again, I balked. I was the girl who'd wanted to live on my own at eleven, largely because it had seemed like the best way to have him in my life, and I didn't want to let him swoop in and be the big man now.

But I still felt incredibly shy around him, especially when it came to telling him no. For a big guy—six foot one and more than two hundred pounds—he was as skittish as a small animal. I felt the need to be gentle with him.

I was cautious when I mentioned the possibility I might move to Portland that fall.

"If you go back to Portland, maybe I'll move there, too," he said.

I didn't say anything. We'd eaten lunch together twice after not having seen each other for nearly ten years, and he was offering to move across the country with me. The last thing I needed was any more pressure on my decision. I stopped telling John what was going on with Scott, especially as I didn't really know, and when I did know—that he was going back to Portland, and that I was not—it was too devastating.

Mom and Craig had planned to take Andrew and me to Ireland that summer. Initially, we had thought Scott would come along, too, but we'd nixed that idea just in time. Our lease wasn't up until September, but since I would be gone for those last two weeks of August on the trip, we decided Scott would pack up his belongings after I left and that when I returned, he would be gone.

Everything in the final days was like breathing, and talking, and walking through mud. My suitcase was packed, and I had to go meet my family. Scott sat on the couch, giving me the same look he had when I'd cheated on him. It hurt.

"Sarah," he said, his voice breaking.

I didn't want to go. I couldn't stay. I picked up my suitcase, and as I walked out the door, I sobbed. I cried all the way to the airport. I got on a plane and spent the next two weeks being soothed by the fact that there was a whole world out there, where my problems were small and meaningless. And, surprisingly, being comforted by the presence of my family, something I'd never really felt comfortable with before. It was the first extended time we'd spent together since I'd gone away to Simon's Rock ten years earlier, and I was moved by how kind they were to me during my first heartbreak. Craig had planned our trip meticulously, with plenty of literary attractions for Mom and me—Ireland loves any excuse to hang a Yeats plaque, and I love any excuse to read one—and the kind of destinations that best captured my imagination. We stayed at a genuine castle and ate the best fried oysters in Belfast. We had fun. It was the first real family vacation we'd ever taken together, beyond camping trips and vacations to visit extended family, and something became clear to me. Mom and Craig had sacrificed a great deal to live a life that was meaningful to them, much like I'd been doing in service to my writing, and I'd learned so much of value from the childhood they'd given me—focus, perseverance, follow-through—that was just as valuable as the inventive, bohemian streak I'd inherited, and overtly celebrated, from my dad. I was finally able to feel really grateful, for everything that had been mine while I'd been waiting at the window for my father to arrive.

Andrew and I shared a hotel room during our trip, and for the first time in our lives, he'd grown up enough that our ten-year age gap wasn't as noticeable. We did the things siblings are supposed to do—occasionally rolling our eyes at our parents being dorky in the front seat of the car, and watching TV together in our hotel room at night. I was genuinely moved when he surprised me with a UK-only CD single by a band, Supergrass, whose first album I'd given him the previous Christmas. We were still very different. And all three of them were more alike than they were like me—I was happiest pushing myself toward some new extreme or telling stories at the center of a gaggle of friends, and they were all quieter and calmer and steadier—but we shared a passion for music and culture and ideas, and a curiosity about the world at large. For the first time in my life, I felt grateful for my brother, and really included in our family.

I missed Scott terribly, questioned my decision a million times, and obsessively fantasized about a happy reunion in New York City or Los Angeles or Seattle, anywhere that wasn't Portland. But I also wondered about the man I'd kissed, whether he would see me now that

I was free. In that wondering I knew, as hard as it was, that I had done what was right.

Returning to our apartment and finding Scott and his guitars and all of his possessions gone was impossible, but it was already done. I did that grief thing where I concentrated very hard on putting one foot in front of the other. My friend Mary and her boyfriend had just broken up, and she and I moved into a big three-bedroom apartment in Jamaica Plain with another friend. When I drank a few beers in the kitchen with Mary, a full pack of cigarettes on the table between us, our conversation endless and soothing, there was a moment when the pain receded. By the time I went to bed at three or four in the morning, I floated, any pain I had felt earlier bandaged in the lovely, familiar gauze of alcohol.

John and I began spending regular time together. He was living in a rooming house a few miles north of the city, and he did not have a phone, so we wrote each other frequent letters; he'd then go to a pay phone and call to confirm the plans we'd made.

In the days leading up to our next scheduled lunch that fall, I again waited for him to cancel. When I arrived at the restaurant, I was surprised to see his familiar shy smile and sloping shoulders waiting for me. It was only after we'd had a few of these dad-daughter dates that I began to relax enough to really savor our time together.

John was still very much the man who had revealed cosmic secrets to me about John Lennon and Wilhelm Reich. He was not surprised by the September 11 attacks and believed they were the beginning of worse global problems.

"There's too many people, too much corruption, too much ignorance and greed," he said. "It's going to get a lot worse before it gets better. I don't want to scare you, Sarah, but there's gonna have to be a mass purge of the population before we can move forward. We're entering the Age of Aquarius, the age of enlightenment, but not everyone's gonna get there. It's a choice we all have to make. Only those who choose to live in a new way will survive."

I was resistant to his conspiracy theories, though not because my worldview was much sunnier. "I don't think the powers that be really need to work so hard to hide their greed, or their indifference to the common good," I said to him. "I mean, look, it's all around us."

"I'm just saying, it could become impossible to get back and forth across the country," he said. "It's time to decide who you love and choose to be with them."

Although I questioned the specifics of John's worldview, I believed him on a cellular level, as I always had. The fact that he'd been returned to me suggested my faith had been valid all along. He was my dad. He knew best.

But I was haunted by John's words. I knew as surely as ever that Scott was the one I loved, but now he was so far away. A solution seemed farther and farther away, as well.

My first few phone calls with Scott were really hard. He was wary of me, and I understood why, but this felt so fundamentally wrong. We hadn't technically broken up. I still wanted to work on things, but he was having a harder time with the idea, since it was unclear what we were working on, especially as we were both uncompromising on the geography front. He agreed to let me come visit in October, and I booked a flight for the end of the month. Our reunion was sweet but left us no clearer on what to do.

Mary and I fell in with a whole group of local garage rock bands and ended up traveling down to New York City for a show at a club on the Lower East Side. While in the city, I arranged to have lunch with Betty and Mimi. Although I was never certain whether Mimi would join us as planned, I went to her apartment at the appointed time. There she was, still regal with her bleached-blond hair and full makeup. The three of us made our way, slowly because of Betty's emphysema, to a neighborhood Chinese restaurant.

"Free wine," Mimi said when we sat down.

I looked at Betty nervously. She'd gotten sober forty years ago, but I still felt uneasy drinking around her. On the other hand, it was hard to say no to Mimi. As Zen as I managed to be when I was out with John, it was impossible not to feel self-conscious with these two. Mimi was fighting a remarkably successful war against her age, having somehow figured out a way to get Medicaid to pay for her liposuction and plastic surgery. She could have passed for her late forties, even though she was two decades older. She liked to be looked at, and admired, and signaled the waiter over to us with dramatic flair. With age, Betty's voice had only grown louder and more cutting, and heads turned to stare. I was on edge, girding myself against Mimi's manipulation and Betty's criticism of my appearance, and yet, I was touched by their interactions.

"Did you take your medicine this morning, Betty?" Mimi asked.

"I took it," Betty said, literally waving away her concern.

"Do you have to go to the bathroom?" Mimi asked her.

"I'm not a child," Betty said. "Do *you* have to go to the bathroom?"

When Betty did get up to use the restroom, Mimi leaned over to me.

"She's incontinent, so I have her wearing maxi pads. It helps."

I smiled as neutrally as possible. I was grateful Mimi was there to give Betty the help she clearly needed, even in her own unique way. At the same time, I could sense it probably wasn't just paranoia on Betty's part that made her distrust her own daughter.

After lunch, we went back to Mimi's apartment, where Mary met me. Seated on the chair Mimi had gestured her into, she glanced down at the item resting near her seat and did a double take. I did, too. It was a prosthetic leg. Mimi had liked the look of it when she'd found it in the street, so she brought it home and painted the toenails bright red.

On another trip my Dad and I made to New York City together in an effort to get Betty into assisted living, the miraculous happened. Mimi's health was not good, causing her to be in a wheelchair. Betty was leaning on her walker more than ever. But we managed to have lunch together—Betty, Mimi, my dad, and I—and everyone came out unscathed. Sitting at the table with them, watching my dad to see whether these female relatives he felt so persecuted by would say something to make him bolt, worrying about Betty's health and yet still wary of her sharp tongue, surrendering to the completely unpredictable diva that was Auntie Mimi, I somehow felt intrinsically comfortable in that strange, ineffable way of family. I had longed for my dad and anything related to him for decades, and now he was here with me, and weirdly, these near strangers were my people.

Next, my dad and I took Betty to a doctor's appointment. Betty was, as ever, pure Betty.

"Why would you ever start smoking at thirty?" Betty's doctor asked.

"My looks were gone, so it didn't matter," Betty said.

I was twenty-five. Apparently, I didn't have much time left.

At lunch after the appointment, Betty did her best to eat her hamburger, even though her poorly fitting dentures popped in and out of her mouth. It was clear the moment for assistance was now, and I was glad I had my dad to help me.

Scott came to visit after Christmas, and although his stay had a few rocky moments, we enjoyed our time together. My period had remained irregular, and I had been diagnosed with an endocrine disorder, polycystic ovary syndrome (PCOS). It wasn't explained to me very well at the time; I was just put on the pill to regulate my cycle. It worked, which was a relief after more than a decade of my body doing its own thing. This also meant we didn't have to worry about birth control. I hadn't been with anyone else, and I didn't ask whether he'd given us a reason to use condoms again. I did my best to pretend nothing had changed.

No matter the underlying tensions between us about what would happen next, or how consistently we avoided talking about it, Scott and I seemed to fit together just as well as we always had. He was extremely affectionate and sweet with me, and we still felt very much like a couple. And yet, neither of us knew how to bridge the geographical divide between us. We got drunk the night before his scheduled return, conveniently causing him to miss his flight. Without having decided, we'd decided. Scott hit it off with two of my new friends and started playing music and working with them. His view of Boston improved, now that he was earning money doing something cool and maybe forming a band.

John came out to Jamaica Plain to have coffee with Scott and me. My relationship with John had been so new and tentative before that they'd never met. Even now, it was so baffling to have John meet my boyfriend that it seemed as if we weren't ourselves. We were characters in a romantic comedy starring Craig T. Nelson as the dad.

Surprisingly for me, I was nervous about what Scott would think of John's rotten teeth and how he talked loudly about topics other people found off-putting. I was so confident in my love for Scott, it never crossed my mind to worry what John would think of him. I was relieved when they fell into easy conversation, both charmed by the bright, inquisitive mind of the other. Sneaking happy side glances at Scott, I felt it was all possible, like we could really build a life in Boston that would make us both happy.

Scott was never great about returning phone calls to his friends and family, and by the time he'd been in Boston with me for five weeks, he hadn't talked to his parents in almost that long. Eventually, they got him on the phone. We were both sitting on my bed as Scott listened to what his dad needed to tell him. Suddenly his whole body tensed. I sat up and put my hand on his back, growing increasingly concerned as he started to tear up.

"Yeah, let me talk to her," he said.

By the time Scott hung up, he was already far away from me again. His mom had been diagnosed with breast cancer, and while her prognosis was good, his family and he had agreed he should go back west during her treatment. Given where we were in our relationship, I couldn't just give up my apartment, my freelance contacts, my whole new life. He got himself on the next flight back. Our second honeymoon was over.

A week after Scott left, Betty called. She was really out of it and upset, but I couldn't figure out exactly why. I didn't know how to help her, even though it was clear how badly she needed assistance. When faced with all she required, and how little my dad and Mimi seemed capable of, I felt young and powerless. I also hated feeling beholden to her, because after my happy reunion with Scott, I was thinking more and more of moving back to Portland. My other grandmother, Grammy, had lymphoma, and it had spread to four places, including her bones. Mom was sad. I was sad. Nowhere felt safe. I wanted Scott to comfort me, but he was far away and in need of comfort himself.

By April, Scott was giving me less to hold on to. After barely returning my calls for weeks, he sent me an e-mail: "I'm in a weird head space, and I don't feel like I can talk to you right now." It was only fair. As much as I wanted to get back together, I'd since had flirtations with another guy. I wrote back a short message saying I respected his request, and he should take as long as he needed. But as I was writing, I got an empty feeling in the pit of my stomach, like I had nothing and no one in the entire world. I applied myself to our time apart like the straight-A student I'd once been, sure if I emerged perfect, we'd find a way back together.

Every time the phone rang, I was filled with hope: Scott. When I heard John's voice on the other end, I was disappointed, which I never would have thought possible when I was a little girl. Betty's condition had worsened and he was traveling to New York the next day. I didn't feel up for the conversation and I had no advice or encouragement for him. Thankfully, he seemed to sense this and kept it short. He called me again from New York, understandably upset. While we had aimed to get Betty into the best assisted-living facility possible, even if it meant being a little less than honest about how much assistance she really needed, we hadn't registered her rapid deterioration.

At the end of April, as I sat where I spent most of my time in those days—at my desk—Scott called me and said we needed to talk. I could hardly breathe.

"I need to end our relationship and get on with my life," he said. "I've been unhappy over you for too long now, and it has only gotten in the way of my ability to get my life together and be happy."

I cried, a lot. As much as I'd been prepared for this, I was completely devastated. I wanted to get away from his words. But I didn't want to get off the phone, because when I did, he wouldn't be my boyfriend anymore. He told me he'd been seeing someone, and even though it had ended, he'd been happier without me in his life. Even though nothing had changed—he was still in love with me, still wanted all the things we'd talked about having together, and still considered me his best friend—he had to move on. Even if I did plan to move to Portland that fall, it was too far away. I was lost, but I could see how important it was for him that he'd finally made some movement.

"I'm proud of you for doing what you need to do," I said. "All I've ever really wanted was for you to be happy, and to be doing what you care about in life."

There was nothing left to say, and we hung up. It was official. After five and a half years, we had broken up. Not only had I lost Scott, I'd lost my fantasy of escaping back to Portland, the small pond with the cheap rent and the dive bars. I had no choice but to be strong now. I vowed to turn my longing into places I'd seen, things I'd accomplished. I knew I had so much to offer, maybe more than Scott was able to see.

Betty's social worker found her in her room, disoriented and frightened, in her own waste, apparently having been like that for several days. Instead of going to a retirement community, she went to the hospital. John rushed down to be with her.

"All she wanted was ice cream," he said from a pay phone, his voice cracked and tired. "It was like she was a child again. And that's all that mattered to her."

John and Mimi quickly resumed their multidecade squabble. He spent the next day at his hostel, arguing on the phone with her—literally fighting about how to best handle Betty's affairs, while both picked at the scabs created by the lack of overt love and affection Betty had shown them—and sulking at Mimi's domineering personality and unnecessarily hurtful words. During all of this, Betty died at the hospital.

When John called to tell me, he was inconsolable over the fact that his issues with his sister had prevented him from saying good-bye to his mother, and now she was gone.

"I'm so sorry," I said.

The loss registered for me like something getting sucked out of the pressurized cabin of an airplane. Betty had been a force in my life, and I'd miss her eccentric zeal. I was glad she was at peace after a lifetime of struggle. But more than anything else, honestly, I was incredibly grateful that none of this had fallen on me, as it would have only a few months earlier.

John was already in New York City. He would stay and dispose of her belongings and make the arrangements for her remains. He would handle Mimi. While John wrestled with guilt that he had not been with his mother when she passed, the experience of helping her, even the little bit he'd been able to when she was alive, and taking care of her estate after her passing, had a visibly positive effect on him. Something had needed to be handled, and for once in his life, he had stayed and dealt with it. His steadfastness made me see him in a new light, too. It made me respect him, a feeling I'd never had before. I started thinking of him, and referring to him, as Dad again.

Finally, he was doing what a dad was supposed to do, stepping up to provide a buffer between me and something I wasn't yet ready to handle. And so when we found out it would cost three hundred dollars to have Betty cremated, although I could have come up with the money, I didn't offer to do so. My dad didn't have three hundred dollars and couldn't raise it. Mimi couldn't or wouldn't help. So my dad borrowed the money from Betty's social worker.

Meanwhile, Dad went through Betty's papers and made some alarming discoveries. There were department-store credit card bills charged up for thousands of dollars. Apparently, she had been entered in several jewelry-of-the-month clubs, and other extravagant purchases had been made on the cards as well. It was possible that an unscrupulous store employee had preyed upon her confusion at the end of her life, but my dad suspected Mimi. Their interactions soured further when he found the paperwork for Betty's life insurance policies. She had two. One benefited Mimi, and the other benefited me. Dad would have only benefited if Betty had died through accidental death or dismemberment, which Mimi taunted him with, as if it somehow signified how little Betty had thought of him. The payout was only a few thousand dollars for both Mimi and me, but that was a lot of money for all of us. I needed that money, desperately, and I was afraid Dad would ask me for some, which my mom had always warned me to protect myself against. At the same time, I wondered whether I was selfish not to offer him any, even though it was Betty's decision to divide the money as she had.

It became a given that my dad and I would see each other at least once a month for our regular outings to the Harvard Film Archive. At the beginning of the month, he mailed me a calendar and had me write him with my pick. He had been appalled by my lack of culture when it came to cinema, even though I'd taken several classes on the subject in college. He'd become a lifelong cineaste when he'd stumbled into a European film at age fifteen and enjoyed the sight of a woman's bare breasts.

When my dad took me to my first Fellini film, *La Dolce Vita*, I was hungover and frayed, as usual, having been out late the night before. I was in no mood for a dad-daughter outing, but I knew I was the one with the power to disappoint now, and I couldn't bear to let him down, so I rose to the occasion.

As Nico sulked onto the screen, all of my worlds came together in a way I found comforting and inspiring. I was transfixed by the story. It followed a journalist who longs to write a great novel but can't because he's too distracted by his job as a society reporter and the many affairs he is juggling. I could not have related more.

After the film let out, my dad and I walked amid the hushed glow of the Harvard campus, talking about Fellini's gorgeous compositions and bittersweet comedy. When he said he'd walk me to the train, as I knew he would, I no longer resented his offer. Instead, I found the gesture thoughtful. As my father leaned toward me and listened closely to every word I said about my newfound passion for Fellini, I bloomed under his attention.

The autumn was hard. Mary started dating the guy I'd rebounded from Scott with, and I was deeply jealous whenever we were all at our apartment. Scott was seeing a new girl. I felt very much alone. He came through town with his band in November, and we fell right back together, even though his new girlfriend had said he could sleep with any other women on the road, except for me. For four days, I completely gave myself over to our reunion, just like I'd done with my dad as a kid. When he left, I was demolished.

My father had begun jotting down possible outings he might take me on, or questions he wanted to ask me: everything from details about how I was writing my novel, to how I felt about Scott's absence, to what MySpace was and how it worked. One afternoon while we were eating in the food court at Faneuil Hall, my father pulled out his little notebook. I picked at the cookie we were sharing. He looked up, looked down at his writing, then looked up again, smiled shyly at me. "I wrote, 'Tell Sarah she has a great laugh,'" he said.

Moments like these were impossibly sweet for me. Even just the fact that he was proving himself to be a reliable companion every other week was a revelation; the fact that he might actually love me and enjoy my company was nothing short of a dream come true. I began to trust him, and I started confiding in him, which involved a lot of heartbreak and anxiety, especially about my writing. Because my father didn't drink and saw booze as an unhealthy form of suppression, I didn't mention my own drinking, which I knew was excessive. I still wanted to be seen as perfect, and I definitely wasn't ready for anyone to suggest I should stop.

We took a day trip on a boat that traversed the city's islands with a picnic of clam chowder from Faneuil Hall. We cruised Boston Harbor on a windjammer. He even convinced me to get up early on a Sunday morning to attend a church service on Newbury Street because it had exquisite music by a live orchestra.

My father was deeply curious, and our excursions were often a part of his attempts to learn and make sense of, well, everything. On a beautiful autumn day, we met in Central Square, got picnic supplies at the natural foods co-op, and walked over to Mt. Auburn Cemetery, where we sat together amid the white birches and marble stones, which were stark against the glowing orange and crimson leaves.

Then he decided we should compare the legendary Mt. Auburn with the equally esteemed cemetery in my own neighborhood, Forest Hills. I mentioned that Anne Sexton was buried there, and he checked out a library book on the poet.

When he rang my bell on the morning of our field trip, I went downstairs to let him in, pausing to hug him, and led him upstairs to my apartment. As I gave him a tour, he looked around in wonder. I was twenty-six, and I shared a two-story apartment with a spacious living room and kitchen, and an extra front room/office/make-out room. My dad was fifty-six, and he lived in one small room in a boardinghouse with a bathroom down the hall.

He was halfway across the warped kitchen floor when he stopped, transfixed by the view of treetops and sky straight ahead. He put both hands out as if to steady himself on a surfboard, bent his knees slightly as if testing the give.

"Far out," he said. "I feel like I'm floating in the sky."

It was unclear whether he was having an actual acid flashback or not, but his enthusiasm was infectious. I laughed then, and on the many occasions after that when I walked into the kitchen and pictured him there caught up in his bliss.

We went to my local co-op and got a picnic and set out for the graveyard. As we walked, my dad drifted into a reverie about Anne

Sexton, speaking as if he had a crush on her, never mind that she'd been dead by her own hand for three decades by then.

"She was just incredible," he said. "Did you know she had a band? She started it with some of her students when she was teaching. They wrote songs, and she read her poems over the music. I would love to find a recording, just to hear what it was like. She was so angry, so unhappy, but so beautiful, too."

When we reached her grave, where she was buried with her husband's family, we saw that previous devotees had left a dozen small koans, stacked stones with a beautiful simplicity that moved me. We built one of our own. Then my father surprised me. He reached into the pocket of his cargo pants and pulled out his current notebook.

"I'd like to read a piece of one of her poems I wrote down," he said.

I smiled at him, loving that he'd been inspired to make this gesture of respect. My friends and I, who made such a show of devotion to the bands and writers we loved, would have felt embarrassed to do something so sincere. His voice still had the lazy inflection of the Trenton hoodlum he'd been, but it was weathered by the decades in which he'd longed to be a poet, and when poetry had eluded him, he'd turned himself toward the puzzle of enlightenment instead. As we walked between graves and stands of ancient trees, I felt closer to him than I could ever remember having been. At the same time, I was incredibly proud of the independence I'd forged at such a great cost and was wary of a father figure, especially one who had essentially abandoned me for the first twenty-five years of my life. I dared a sideways glance at him and hoped we would figure it out.

chapter twelve

KRYPTONITE

I was at once heartbroken and on overdrive. I longed for Scott, and yet I was determined to suck every bit of marrow out of the life for which I'd sacrificed him in order to find myself. The unbending deadlines of freelance journalism gave me a convenient place to hide out when my feelings overwhelmed me.

Mary and I were out at my favorite local club, the Middle East, when she ran into one of the *Globe*'s staff music writers, Steve Morse, whom she knew from working nights at the *Globe*'s website. He stopped to chat. I told him I was a regular freelancer for the *Globe* and wanted to start writing about music. He was gracious and gave me an entrée to do my first CD review for the paper.

I loved covering music, but my central obsession was always my own writing. I felt guilty, that I never got enough done. I was sure I was falling behind. More than anything, I wanted to distinguish myself, to create a novel that spoke to all of the musicians and writers and artistic-minded friends I felt had literally kept me alive.

I usually had three or four articles going at a time, plus pitches for more work, and I always wrote up until the exact last minute before it was time to go meet my dad or anyone else. The next thing I knew, I was fifteen minutes late and still had to put on face powder. Then I was twenty minutes late and at the mercy of the bus or train.

I arrived, out of breath, sweating, and found my dad pacing in a slow diagonal, holding a plastic shopping bag with whatever he'd brought that day—free real estate listings or health food circulars that had caught his eye, a newspaper piece I'd written, a photocopied article about the film we were going to see. I hated being late, and I was cranky in that guilty way. His face opened up in an expectant smile. Suddenly, as if I were once again the moody teenager he'd barely known, I wanted to crush him.

"Did you have to wait long for the train?" he asked.

"No, I'm on deadline," I said. "I shouldn't even be here."

"Oh," he said, sounding hurt. "Are you working on a story for the *Globe*?"

"I'm always working on a story for the *Globe*."

He stood there smiling, not provoked at all, and it was hard for me to stay mad. He never got upset with me for being late, and he was never anything but interested in everything that was going on in my life, even when I claimed it made me too busy for him.

One night, when I rolled up at seven fifteen, out of breath, my dad was outside, beaming.

"Sorry I'm late," I said, already defensive.

"We've got plenty of time," he said. "The movie doesn't start until seven thirty."

"But you said—"

"I said seven o'clock, so you'd be here early."

I stopped short, shocked and indignant. And then I laughed. His solution was so elegant, and there was no judgment in his tone. Without having to scold me or complain about my tardiness, which only would have set me off, he'd gotten me there early for the film.

If I had previously worried that he might suddenly try to exert a father's discipline or control over me, I soon relaxed and began to adjust to the father he really was, not the fantasy I'd created in his absence. It would have been hard to see him as a traditional father anyhow. When we grew close enough to talk about personal topics, including my breakup with Scott, his advice was unlike any I'd ever heard of a dad giving his daughter.

"I think you should take a lot of lovers," he said.

I didn't respond, or even look at him, embarrassed to find myself blushing, even though I prided myself on being able to talk tough with my male friends.

"The younger the better," he continued. "That way you can figure out what you want and don't want."

I nodded my head instinctively. On a purely intellectual level, it made perfect sense, and it was basically what I'd been doing in the wake of my breakup.

"I mean you have to be responsible. You have to take responsibility for your relationships. Otherwise you're just an asshole."

I laughed. Not only at his frank way of speaking, but at the idea that I'd ever be such a master of romance. I could take a lot of lovers, sure, but I was terrified that each and every one of them was going to abandon me. And that insecurity was fueled by obsessiveness, even about men I didn't really like enough to want to stay. I was fucked up. I knew that. And my dad knew it. But we weren't quite ready to look at how I'd gotten that way or what could be done about it.

As my dad and I warmed to each other, he often complimented me, even about things that weren't obviously positive. I discussed the breakup with my dad, saying that if we could just find a way to both make ourselves happy in the same place, then we'd be able to enjoy all of our love and mutual attraction.

"A lot of people would have given up by now," my dad said. "They'd already have moved on to multiple other relationships that would have just re-created the same problems they had in their first relationship that didn't work out. But not you. You're really sticking to it, and wrestling with it, and you're determined to figure out what went wrong and how to learn something from it."

I smiled shyly at my dad as he spoke. I did want to discover something through what had happened with Scott. Now that I was over my fixation with the other man I'd kissed, I was deeply ashamed of how I'd behaved and how much it had hurt Scott. I wanted to get to a place where I knew myself better, was taking more responsibility for my life, and not causing so much collateral damage. I was convinced if I was honest and courageous about who I was and what I wanted, Scott would forgive me.

I wrote him an impassioned love letter, telling him that he was the only man for me, and letting him know that I would be there on the other side of whatever he was going through. And then I waited for his reply. And waited.

He e-mailed me a few times in January and left me a message on my birthday, but he never mentioned my letter, and I was too afraid to ask. In February, my phone rang at eleven in the morning. It was Scott. Although it was eight o'clock in Portland, he was still up, and very drunk. He said it was a beautiful letter, he still loved me, he still wanted to be with me, but he had another girlfriend. I chose to focus on everything before the "but."

The night after I had this conversation with Scott, I went to a show downstairs at the Middle East. I'd been trying to at least distract myself with other guys in the wake of Scott's return to Portland, even if my heart still belonged to my first true love, but I'd yet to meet anyone who'd even begun to compare to his charm and intelligence. That night, I was introduced to Anthony, a tall, lanky young man with a thicket of dark curls and chestnut eyes. As soon as we met, we were instantly flirting. Our wits easily dovetailed, and his presence numbed out the painful memory of Scott's call.

The next time I saw him, he told me he needed a place to live, and I hooked him up with some friends whose house was my main hang out in Jamaica Plain, giving me easy access to him. When he brought me up to see his room a few weeks later, he surprised me. He was funnier and smarter than I'd anticipated, and I hadn't expected him to be so perceptive about the kinds of tiny nuances I noticed but most others didn't. When we were alone together, he turned to look at me. Laughing, he tugged his earlobes.

"What's up?" he said.

Only then did I realize he was mimicking me—I was tugging my own earlobes. I quickly stopped, half-embarrassed, half-flattered he'd been watching me so closely.

"It's something I do when I'm nervous," I said, demonstrating.

"Are you nervous now?" he said, his voice devilish as he yanked his ears again, and then he kissed me, hard. We ended up talking and kissing until dawn.

A week later there was a big party at Anthony's house. I walked into the kitchen and the whole room erupted into a chorus of "Duchess." Everyone in that group of friends had a nickname, and mine was "Que Sarah, Duchess of Rock," soon shortened to "the Duchess," which, of course, I loved. The room was already noisy, and smoky, and full of people and laughter and music. He grinned at me, and I felt the promise of an imminent rendezvous. After a few beers, I made my way to his room. He turned, pouch of tobacco in hand, and kissed me. It was still new and exciting, and yet, I knew his body a little bit now, and I felt entitled to lean into him and put my hands in his thick, dark hair.

We fell onto his bed. His pleasure, when I got him off, made me happy, made me feel powerful and sexy. He pushed me back and tugged down my jeans and underwear.

"I'm reciprocating," he said, laughing.

He put his lips on me with gentle attention. It felt as if his mouth had been made for this. A sigh escaped me like a silk scarf fluttering. When I came, in only a minute, maybe two, it was fast and hard, like I had seen it be for boys. When he pulled away, I realized my shoes were still on. I lay there for a delicious moment before I stood and dressed.

His room was neat and cozy, like the cabin of a ship, and I didn't want to leave. He smoked a cigarette, sitting on the edge of his bed. I closed my eyes and drifted.

"Sarah, you have to go," he said.

I rolled away from him toward the wall and lay there until I felt him give in and lie down next to me. My fake sleep gave way to the real thing. In the morning, I couldn't face my messy room, my deadlines, and the sounds that came through the wall of Mary's bedroom, reminding me of the boy who had chosen her over me, so I let myself drift back asleep in Anthony's bed. Even when I heard movement at the foot of the bed, I kept my eyes closed. I recognized Anthony's bandmate, who'd come to get the keys to their van.

"Who's she?" Ken asked.

"No comment," Anthony said.

Not exactly a term of endearment, but I knew the crude jokes and stupid nicknames guys in bands often made up about the girls they fooled around with—and I was relieved he hadn't let his anxiety about the situation cause him to be cruel.

I didn't think about Anthony as a potential boyfriend or wish he would call and take me to dinner. I didn't think about him rationally at all. I just wanted him. It wasn't only that he was tall and handsome and played "Blackbird" for me on his guitar, laughing at himself a little as he did, before segueing into new songs he was writing, or that we had the kind of sexual chemistry that had inspired me to nickname him my kryptonite. He had a natural grace and sparkle that made everything an adventure, made it feel as if the whole big world was right there with us, and I was living in it, just by being in his bed.

I was hanging out with Anthony's roommates one night, and when he got home, late, even though we hadn't hooked up for months, he swept me up to his room. We had sex, and it was as seamless as I'd known it would be. He kept me up long enough that I missed my morning bus to Cape Cod, where I was to be a bridesmaid in Marya's wedding. Stuffing food into my mouth on a later bus in hopes of soaking up the remaining alcohol in my system, I smeared avocado all over my jeans, which only made me look more like the Cameron Diaz character in a screwball romantic comedy.

Cleaned up and halfway presentable a few hours later, I joined the rehearsal dinner. It was a lovely night. As I stood outside the group, drinking bourbon, a man stood beside me and rested his hand on my back in a friendly way. It was Marya's father. His small, kind gesture went unnoticed by others but filleted me. *So that's what it feels like to have a normal dad.*

In that instant, I understood, almost on a molecular level, exactly what was still lacking, even now that my father and I had reconciled. He had no interest in putting aside his counterculture lifestyle for even one night to do the ordinary things dads do. Intellectually, I respected him for this, but there's nothing logical about the heart's desires.

I looked across the deck at Marya, laughing and talking amid her wedding guests. She was tall and beautiful and poised. More than that, I knew it was what was inside of her that mattered. She had a sense of her own worth. She knew she deserved to be happy.

That was why she was getting married, and I wasn't.

It wasn't that I cared so much about marriage specifically. Since Scott and I had broken up, I'd started saying: "I don't have a baby clock; I have a book clock." And it was true that I'd let Scott go back to Portland mostly because I didn't see how I could sustain our relationship and my writing at the same time. But I wanted to be worth marriage. I wanted to know I deserved to be happy, even if I wasn't about to admit it to myself yet, and if you'd asked me—But don't you want to be happy?—I would have rolled my eyes, lit a cigarette, and said *Bang bang shoot shoot.*

My longing for worthiness had been imprinted on me when I was a baby, forming the foundation of my personality, as seamlessly as I'd learned to recite my alphabet and tie my laces. Having my dad back in my life for a year wasn't going to instantly heal me.

The next time I went to a party at Anthony's house, he was in his room, practicing for an audition in New York City to play with an up-and-coming band whose first album I'd adored when I reviewed it. As much as he partied, he was also focused and devoted to his music, which he wanted like I wanted to write. He got the gig, as I'd known he would. I didn't see him before he jetted off to Europe. I was jealous: He got to stop painting houses and do what he loved and was good at, travel, and get paid. He took what he wanted. Meanwhile, I was left juggling deadlines, rolling quarters to pay my bills, and not hearing from Scott. I made a vow to take what I wanted, too: I would finish my book.

I was as swamped with deadlines as ever, but when I was done writing articles and reviews, I pulled my laptop over to my bed, poured a glass of wine, and worked on my novel, which was slowly but surely taking shape. When my resolve wavered, I drew inspiration from my kryptonite, distilling my goal into a simple mantra: Be like a boy.

I had continued to enjoy the deeper relationship with my family that had blossomed during our trip to Ireland. My brother was attending Boston University, and I often took him as my plus-one when I was sent to cover bands he liked. Even though it was happening ten years later than it normally did for siblings, it felt good to be his cool older sister. When my mom and Craig came down to visit him, they took us both out for meals, and I appreciated how nice they were to me following my breakup with Scott. Still wanting to be perfect, and to protect them, I hid my heavy drinking and entanglements with boys in bands from them, although I'm sure they sometimes noticed my epic hangovers.

Despite my newfound focus on writing and my enjoyment of my family, by the time my kryptonite got home from touring in late September, our affair was one of the most vibrant parts of my life. He continued to have this way of really seeing me, careless as he could be.

During a phone conversation about my writing, he started unfolding a fantasy about how I needed a male intern who would work naked. In the morning, I would wake up, put on a silk kimono, and have my intern pour me a martini. Then I would light a cigarette and say (pausing to drag on my cigarette):

"Intern, take dictation. I had a bird. It flew away. It was my father."

Stunned that he'd been paying attention all along, I smiled at his words.

Happy to finally be in his room with him once again, our bodies close together, my skin singing, I talked with Anthony about his music, my writing, and the big world beyond Boston. He took me to bed and stripped me. His skin was tan and smelled like sunshine and the dusky scent of tobacco. I was freer with him than I had been with Scott for a long time, maybe ever. We drifted off to sleep, entwined, at dawn.

The next morning, I stopped in at the Dunkin' Donuts on my way home because I wanted something sugary. I felt dirty in that happy way, with his smell on my skin, and my writing waiting for me, amid all of the commuters who were going to the coffins of their desks. Not me. I felt like maybe I was creating a life for myself that supported my writing and my desires. Marguerite Duras had lovers. Patti Smith had lovers. I had a lover. I was maybe becoming an artist on the cusp of the big life I'd always dreamed of having. I went home, alive, to write.

I'd been writing CD reviews for about six months, and I'd developed a nice rapport with my editor. As I earned his trust, he gave me more power to select the albums I covered. In the middle of October, I noticed that the guy I'd had a crush on when I was seventeen, Judah, had a new album. I pitched a CD review and landed the assignment.

The album was an ode to the singer's best friend, who had died suddenly the previous year. It was perfect for my mood that fall. As much as I was enjoying my affair with my kryptonite, we only spent about one night a month together. I missed Scott. And when I heard Mary and her boyfriend through my bedroom wall, I envied what they had. I listened to the album, again and again, crafting my review carefully, as if I were writing a love letter to the singer, which, in a way, I was.

I pitched a feature to preview Judah's band's upcoming Boston show. My editor had been impressed with my CD review, and I was assigned the piece. On the afternoon of the interview, my heart hammered in my chest, even though I did phoners all of the time and I'd already covered people who were more famous than he was. We felt each other out for the first few minutes, before we both relaxed. I couldn't help but flirt.

"So what's a typical date with you like?"

"I'm a great date. I'll do anything except go see a Merchant Ivory movie."

He laughed, a delicious, sexy shuffle. I laughed and felt something happening on the phone between us. I wasn't even surprised. It felt right. I was too hardwired to move toward the promise of the elusive rock star, no matter the potential risk, to remember my mom's prescient warning to me in her graduation letter. I couldn't give myself value. Only he could.

The conversation shifted to his reputation, which was formidable.

"You've got to keep your fists up, Sarah," he said.

It was a one-off comment. He didn't really know me. I knew this. But his words were so true. I'd always been drawn to something in his music. It was dark, raw, brutally honest about human nature, desire, and love. Some people considered it misogynistic. I'd always seen it as power, which was something I wanted for myself, especially now that I was on my own. No Simon's Rock. No Bard. No Claire. No Scott.

I'd earned access to this man who knew how to be this force in the world, and I wanted more of that for myself. I told him I'd be at his Boston show.

"Come back and say hey," he said.

I was nerved up as I approached the venue, but it never occurred to me to not go. Everything that scared me was always what I desired most.

The room was crowded, his fans devoted as usual. I ordered a Maker's Mark and soda, and then another, hovering at the bar while I drank them quickly, almost afraid to approach the stage. I pushed myself into the crowd so I could see him. The music was sexy. It throbbed and glistened. He had put on weight since I'd seen his old band in Portland nearly eight years earlier, but he was still light on his feet, elegant yet forceful in the way he stretched at the mic, telegraphing every emotion.

I thought about our conversation, and the article I'd written, and enjoyed the thrill of feeling as if this public man was a little bit mine, especially when he sat at his keyboard for a medley that included a bit of Fleetwood Mac's "Sara." At the end of the show, I was nervous but walked into the green room like it was no big deal. Judah was sitting in the corner, a white towel over his head, like a boxer postfight. His bassist nodded at me, then left us alone in the small room crammed with gear. I introduced myself.

"How's the rest of the tour been?" I asked.

"I always say you don't have to pay me to play. That I'll gladly do it for free. It's the other twenty-three hours of bullshit you have to pay me for."

He laughed, gravelly and genuine, the kind of laugh it was a pleasure to join. His gaze was knowing and cryptic like a cat's. We talked easily for a few minutes, my whole body thrumming with the old excitement of my teenage crush. Suddenly, I was sure I'd kept him too long, that he wanted to get on with the rest of his night.

"Here, take my card, so we can stay in touch," I said.

"Stay in touch," he said, teasing me, as he took hold of the other end of the card.

"Yeah, I'll be in LA in January," I said, making it up on the spot.

"You've got my number."

I offered my hand. His grip was firm. We held on to each other a little too long, our gaze locked. It was almost enough to make me blush. As I turned and left the room, I was very aware of his eyes on me, tracing my hips. The chilled night air hit my feverish skin all at once. I walked home over the Mass Ave Bridge, singing his songs, ecstatic.

As I rang in 2004, my life was a constant up and down. Just as with my childhood survival technique where I'd focused on my dad's small gestures of love, rather than his gaping parental deficiencies, I held on to the slightest affection from my kryptonite, Anthony: when he kissed me at a bar in front of friends; when, after the New Year's Eve party at his house, his ex-girlfriend went home, and he and I ended up drunk in his bed together.

And I glossed over the moments just after the sex, when the affection evaporated as quickly as the sweat on our skin. He jumped out of bed and sat down on his couch to roll himself a cigarette. I sat up, the sheet pulled to my waist.

"Sarah, you have to leave."

"You don't respect me. You don't like me because I'm smart."

"I like you because you're smart. And you have great tits."

I laughed. It was so stupid, and yet, I felt complimented. Again, I preferred to only hear the positive and ignore any harshness. He lit his cigarette and lay down on his rug, smoking, staring up at the ceiling, looking drunk and exhausted and done with me. Something snapped inside of me: in that moment, I wasn't a twenty-seven-year-old woman with a successful freelance journalism career and a life lived on my own terms, but a woman hungry for the great love it felt that life had cost me.

"Please, let me stay," I said, beyond pride, beyond everything. "I want to stay."

In the primal, childish way of temper tantrums and doomed love affairs, all my pride and obstinacy kicked in, but instead of that carrying me out into the night with a vow to start a new year in which I only allowed myself to be treated with kindness and respect, I focused on getting what I wanted in that moment: to sleep beside him. I had a lover, and to have passionate sex and then sleep beside each other was what lovers did.

And I got what I wanted. I spent the next two nights with him, smoking pot, drinking, and hanging out with our friends. His house had become a magical place, like the Island of Misfit Toys, where a small group clung together against the treacherous rapids of adulthood. He ripped my shirt over my head. I kissed his skinny chest, tugged off his jeans, already ready, always ready, for him. He was moaning and talking. He liked to talk dirty to me, and I liked to talk back. But this time, his words were different, and I tried to block them out. "We have to stop this," he said. "It's starting to feel too good. We know what to do for each other."

We didn't stop. In the morning, I dressed and got ready to leave without having to be told. When I stepped into the bright sparkle of the winter sun, the cold air slapped me awake. I'd spent nearly three straight days and nights with him, and he was thick and syrupy in my system. But even as I felt triumphant that I'd been allowed to stay, I knew it was a temporary communion. He would soon be going away again, and leaving me far behind, geographically if not creatively. I wanted more for myself: I wanted the whole big world.

chapter thirteen

I LIKE YOUR BRAIN

In mid-January, I traveled to Los Angeles. A good friend had been trying to convince me to visit since she'd moved there the previous year, and now, full of the possibility of my rock crush, Judah, I made it happen. As soon as I arrived, I was smitten with the city.

The night I worked up the courage to call Judah and leave a message: my friend was having a party at her bungalow. I stayed mostly sober in case he called back. At five in the morning he did, and when we realized I was staying just a few blocks away from his house, he sent someone over on foot to get me. I didn't find this at all strange. I walked out of my friend's bungalow and stood in front of the Silver Lake Lounge, enjoying the secret feeling of being awake when no one else was, loving the palm trees and vast sky, and wondering what would happen next. After about ten minutes, a short Asian woman, Alyssa, strutted toward me across the street. She was pretty, with long, flowing hair, and she was dressed casual-sexy in low-slung jeans, high-heeled sandals, and a halter top with no bra.

It had never occurred to me that he'd send a girl. As she led me up into the hills where he lived, I darted sideways looks at her, trying to figure out who she was and what she was to Judah. I scattered bright, happy chatter around us, wanting her on my side.

Alyssa knocked quickly as we entered. I stopped just inside the threshold, suddenly nervous. It was a space with gravitas, low lit, the end of a fire burning in a tiled fireplace to my right. Judah sat on the couch, facing a low coffee table covered in clusters of lit candles, ashtrays, packs of cigarettes, lighters, pill canisters, a bottle of baby oil.

"Welcome," he said. "Come on in."

I smiled and bowed my head toward him, the master of the house.

"Good morning," I said. "Thanks for having me. My friend couldn't live any closer to you. I think her apartment may actually be inside your house."

"What brings you to LA? Business or pleasure."

"A little of both."

"Good answer."

I was still trying not to do anything to make Alyssa turn against me, so I let her slide onto the couch next to Judah and chose an armchair across from them. He picked up his phone and looked at it. He had us wait in the bedroom while a man came with a delivery, and then he offered us one of the cans of Tecate beer the man had brought.

Judah was wearing sunglasses, and he and I were circling each other slowly. This was what I had always dreamed of—time at home with an artist I admired—still, nerves rattled me. I was trying to soak it all in, not just the smell of incense and the silky black cat rubbing himself against my ankles, but also the gilded glisten of the air as it soaked into my pores.

Judah suddenly looked at me head-on. With a well-practiced motion, he pulled out a small baggie, dumped out a pile of white powder, and began to rack up lines. I had done some coke but had always felt like I was doing it wrong.

Judah cut a plastic straw and nodded me over, holding it out. "Come do a line."

"Thanks but not yet," I said.

"Come do a line, or how do I know you're not a narc?"

"I will, in a minute," I said.

He stood and looked at me with force. Alyssa sat on the couch, watching as we went back and forth like this a few times. Judah and I faced off against each other for a long moment, and then we smiled, both satisfied we'd made our point. It was six in the morning.

I took the straw from him, kneeled on the floor in front of the table, and snaked the coke up into my nose, then closed my nostril with a finger and inhaled deeply. My skin glittered, my thoughts glistened, and I smiled at him. Judah moved with the concentrated nonchalance of someone who'd spent more than two decades onstage. As he cut lines, he spun stories of life on the road. I pushed back from the table and looked up.

"I'm good for now, or you're about to have a very fucked-up girl on your hands."

He smiled at me and nodded. Somehow I had propelled myself out of my regular, small life to sit with this man I admired. Judah brought out a bottle of Maker's Mark and ordered Alyssa to the kitchen for ice. I watched them closely, still unsure about their relationship and what it meant for me, determined to talk with the men, not serve with the women. And yet, I wasn't silky and well put together like she was, and it seemed possible he was going to send me away when the drugs ran out, with the promise of tickets to his next Boston show. The light around us was Southern California gold. I was very, very high.

"Maybe you girls should take your tops off," Judah said.

"Okay," Alyssa said, giggling, instantly topless.

Her skin was caramel, and her breasts were pretty, and she had a little potbelly that made her look younger than she was. I looked at Judah for a long moment.

"I'm going to keep my bra on," I said.

He laughed. "Okay," he said.

Slowly, embarrassed, I opened my shirt, button by button. Judah watched.

"Now go stand over there together," he said, pointing. "Let's take a picture."

I handed him the disposable camera from my purse.

"Hug each other," he said.

Alyssa knew exactly what to do and wrapped her satiny skin around me. She was much shorter than I was and her face nestled near my breasts, bound in their black bra. We were both still wearing our sunglasses. I smoked my cigarette, unable to contain the wolfish grin roaring up inside of me. So he wasn't going to send me home after all. But I didn't want to share him. After he snapped photos, I kneeled at the table again. Judah seemed to accept this. Around three in the afternoon, Alyssa went to sleep in his room.

"Why don't you slip into something more comfortable?" he said.

I smiled at him and followed him toward the kitchen. He reached into the dryer and handed me a pair of black boxer briefs. I held his eyes with mine as I unsnapped my button and slowly slid down my fly. He stepped close to me and helped me tug down the stiff fabric of my jeans. My skin was instantly hot. I leaned into him. He didn't touch me anywhere except where his arm circled my hips, which made it even hotter.

"Now put these on," he said, his voice low and raspy.

I felt like I could get off, just standing there by his dryer with him.

Without thinking twice, I followed him outside in my bra and his underwear at three in the afternoon on a Saturday. It was a perfect Los Angeles day. I was dimly aware of at least one neighbor in a nearby yard, but everything outside our lovely, gauzy cocoon was distant from me. Until I glanced up and was immediately filled with delight: the mythic white letters of the Hollywood sign crowned the hillside in the distance. The love I'd felt for Los Angeles throughout my visit crested to a perfect blissful glow.

He held me on his lap and had me inhale nitrous, which washed me up into a remote part of myself where it felt like nothing bad had ever happened.

"Have you ever been fucked by a man on Viagra?" he said.

I shook my head no, not telling him I could nearly count all of the men I'd ever had sex with on two hands. We smoked and drank and kissed. His hands were heavy on the bare curves of my hips, his mouth on mine, the sun warm on my shoulders and back. Every time his fingertips grazed me, it was as if sparklers lit up along my skin.

He led me back inside, and I walked into the kitchen for a glass of water. He was touching me, leaning against me from behind, bending me over the counter, pulling down his underwear, and my underwear, and sliding himself inside of me. I pushed back into him, urgent with wanting. It felt like a perfect fit, which was something he sang about, and I heard his voice in my head, but no, it was just by my ear.

"Sarah," he said. "Sarah."

The sound of my name reminded me where I was, and who was fucking me, and the story he'd told me earlier in the day about a stripper/drug dealer he'd fucked under the stage when his band was opening for one of the great stadium rock bands of his youth. How he'd made his reputation on fucking almost as much as on music. I kicked my way up out of the undertow of pleasure in which I'd been swept out to sea.

"Do you have a condom?" I asked.

"No."

"You can't fuck me without a condom."

"Don't you want to get fucked?" he breathed into my ear, pushing into me.

"Yes," I moaned. "Let's find a condom."

"No," he said, and like smoke, he'd slid out of me.

I stood for a long moment, bereft, empty, abandoned, wanting to do whatever it took to make him fill me up again, now and forever, to be his good girl and make him like me. I turned to look at him, pulling up my underwear.

"Judah," I said.

He was already walking back to the living room, lighting a cigarette. I followed behind him nervously, preparing to be cast out. As with my dad, and my kryptonite, I never thought about leaving. I would do anything to stay and have the experience, even when it didn't go my way. But he simply cut new lines and handed me a fresh straw.

The afternoon unfolded like an extended game of Truth or Dare, with his telling me to do something, and my either saying yes or no. After a few rounds, I relaxed, realizing I'd finally found a man who was confident enough to withstand a no.

Time drifted to and fro. I looked up at his bookcase and saw my business card propped against a book, which made me happy. Next to it was a photo of a blond woman. It made me think of his most famous release, a breakup album.

I mentioned the title to him. "Who'd you write it for?" I asked.

"I wrote it about her," he said, standing and retrieving the photo near my card.

I looked at her. She was pretty, but there was nothing in her face to indicate that she was going to end up on his bookshelf a decade after the release of the album she'd inspired, an album I'd listened to obsessively for years, whose lyrics had informed my thoughts on relationships and sex. I held on to the photo, not because I was jealous, but because I was learning something important about where art came from, and how I might turn Scott, my kryptonite, the shooting, and everything else into something, maybe as beautiful and raw and alchemic as his album had been for me and so many others.

As I handed the photo back to him, I saw his copy of *A Book of Dreams.*

"Peter Reich," I said. "I've always wanted to read that. My dad took me to see Wilhelm Reich's cloud buster when I was little."

"I covered 'Cloudbusting,' and I read it to understand the song before I sang it."

"That's right," I said. "We talked about it in our interview."

I grew happy then, as if I had stumbled upon the true path of my life and was finally learning what I needed to know to become the artist and the woman I wanted to be.

"I'm writing a book," I said.

"You are? Do tell."

I told him the whole story of my novel, *Because the Night*. He listened intently, asking questions in the right places, but not trying to dominate the conversation or tell me how my book should be, which I appreciated.

Even though I'd seen the light leak out of the sky through the windows as we'd talked and made out, when Judah led me outside at nine o'clock so he could go to the recording studio, the darkness surprised me. I was getting that Sunday night feeling, but I tried to fight it. He drove me in his new car into the hills, which were shadowed and lovely. We made out and did bumps of cocaine off his key, and he slid my red satin underwear off me to bring with him on tour in Europe. He pulled into the little alley near my friend's bungalow.

"Thanks for having me over," I said with a smile.

He laughed.

"You'll always remember me because I was the first woman you made out with in this car," I said, repeating words he'd spoken earlier, certain everything was about to disappear forever. I felt like I was always building everything from scratch.

"I'll always remember you because you're my friend, and sometimes lover, and the woman whose novel I'm going to write an introduction for."

"Really?" I said, too happy to even play at cool.

"Really."

"I guess I'd better finish writing it then."

He laughed again and kissed me quickly on the lips.

"Ciao, bella," he said, and he was gone.

Late that night, my phone rang. This was the big life I'd always dreamed of. But when he invited me over, his voice reminded me of those people on *The X-Files* with the black tar in their eyes, as if the cocaine and the sleeplessness had replaced his essence with something dark, and I refused him, even though I feared that would be it between us. I hoped he would forgive me for leaving him alone late at night, even hoped he had someone else to be with, because I knew well the kind of loneliness he was calling in reinforcements against.

I'd fallen hard for Los Angeles—it was like falling in love with a person—and I'd hated to return to Boston. It was the first year Scott hadn't called to wish me a happy birthday, even though I'd called him eighteen days earlier on his. On my kryptonite's birthday a month later, he left his ex-girlfriend asleep in his bed and took me downstairs to the basement, where we fucked on the washing machine and a chair in the low-ceilinged, dingy room.

During all of this, I'd sent Judah an e-mail. Taking inspiration from an erotic website he'd shown me during our night together, I wrote a short piece with one of the songs we'd listened to together as the soundtrack. In it, I wore red satin underwear, just like the ones he had with him in Europe. He wrote back that he liked my story very much.

One day early that spring, he called me three times before I finished my day's deadlines, and I gathered the nerve to answer his fourth call. I knew enough about cocaine to understand the drug was behind his focus and intensity, but still, I was fluttery with excitement when I heard his deep, hypnotic voice on the line.

"What are you wearing?" he asked.

"Nothing," I said, catching on quickly, even as I heard a loud crush of voices behind him. "What's all that noise?"

"I'm at a Lakers game at the Staples Center," he said. "It's halftime and my friends are inside while I'm outside smoking a cigarette."

We both laughed at the naughtiness of this. He got me off with his voice and went inside to watch the second half of the game. After that, he called me several times a week, often several times a day. He'd call me after last call at his bar, or when he'd come in late from the studio, around six in the morning, in Boston, so often that I began sleeping with my cell phone on my chest, just above my breasts. We talked our way through elaborate fantasies, like one in which he played in Boston—as he would in six weeks—and he went backstage between songs, where I waited for him with an eight ball and got him off.

He wanted to know everything about my sexual history, and he was always just as transparent with me. Because he never got more romantic than a good-bye, "Ciao, bella," I wasn't jealous of the other women he mentioned. I knew he didn't want a girlfriend and understood why. When we talked for hours, I knew there must be something in me that was clever and charming and sexy enough to interest him, and it made me feel a little more of those things in my daily life. He was eleven years older than I was, and he was giving me an education, exposing me to his sensual world, which thrilled me.

At that moment in my life, I was obsessed with figuring out what it was an artist "did"—reading Patti Smith's journals, in which she described her songwriting process, talking about the craft over glasses of Maker's Mark and soda with my writer friends Cathy and Erin.

So I was deeply curious about the ins and outs of Judah's daily life as it applied to his music. He had played me the early sketches of some songs when I'd been in LA, and I wanted to know how he was expanding these and other ideas into full songs, when and where he was going into the studio, and what else he was listening to and reading. Mostly we talked about sex, but even that was cerebral. One night, very late, in the midst of a passionate exchange, he asked me, "Do you like that we have this?"

"Yes," I said. "I like your brain."

"I like your brain, too," he said, laughing.

I did like what we had, very much. As the date of his next Boston show approached, he began to plan our next assignation with great attention to detail. He wanted drugs, a lot of them, and it was up to me to get them. He wanted me to be waiting for him in his hotel room. Wearing lingerie. We would do the drugs. We would fuck. He would go to the club and play his show. I would attend as his guest.

There was just one problem, which I was not about to volunteer: I had never bought drugs before, except a little pot and acid. But I had a friend who would help me.

As I counted the days until Judah's show, anticipating our reunion eagerly, Judah suddenly stopped calling. I allowed myself to call and e-mail him once. After that, I was cut off. I wasn't going to be the girl who got clingy or made a big fuss.

I was in my pajamas, at my desk, sluggish with a hangover, when my phone rang. It was Judah. We hadn't spoken in several weeks, by far the longest we'd gone without contact since LA, even when he'd been in Europe. After a few beats of awkward small talk, he said, "I'm sorry I disappeared."

"Yeah, thanks, is everything okay?"

He told me a story about a personal loss that had prompted him to stop doing coke. I was moved for him, but I struggled to adjust to this new him, without the fantasy, and the air of debauched bliss. Even as I wanted all of that back, I was honored to be a friend he trusted enough to confide something private.

"I'll call you again before we hit Boston," he said.

"Okay, be safe out there."

When I hung up, I crumbled. There had been no flirtation in his tone, no sex at all. Even though, intellectually, I appreciated his friend-ship, emotionally, I felt abandoned. I knew it was a sign of great respect that he'd let me in on what was going on with him. Here was a man I'd admired since college, and now he was treating me like one of his closest personal friends. I valued this, especially as the girl who always wanted to make people feel better. But real intimacy was terrifying for me. And I could only handle it in rare cases: with Scott, who had the constancy to make me feel safe; with Anthony, who quickly minimized any real connection we formed by disappearing for long stretches of time. Without Judah's consistent advances, it felt as if he was about to disappear. I desperately needed to talk to someone who'd get it.

That week, I was out with my dad on one of our by-now-established father-daughter dates. As usual, we spent much of our time talking about film and writing and art, and I'd recently begun mentioning discussions I'd had with my "friend" Judah about the same. I'd just always left out the sex parts, not that my dad would have minded, but I had a natural instinct toward at least some boundaries, even if he didn't.

As my dad and I sat over lunch at an Indian restaurant in my neighborhood, I told him the whole story and confessed how hurt I was.

"Sarah, let him be," he said.

"What?" I asked, surprised. Normally, my dad wanted whatever I wanted.

"He's dealing with something way beyond your experience," he said. "You've never been an addict, have you?"

"No," I said, as if that were some failing on my part.

"He needs more than you can give him right now. He needs friends who have gone through recovery and can support him."

"But I really care about him."

"Then be his friend and support him by letting him do whatever he needs to do to get through what he's going through right now. This isn't about you."

It was just what I needed to hear. I wanted to be better than I was. I wanted to be able to meet Judah where he was. Full of unexpected wisdom, my dad's words helped me to at least get closer.

My dad had just received a letter from my younger sister, Asmara, much like the one I'd sent prompting our reunion. She was sixteen now, her English was quite good, and she was looking for answers about her dad, and maybe even a relationship with him. He was so pleased that he photocopied her letter and brought the duplicate to our next lunch.

I had mixed feelings as I read her elegant European cursive. Part of me wanted my dad all to myself, as I always had. Plus, she might get to have a meaningful relationship with him at age sixteen, which was almost exactly the age I was when he'd totally disappeared on me. But I knew I couldn't let my jealousy cloud my judgment.

"You have an amazing opportunity here, Dad," I said. "Imagine if you and I had patched things up when I was sixteen instead of waiting until now."

"I know," he said. "I thought the same thing."

He had written her back to encourage their burgeoning relationship, and now he was eagerly awaiting her reply. When I saw how excited he was, almost like a lovesick teenager, the green uglies reared up again. I resolved to be happy for them, but it was a struggle.

On the afternoon of Judah's Boston show, just when my anxiety had reached its zenith, my phone rang. He was at his hotel, and although he wasn't feeling well, he'd wanted to check in with me. "Did you ask to get listed for the show?" he said.

"Yeah, is that a problem?"

"No, I was gonna put you on the list."

"I figured you were busy," I lied.

I waited for him to invite me to his hotel. I waited for him to ask me about the sheer pink baby doll nightie I had bought just for him. I waited for him to want me to be backstage before he went on. When none of this came, I tried to remember my father's words, tried to be neutral. I tried to be Judah's friend.

By the time I walked up to the club that night, I was feeling raw. But I also felt sexy and more grown-up than ever before. I'd dressed carefully, put on red lipstick. No matter what happened, I was a woman with a lover. He had called me that day. I'd made this life of adventure happen.

His tour bus hulked outside, like a big bug, its reflective eyes watching me. I wanted to knock, claim my right to him, but I knew better. I went inside and found my friends to the left of the stage. The mood was tense and expectant, and rumors flew that Judah had over-dosed and was calling the show. I checked my phone: nothing. The minutes dragged into an hour, and then an hour and a half. A new friend, Rebecca, who knew Judah's circle in LA, talked about what an asshole he was. A friend who worked at the club said he'd threatened one of his musicians during sound check. I used my selective hearing and focused on the fantasies Judah and I had woven.

Almost two hours later than the band's set time, the lights dimmed. People cheered and whooped. The band took the stage. A slinky beat unfolded like a low-rider strut; Judah stood at the mic, smoking as usual, his voice as sexy and sure as ever. He was all right. I was so relieved that I didn't think about anything else. It was impossible not to enjoy the show—he was a consummate showman, no matter what else.

Afterward, I walked outside to smoke and hopefully catch sight of Judah. As I turned back to the club, a tall, thin man, who looked famil-iar to me, approached.

"Are you Sarah?" he said.

"Yeah."

"I've got a message from Judah. He's very sorry, but he can't see you tonight."

My face must have registered the blow.

"Do you want a hug?" he asked.

Stunned, I let myself be hugged. But I pulled myself away from him quickly, hating that I was allowing myself to be so overtly handled by Judah's entourage. I would not cry.

Later, blissfully drunk, I climbed into my bed, where I had talked with Judah so many nights. Listening to his voice mail greeting, I com-pletely fell apart, crying into the phone: "That's no way to treat a per-son," I said. "You should have called me."

In the morning, he hadn't called. I didn't feel neutral anymore.

chapter fourteen

I'M YOUR FATHER

I started waking up with a feeling of crushing dread every Sunday morning. My CD reviews were due that night at nine o'clock, and I was suddenly convinced I wouldn't be able to pull them off, even though I always did, and they were getting edited less and less. But this anxiety inspired me to see a therapist.

My dad completely supported the idea of therapy and had recently bought me a book by a therapist who ran with his patients, after I described something that had begun happening nearly every day on my run. When I had time to do a full loop through the Arboretum, which took about forty-five minutes, as I descended the final hill I had a recurring fantasy that I punched Scott in the face. In truth, I didn't want to hurt Scott—not after how much I had already hurt him emotionally—so the image made me feel guilty and bereft.

My dad excitedly ran through the book's explanation: "The brain has four states. Beta, Alpha, Theta, and Delta. Theta is like a meditation state. Well, when you've been running for forty-five minutes, your brain goes into Theta, which means you're actually entering your sub-conscious. It's wonderful that you're able to create that for yourself. That's why I want to get a biofeedback machine at home, so I can read my brain waves and see how they change when I do my breathing with my snorkel."

My dad was eager to explore his subconscious on his own terms and regarded therapy as a positive experience that everyone should undergo if they could afford it, pointing to one of his heroes, Woody Allen, as a model. He was slippery, though, about whether or not he needed therapy himself. He was down on Gamblers Anonymous—which he'd used to try to quit gambling, and failed—and the other AA incarnations, basically comparing them to brainwashing. But in my own moment of acute emotional stress, I was just trying to stay afloat and seeking anything that would work.

My therapist and I talked about my deadline anxiety, my money worries, my dad. It never occurred to me to mention the shooting because that was so long in the past, and I didn't mention either Anthony or Judah because I didn't want to be one of those girls who just talked about boys. At the end of a few sessions, he determined I wasn't clinically depressed. I was actually a bit let down. I knew something felt broken inside of me, and if I were simply depressed, then there would be a diagnosis and a cure, to which I could apply myself like a good A student. Instead, he focused on trying to get me to worry less and feel more self-confident based on genuine accomplishments. But that did nothing to stop me from feeling at the whim of the world.

I was at my computer working one day late that spring when Judah e-mailed me an apology and an olive branch of friendship. I was glad and felt respected. But I also felt disappointed. As with Anthony, if he wasn't coming on to me, I didn't know what he wanted from me. I wrote back, keeping my response light, all the while hoping for more of everything from him. But in the following weeks, there was no reply.

✦

Beth and I decided to rent our own apartment in the South End, closer to where she was bartending. One day not long after we'd signed the lease, my dad and I had lunch at the Thai restaurant we liked near Berklee College of Music. I was excited to show him the majestic brownstone that would be my home, and we walked down Mass Ave toward my new neighborhood. As we left the upscale avenues around Boylston Street and approached the more downtrodden area near the hospital, my dad grew quiet. He was such a constant and consummate talker that this was never a good sign. When we reached my apartment building he nodded politely, but that was about it.

As we turned and walked toward the bus stop that would take me back to JP, I snuck glances at him. "Why don't you just say whatever it is?" I said.

"It's not a very safe area. I'm your father, Sarah. It's natural for me to worry."

I was so mad I almost stopped short right there. Instead, I threw my anger into my walk. How dare he worry about me *now*? And how dare he plant the seed of worry in my mind when I was otherwise so excited about my new apartment and new life there? I certainly wasn't going to yell at him. That was too scary. I'd never yelled at anyone in my adult life. But, for once, I did open my mouth:

"It's kind of upsetting to hear you say that now, when you weren't around to worry about me during all of the years when I really could have used a dad."

"I know, Sarah, I'm sorry. But I'm going to make it up to you. What if I told you I had a key, a metaphysical key, and if I gave it to you, and helped you to master it, it would allow you to get anything you wanted?"

Judah. His name flashed up to the surface of my mind, even though I hadn't ever let myself think I wanted him truly, not beyond a casual lover.

"No, don't do that!" I said, genuinely alarmed.

He started to laugh.

"Most people would want to get everything they want," he said. "But not you."

"I'd just use it to try to get Judah back, and that would be a disaster," I said.

"Why?" my dad asked.

"All his drugs, the other women."

"I thought you said he got clean."

"Yeah, but he doesn't want to be anyone's boyfriend. It wouldn't be fair to him."

More than that, though, I was afraid to put one of my dad's cosmic theories to the test. I knew he believed we all have an energetic relationship with the universe that, when mastered, could result in something like manifestation, or "the Secret," which would become all the rage the next year. I'd watched him do affirmations and seek enlightenment my whole life, all while he lost women, children, jobs, and thousands of dollars at the track, and yet, I still wanted—needed, even—to believe in him. And so my father did not give me the key, and I distracted myself from Judah's silence with writing and music and booze and boys in bands.

My newly intimate conversations with my father were opening up in strange and surprising ways. I was still getting used to having a dad around at all, and what a dad he was. We both loved to walk and often did so instead of taking public transportation because we both preferred the open air in all weather. His back was stronger than ever, but it still gave him trouble sometimes, and the walking helped. One day that summer, we crested the top of the Arboretum and sat down on a bench there.

"I really believe there's a nationalistic urge in people," he said. "Like an instinct toward their own people."

"Yeah, what do you mean?" I asked, idly admiring the pastoral view.

"Like, well, I found this one porn," he said.

As the words left his mouth in his loud, booming voice, two sporty hikers ascended the top of the hill on which we were perched and headed toward us. *Just another dad-daughter day,* I thought.

"Hungarian porn," he continued.

"They make Hungarian porn?" I asked, too curious not to engage with him.

"I know," he said, laughing, genuinely amused. "They make everything, I guess. But I was more attracted to these women than I've ever been attracted to a woman before. I think as a species we're attracted to those people who are the most like us."

My dad had already told me on several occasions that he knew how to have tantric sex, and that he'd decided he was not going to have any more relationships in this life. His decision seemed like a sound one to me, given his history with women. Having my dad talk to me about sex didn't make me uncomfortable exactly. But with my dad, talking about feelings was more complicated. There was no one's attention I craved more, but his honesty could be off-putting.

One day we walked over the Mass Ave Bridge between Cambridge and Boston, talking about our relationship. "Well, I broke you, so it's my responsibility to fix you," he said. I balked. Judah had a lyric like that. Something in the idea felt true to me; it was why I'd dared to write that letter to my dad in the first place. But it was an assessment of our relationship that gave him all of the power, and I wanted to have that power for myself. None of my struggles would be worth anything if I never felt free.

"You don't have to do anything," I said.

"But I want to," he said. "These issues you have with men. And work and money. They all come from your relationship with me. That's how it is with fathers and daughters, just like it was with Betty and me. She never knew how to give me love. And so she fed me. That was how she tried to get me to do what she wanted. And when I was older she let me smoke cigarettes and drink and do drugs. Because she knew if she gave me a place to do that, I wouldn't leave her, and she could get me to do what she wanted."

I stared straight ahead, trying to unravel what he was saying and what it meant. He was my dad. But he was also a grown man who still blamed everything on his mother. I did not want to still be blaming him at that age. This was our moment to fix it, and we were both finally willing, but I still didn't know how.

My dad was obsessed with the fact that Asmara was coming to visit him for the first time since she and her mother had moved to Germany. When he first brought it up, he circled around the topic for nearly an hour, as I was beginning to learn was his way when he wanted to ask for something he was afraid he wouldn't get.

"I was thinking," he said. "She could stay with you and Beth."

"What?" I said. "Where?"

"On your couch in the living room."

"Dad, I work in our living room."

"Well, she's your sister, and I want you to spend time with her."

My mind went red with rage. How dare he act like the responsible father, who only wanted what was best for my sister and me? She was basically a stranger.

"Let me talk to Beth about it," I said, masking my real reaction. "She gets home from work late, and I don't want to put her out by having someone on our couch every night."

I discussed it with Beth and Claire and a few other friends, feeling guilty for being a terrible sister, and also for letting my father down. But I couldn't find it in me to say yes.

"I'm sorry, Dad, I just can't," I said. "It's too much."

I had feared his wrath, prepared to be defensive in return, but he was extremely neutral, as usual, so I got defensive about that—what, didn't he really need me? Apparently, he didn't. He found her accommodations that he could, barely, afford.

When we met for lunch, he spent hours going over his preparations for her arrival, which did not help my jealousy. He did a dry run out to the airport on the subway to make sure he would be able to get there in plenty of time to pick her up on the day her plane arrived. He even went to the American Express counter there and got information about exchanging money, in case she needed to do so. He obsessively revised his list of outings he was going to take her on, and he requested my presence for at least two dinners and one trip to the aquarium. I agreed but resented it.

I knew better than anyone else what my sister was going through as she tried to build a relationship with our dad. As her older sister, I should be nothing but supportive. And I was supportive, really I was. I just couldn't share him with anyone, even her, given how little of his love and attention there'd always been to go around.

I was a few minutes late when I rushed into the Ethiopian restaurant my dad had carefully chosen for dinner because, like my sister, it was named Asmara. My dad stood up when I walked in. A smile nearly broke out on his face, but he was too self-conscious about his teeth. My sister stood, too. She was lovely, like a dark-haired, Bavarian Brigitte Bardot. My father beamed at her as if she were a movie star. I suddenly felt sweaty and windswept and could hear the Big B's voice in my head: "Comb your hair! Put on more makeup!"

There was something inherently familiar about her. *Dad has a type,* I thought, as I noticed her figure was curvy in the same places as mine. And yet she was a stranger. As she endeavored to answer my questions about her flight, she grew flustered.

"But your English is very good," I said, trying to encourage her and let her know how impressed I was with her courage in coming to America to meet her family.

As we ate, my father pulled back a little and looked at both of us.

"I'm just so happy," he said. His voice cracked, his eyes misted over, and he stopped speaking and looked down. "The fact that I'm here having dinner with my two daughters. It's more than I ever could have expected."

I smiled at him, hushing the dark nasties in my heart, letting him have his moment. He had earned it. Whenever I told friends or acquaintances how I was rebuilding my relationship with my dad, I inevitably happened upon someone who got a wistful look on her face as she wondered whether her own dad would ever be capable of such a thing, and then a crestfallen echo as she realized he would not.

Asmara studied him and then, maybe uncomfortable or embarrassed, looked away. I softened toward her. I had been lucky to know my father as little as I had as a child. She hadn't even had that. She'd never met Betty. Would probably never meet Mimi. I had no reason to be jealous.

When I later met them at the aquarium, my sister seemed exhausted and stressed. I had spent enough time with my dad to know that feeling well. When he went to the bathroom, I pulled her aside, feeling disloyal to him but wanting to help her.

"Is everything okay?" I asked.

"Yes," she said. "It's just, John, he can be so much the child."

"Yeah, I know. He's just so happy you're here. And he doesn't always know how to behave. But I hope you know I'm here for you if you need anything."

"Thank you," she said.

We quickly stepped apart as my dad rejoined us. When we walked through the North End, looking for an Italian restaurant for dinner, I felt closer to her, like maybe I'd found an ally. But as much as she and I were alike, we were also very different. While her mother had repeatedly taken her to an ashram in India as a child, she was very rooted in her Bavarian upbringing, with its lack of rebel counterculture. When I spoke about my novel, she looked at me. "But what will you do if it does not sell?" she asked honestly.

Kill myself.

"Write another one," I said. "Many writers never sell their first novel."

I was glad to have met her. But I also felt glad to get away, not because of her but because of my father, who was clearly enmeshed with her.

"I'll give you Asmara's address so you two can write letters," my dad said as I made my farewells and prepared to walk home. Write, I would be happy to do. I just wanted a little distance from how I felt when I saw them together.

Although I never could have admitted it to her face, Asmara's question about my novel had been on point. I'd contacted nearly a dozen agents, several of whom had been interested in reading the opening of my book. As I sent it off to them, I was buoyed with hope. But just as quickly, I was overwhelmed by polite rejection letters and despair. Cathy gently tried to suggest that maybe, just maybe, I shouldn't be too hard on myself because I'd essentially sent out a first draft of my book, and everyone knew the publishing world was incredibly competitive and maybe, just maybe, if I revised it a bit more, I'd have better luck. I appreciated her kindness and her courage to tell me the truth, even when I was glowering at her about how it didn't need to be revised. Either all or nothing, I thought it needed to go in the trash.

That fall Beth and I both rented our own studio apartments, mine in Cambridge. Mom and Craig visited soon after, and they brought me housewarming gifts, and my brother put together my new desk chair. I loved my neighborhood. Now I could stay out at the bars until last call every night and stumble home. And I did. Often it was fun, but things were getting darker. Two years earlier, when I'd first started as a music journalist, I'd been drinking a lot, but with my roommates, good friends, and casual acquaintances with whom I shared a great deal of affection, sometimes even with my editors, who always made sure I got home safe. Now many of those friends had moved away or were in relationships and leading quieter lives.

One night, I was out with a female friend who liked to drink even more than I did. We did shots, which I didn't normally do, and she left me in the back of a cab with a straitlaced, heavyset man she'd met outside the club. I suddenly felt very drunk. I was going in and out of focus, and then I was in the guy's apartment. The shadows of tree branches climbed the walls in the dim room. I didn't know what street I was on, or who this guy was. *This is how girls disappear,* I thought. *This is how girls die.*

I was afraid, really afraid, as I'd only been once before in a decade of partying, often on my own. I'd always been a part of a web that had kept me safe—all of those bouncers and bartenders who were like older brothers to me, and the girlfriends who kept an eye on each other. I wanted to get away from him, but I didn't want to make a scene for fear of embarrassing him.

He was close to me. His hand traced up my leg and under my skirt. His fingers slid inside my underwear, which embarrassed me because they were old and ratty—even though I didn't want him or this—and then he was touching me. I didn't want it. I didn't know what to do. I was so drunk I had lost coherent thought and language. The shadows fell across our bodies like the long claws of a big animal. I was trapped.

Suddenly, it was as if he'd just come to with his hand inside my underwear. I felt him mentally pull back from me and his role in the situation, and then he pulled back, literally, and stood quickly, like he wanted to get away, too.

"I'm going to get something to eat," he said.

I stood and followed him out onto the street, focusing so hard on stepping one foot in front of the other that I had no mental space left for words. I wanted to run, but I didn't know where I was, and I was beyond reading signs, or using logic. Worst of all, if I let him see I was afraid, he might realize the power he had over me. I had to hold it together until we got to a street I recognized, and then I could get away.

He didn't talk to me, and I walked a little behind him, hating him and yet feeling so grateful he'd pulled himself back from the brink.

Finally, we walked out onto Mass Ave, and there were lights and people going in and out of the 7-Eleven. He stopped just outside the door and turned to me. I didn't stick around long enough to find out what he was going to say or do. I turned and walked away from him up Mass Ave toward my apartment.

When I got a few feet away, I fell down on the ground, landing on the palms of my hands and my knees. For a split second I rested on my scraped skin, so humiliated I wanted to cry. But I pushed myself to walk without looking back, even though I was bone-sure he would come up behind me at any moment, put his arm around my shoulder, and try to force me back to his place. When I got to the next block, I started to feel a little better, but I still didn't look back until I'd reached the block before my apartment. There were not as many people here, and if he was behind me, I didn't want to turn onto my street, because I would be vulnerable there, and because he would know where I lived. My heart racing, I willed myself to look back. The man was nowhere in sight. I started to shake, but I didn't stop, not until I'd reached my apartment and locked the door. I crawled into bed without washing my face or brushing my teeth, needing to be safely cocooned in my blankets.

I considered myself profoundly lucky that I'd drunkenly stumbled into a nice guy, or a bad guy who was so drunk that he really just wanted a taquito. Either way, I saw it as a warning. I didn't talk much about what had happened, as I was embarrassed by it, and because nothing, really, had happened. I pulled back from the friend who'd left me in the cab with the guy. I began to leave clubs and parties earlier. I lined up rides. I drank a little less.

But even after a normal night out that fall, when I'd supposedly had fun, I came home alone, got down on my knees, rested my head against the carpeting, and screamed a silent scream, unable to even call out in my frustration, for fear I might bother my upstairs neighbor. Something was wrong, but there was always another show, another party, and I was supposedly having the time of my life.

Scott's band came through on tour just before Christmas, and they planned to take four days off in Boston. This was his third visit since we'd broken up, and we'd fallen into a routine of falling back together. After his show, we rushed to an Irish pub, J. J. Foley's, and the retirement party for my mentor, Steve Morse, who had assigned me my first CD reviews for the *Boston Globe*. Steve had just arrived at the bar after going to see U2 play, and there was a rumor the band was going to show up to thank the music journalist who had helped break them in America by giving them an early rave in the *Globe*.

After I greeted Steve, I paused near an older man in a woven tie who was standing alone in the middle of the room. I started talking with him to be polite, but then I realized he was Paul McGuinness, the band's legendary manager. I charmed him with the story of how Mom was such a big fan that we'd almost gone to the band's Slane Castle show as a family, and coaxed stories out of him in turn. We were laughing like old friends when the bar's barometric pressure shifted. Just like that, next to me, stood Bono.

Even in the straw hat he was wearing in those days, he was several inches shorter than I was. He beamed up at me from behind his purple shades as the three of us made small talk about Steve and what a contribution he'd made to the music scene. Then, it was as if the atmospheric disturbance had spread out around me. A pint was handed to me, to hand to Bono, and then another, and another. He smiled graciously as I passed each one to him and lined them up on a shelf behind him. Steve greeted his old friend.

"This is my protégée, Sarah," he said. "She'll be the one asking you questions now."

Bono took my hand and kissed it. "I look forward to it," he said.

I glanced over to where Scott was waiting for me to join him.

Later that night, Scott told me he was going to marry his girlfriend and then took me to bed. When we were alone together, it was as if no time had passed, and I was able to forget what he'd said and how it had made me feel. But the visit, and all of our conversations, had developed a bittersweet inertia.

When I drove him to meet up with the band a few days later, I wasn't as devastated as I'd been all of the previous times we'd said good-bye. But as he turned and waved before he went inside, it hit me: I still loved him and wished he would stay. I couldn't really imagine him being a part of my new life now, and yet I couldn't fully accept that my life had gone on without him.

That winter was a stressful time for my dad. He'd just been informed that the rooming house where he'd lived for the past ten years was being sold. When he began looking for alternative accommodations, he found that the small disability check he received from the government was not going to be able to afford him an apartment anywhere in Boston, or even in the suburb where he lived. He needed to get on the federally subsidized housing program Section 8, which would allow him to live in an approved apartment rent-free. But the waiting list in most communities in and around Boston was two to three years long. He began applying, but it wasn't looking good for him to get accepted before he had to leave his current living situation.

My dad invited me to visit him at the rooming house only once. I was nervous as we passed through the narrow hallway to his room, afraid of what I might see, and how it might make me feel about him. He had complained to me about a variety of characters seemingly ripped from a Bukowski story, who drank and fought and schemed in the rooms around him. It was undoubtedly a depressing place, but it was also relatively well kept and orderly, and he clearly felt comfortable there, pointing out this and that special feature as anyone might do at his home. I was relieved that no one cursed or screamed or harassed us while we were in the hallway, and when he opened the door to his room for me, I was happy to see it was tidy and snug, filled with towering stacks of books and movies and notebooks, much like my rooms always were. His only friend, Bobby, who wanted to meet me, was funny and kind, a Joe Pesci–type man. Bobby managed the rooming house, which made my dad's living situation there much better than it would have otherwise been.

I could see why my dad was anxious about leaving this place and nervous he'd end up somewhere he didn't like nearly as much. On the other hand, if he was proactive and got approved for Section 8 housing in the right community, he could set himself up for the rest of his life. I had just been given Craig's mother's car, an old Dodge Omni with fewer than twenty thousand miles on it, and my dad and I decided I would drive him out to look at several towns where he thought he might feel at home. His only requirements were that his new community be a place where he could take his long daily walks and be near an isolation tank or hot tub, which he planned to use as part of his meditation program. Invented by the scientist John Lilly in 1954, the isolation tank could be used to speed up my dad's metaphysical work, he hoped, as he tried to achieve enlightenment without LSD and actualize a vision of his. He had never told me about the entire vision, as he claimed it might be too much for me to handle, but he hinted at it regularly. I chose not to press him for details, as I was irritated by such moments when he withheld information from me, as if he were a spiritual Svengali.

My dad had asked me several times to show him my writing, and I'd given him an essay about Auntie Mimi serving juice, which he'd enjoyed. So in advance of our day trip to Amherst, I sent him the first few chapters of my novel. But then he canceled our first planned outing because of his bad back, leaving me with the same feeling of powerlessness and frustration as when I was a little girl. On the day of our second attempt, we hit the highway, and my dad settled into the passenger seat and retrieved my pages.

"Well, Sarah," he said. "I have to start by saying it's a little disconcerting to read a story where a character with my name dies on the first page."

We went into a used bookstore, but even this wasn't enough to make him feel as if he'd found his spot. Now I was worried. It was one thing to turn his nose up in theory. I got it. I did. I had left rural Maine not only because I'd been hungry for a big life, but also because I'd grown tired of being viewed as a freak. But the boardinghouse was going to be sold, and if he didn't find an alternative, he would be out on the streets. My dad had prepared himself for this eventuality by spending several nights in homeless shelters, and he said he'd been fine, but it wasn't something I wanted to think about. He was almost sixty years old. Boston had brutal winters. Even if the citizens of Northampton weren't quite ready for him, it was surely better than homelessness. But I knew it wasn't my decision to make. And so, I just hoped he would choose a new home.

Like my dad, I was struggling to figure out where I was meant to be. I'd nearly moved to New York City the year before, only staying in Boston to write a weekly music column. But now, so much of what I'd loved about my life in Boston was gone. When I'd first moved there, it had been the big city of my childhood dreams, and I'd loved exploring its streets and writing about its happenings. But after six years, I felt as if I'd walked down every street, and I wanted the kind of life that could stay big even as it became more stable. It felt as if everyone had moved on but me. Something had to change.

The *Boston Globe* began searching for a new staff music writer. Although I'd started out in journalism as a trade, I'd become passionate about my music writing. Not to mention the fact that Bono was expecting me to call him any day.

I spoke with my editor about my interest in the job and went through the application process. I tried not to get ahead of myself, but given the constant state of financial worry in which I'd been living for the past four years, it was hard not to think about how great life would be if the job were mine.

One night I saw a fellow freelancer who'd always been like a big brother, and he asked how I felt about the *Globe*'s choice for its new music writer. They'd hired someone else and never called to let me know. Just like that, I was done with journalism. I was done with Boston.

When my lease ran out that April, I moved in with friends in Jamaica Plain, cutting my rent in half and giving me the freedom to leave the city whenever the time was right. And then, a woman ran a red light and hit me, totaling my grandmother's car. I was stuck in all new ways, and I felt it keenly. I gave up my columns and regular contributions to the paper, though it was hard to relinquish control. I considered it a privilege to write about bands I loved and help bring them to the attention of a larger audience, and it thrilled me to see my byline in the paper I'd grown up reading. But as with a love affair that has run its course, I had to move on; I had gladly chosen the poverty of the freelance life for the privilege of being mentored by the talented editors at the *Globe,* but in the end, I'd been just another freelancer to them. I had to leave. I had to find my place.

Claire had moved out to LA, and I stayed with her and her boyfriend for a week, excited to find myself reunited with a city I had come to love. She was the best kind of hostess, planning outings and carefully curating the books in the guest room. But I wanted more than the slice of LA she told me to want, including Judah, whom I'd maintained a flirtation with on and off over the years, and the other musicians I knew out there. I felt restricted. Claire felt underappreciated. We still had the intense relationship we'd had at sixteen, but it now felt uncomfortable in our adult lives.

That spring, Scott came through on tour again. When he got in touch to give me a heads up, I felt that familiar uptick of excitement. Even four years after our breakup, I was eager for the oasis of sex and love and comfort he offered. But when I arrived at the venue a little early so we could have dinner, he had a surprise for me.

"I have to tell you something," he said. "My girlfriend is on tour with me."

I was shocked. He and his girlfriend had broken up instead of getting engaged. Who was this new girl who wasn't me? Even if I knew in my heart I couldn't really move back to Portland for him, it didn't mean my heart was any less his.

"How did you not tell me this?"

"I'm sorry," he said. "Do you still want to have dinner?"

We walked around the corner to the Middle East and there she was: his new girlfriend. She was a European rocker he had met on tour, with platinum blond hair. She wasn't smiling. Neither was I. The three of us awkwardly got through dinner. When she left to set up the merch booth for the show, I sat in stunned silence across from Scott, unable to say anything, unable to get up and cleave us apart. Even this small moment alone together tugged at me. I drank whiskey steadily all night. The band was sweaty and wild, and I sang along, even though I wanted to run away. Before I knew it, the night was over. Scott and I stood at the center of the rapidly emptying club.

"What are you doing now?" Scott asked me.

"Going home," I said, grateful it was almost over, as much as that hurt.

"I could go with you," he said.

"There's not enough room for both of you," I said.

"I could come and hang out," he said.

The possibility of ending the night alone with him was such a relief after the painful surprise of his new girlfriend's presence. I leaned toward him a little. It struck me how impossibly awful that would be, to abandon this poor woman who had flown from Europe to sell T-shirts in grungy clubs just to be with Scott. I started to cry.

"I don't know what you want from me," I said. "What the fuck do you want? Tell me. Please. Because I don't understand anymore."

"Sarah," Scott said.

My name in his mouth was still so precious. I cried harder, fought temptation.

"I have to go," I said.

He hugged me, so I was crying in his arms, and it felt so safe, but then I got it that this *really* was the last time, and I cried harder still. "Good-bye, Scott," I said.

As soon as I got out to my friend's car, I let go completely. It hurt as if we were breaking up for the first time. There hadn't been a time in the past ten years that Scott and I had seen each other without going to bed together. But that hadn't happened tonight, and wasn't going to happen, not ever again. It really felt like everything I most loved was gone. I had no idea what to do next.

I received my insurance settlement from the car accident and bought a very used Honda. With a reliable car at the ready, I acknowledged a dream that had been rising in my heart for nearly three years now: Los Angeles. I was smitten with her.

The thought of my new life made me ecstatic. There was just one problem: my dad. I was nervous about telling him, as if he might see my departure as a betrayal. And I was afraid that without me there to drive him to Section 8 properties and make sure he didn't give up on the paperwork, he'd end up homeless. Still, I broke the news.

"Los Angeles," he said. "Far out. How are you going to get there?"

"I'm going to drive."

"Yeah? I used to love to drive."

"I know you did, Dad."

"Well, I fully support you getting everything you want," he said.

It was a double-edged blessing. I was grateful for his support, but as usual, his neutrality made me feel like he had all of the power. I secretly longed for him to be a little more broken up about my departure.

I went up to Maine to store a few belongings at Mom's house and say good-bye. Some things hadn't changed: I was eager to go, but the morning I was supposed to leave, I stood just inside the doorway, hugging Mom and crying. She and Craig had created a beautiful sanctuary, and I always hated to go away, but I knew I couldn't stay.

chapter fifteen

DON'T EVER DATE HANDSOME MEN

As usual money was an immediate and constant worry in Los Angeles, but money had always been a worry, so I made do. My friend Rebecca had taken me in, giving me a room in the house she'd just bought and charging me very little rent, in part because I was helping with her dog, and in part because she believed in my writing and became my patron of the arts. I woke up, diligently worked on a short story or journalism pitch, went running, and then the whole afternoon yawned in front of me until Rebecca got home from work and we cooked dinner together, or I went out with one of my few friends.

There was one person who was home during the day and had no job or other obligations to distract him from my need for reassurance: my dad. There was just one problem. He didn't have a phone. There was a phone in the boardinghouse, but it was down the hall from his room. So my dad and I began scheduling calls in advance, either by letter or at the end of a conversation. At our agreed-upon time, he would call me from one of the pay phones he had scoped out around Boston.

He bought those inexpensive phone cards favored by immigrants, so we could literally talk for hours, and we did. In my loneliness, I was more candid with my father than I'd ever been. I spoke of my past affairs, describing the men I'd fallen for, and how none of them had fallen for me the way I wanted.

"You should never date handsome men because they don't have to develop any other aspect of their personality, and so they don't."

I laughed, even while protesting, but I knew he had a point. As he did when I told him most of the men I'd been involved with of late had also been involved with cocaine.

"You should never try to compete with cocaine, Sarah," my dad said. "It's designed to be the best feeling in the world. And you can never win."

I knew his words were accurate. But it wasn't in my nature to let go. And, at least in the case of my father, my stubbornness had paid off. If I had given up on him, he and I never would have reconciled. Because I hadn't stopped believing, we had a relationship.

My dad applied himself to my love life with the same intensity and thoroughness with which he approached his own quest for enlightenment, and even more than that, with a renewed acknowledgment of his part in my personal issues.

"I broke you, Sarah," he said to me again. "It's up to me to fix you."

Part of me believed it to be true. I had tried to fix myself with perfectionism, and writing, and running, and booze, and other men, and none of it had worked. Much of what he said about our dynamic made sense, but his requests to "run" my past lives or redo our childhood interactions made me nervous.

"Because I wasn't there for you when you were a little girl, you think you're undeserving," he said. "But we can fix it. We can go back and start again. You can be the child again. You can say anything to me. There's nothing to be ashamed of, there's nothing that will upset me or make me go away again."

I heard him. I was grateful. But his offer also made me deeply uncomfortable. He might as well have told me it was okay for me to suddenly be fluent in French. Sure, it was a nice idea, but if I'd never been taught, there was no way I could feel comfortable speaking it to someone else. I couldn't say that to my dad, though. And so I said, "Thank you."

Going into the holidays, I was invited to a party at Lucinda Williams's record label by a friend who knew Lucinda was the inspiration for the heroine of my first novel. By the end of the night, Lu and I were drinking wine together, bonding over the important topics of the universe—poetry, men, our fathers, and shoes.

The next night I had dinner with Claire and tried to rally through my hangover to enjoy our conversation. Things had been strained ever since my last visit. It was wonderful to have an old friend in a new city, especially one who was also driven to succeed as a writer, but I felt wary around her; it was like she always wanted me to be someone else. After dinner, she urged me to have another glass of wine. I demurred.

"You'll get drunk with Lucinda Williams, but you won't get drunk with me?"

I stared at her, surprised by her genuine anger. I ordered another glass of wine. And then went to another bar for more drinks, even though I was worried about driving home. By the time I made it to my car, I was tipsy and glad to be free of her. We met for dinner and drinks once more, but it was clear that something was seriously wrong, and neither of us had the energy to find out what. I didn't want that seemingly constant level of intensity—fighting, reconciling only after long, difficult conversations—for me, or for her. I realized I'd rather love her from afar than resent her and fear her as a friend. We never spoke again.

I was getting some regular work for the *Los Angeles Times*, but they had recently declared bankruptcy and cut their freelance rate—already not a lot—by fifteen percent. The downsizing of the newspaper meant fewer pages, which meant fewer assignments to go around, which meant less money. I started tutoring kids for the SAT, but that still wasn't enough to live on, and so I started working for a catering company.

It was hard not to feel that I'd taken a step back. In the five years since grad school, I'd managed to support myself with my writing, and here I was wearing a black tie and searching out straws for rich socialites so they wouldn't muss their lipstick while sipping overoaked chardonnay. And, still, I wasn't making enough money to survive.

I'd always assumed I would eventually sell a book, which would be the foundation for my financial life as a writer. It seemed clear, though, that my first novel was never going to find a home without major revisions, and that meant supporting myself long enough to complete them. So I hobbled along.

One day, a manila envelope came for me in the mail. I still received quite a few press CDs, so this was nothing unusual. But when I opened it, I found it was a book: *I Deserve Love: You deserve love and sexual pleasure—and you can get exactly what you want!* by Sondra Ray. I laughed, wondering which of my friends had sent it to me as a prank, but I read through the hundreds of sex-positive affirmations inside.

"Did you get the book I sent you?" my dad asked during our next call.

Of course it had been my dad. How had I not realized it immediately?

"Oh, that was you," I said. "Yeah, thanks."

"I did all of the affirmations before I sent it to you. It's really good. I really recommend that you pick a few of the affirmations and write them out."

"Okay," I said, trying not to think too hard about my dad writing out the affirmations, such as "When I put my penis in a woman's vagina . . ."

"And have you given any more thought to having me run you?" he asked. "I don't want to put any pressure on you, but I think it would be really good for you."

I paused for a long moment, looking out the window at the over-exposed sunshine on the palm trees and stucco houses, willing myself to find enough nerve to push back, even a little bit. He was speaking of "running" my past lives as a way to identify traumas that were creating problems in my current life. I knew it was something my dad, and even my mom, had done in the seventies, and my dad still believed in it deeply.

"I'm not sure, Dad, let me think about it," I said.

"Okay, well, we wouldn't do it until you're home at Christmas anyhow," he said.

It wasn't that I didn't appreciate my dad's desire to help me. All I had ever wanted, after all, was his time and attention. But I knew enough about therapy to understand that one of its central tenets was the need for an impartial healer. On my good days, I feared my dad was so interested in my progress that it would be impossible for him to actually help me. On my dark days, I was struck by the fact that my father, who had spent his life searching for a mother, had found himself with two daughters and had decided he was the only person who could heal them. Deep down, I feared he wanted to keep me broken so I would never outgrow my need for his help.

My father was constantly hungry for an ever-expanding list of books, from the new age healers of his day, such as Sondra Ray and Louise Hay, to *On the Road,* which he decided to reread, and works by Freud, whom he read in his entirety, and movies, from the pulp directors he adored, including John Carpenter and Dario Argento, to the greats he had introduced me to, particularly Bergman and Fellini, whose creative process fascinated him. He was forever on the lookout for treasures at his favorite thrift stores around Boston, and he happily told me about finding his coveted items for two or three dollars, as well as surprise treasures he had only bought because of their price or cover.

"You have to see this movie," he said. "It's amazing. I picked it up because I remembered the actress. And it's just incredible. I mean she can't really act, but she's just so natural on the screen. It's like you can really see who she was. Actually if you could look up her bio on IMDb and send it to me, I'd appreciate it." At various times, he asked me for IMDb bios on everyone from Fellini's muse, Giulietta Masina, to Jennifer Aniston.

I sniffed, partly amused, partly jealous. He had a profound respect for actors as artists, and he truly believed it was possible to see a resonance in Drew Barrymore's romantic comedies that could be traced back to the natural talent of her grandfather, John Barrymore, whose catalog he'd seen in its entirety.

And so my father meant it as a compliment to me when he said, "I think you're going to meet an actor at a party and know a love like you've never known before."

In the meantime, when I turned to the used-book dealers it was possible to access through Amazon to feed his voracious appetite for books and movies, he became very interested in the site. During every call, he asked me to find a copy of some obscure film or self-help book, cackling with glee when they could be bought for one penny, plus shipping and handling, and often having them sent to me so I could enjoy them first. If our dad-daughter outings in Boston had been our re-creation of the childhood relationship we'd never had, now I had reached my teenage years with him, chafing at his attempted influence. I often waited until he started nagging me for the book or movie after several months and sent it to him without ever having read or watched it.

Of course, when I did watch the movies he sent me, they were always brilliant and moving, or at least cool. But sometimes they were hard for me to take. My father became obsessed with Dario Argento's daughter Asia and sent me a double film set that included her directorial debut, *Scarlet Diva*. I was freaked out from the first moment I saw the DVD cover, which featured a photo of Asia topless, coyly covering her breasts, because I saw a striking resemblance between her and my sister. The movie itself was a very dark look at a young Italian actress who'd been screwed up by her parents and spins out of control in a wash of drugs and sex. It included an explicit scene with a musician in which the dialogue was an almost word-for-word duplicate of what I'd experienced with my most recent rock star, whom I'd spent the night with in LA following his Grammy win.

As I watched the scene unfold, I felt queasy. I'd spent years seeking books and music and movies that made me feel less isolated, so there was no way for me not to be moved by her story. I could have been touched by the fact that my father had sent it to me, maybe even as a way to connect with my experience, which he was well aware the film mirrored. "You were never a groupie," he once said to me when trying to help me put my time in the rock world in perspective. But there was something off about the scenario. I knew he was fascinated and moved by Asia and her movies because it was too painful for him to get close to the parts of my sister and me that had been damaged by his absence. There was something comforting for him in caring for this lost girl. Again, I knew I should have felt moved by this. But instead, it made me furious. He had the luxury of choosing to look at my pain or of understanding it through films. Of course, I didn't say any of this. I tamped it down and carried on as I always had.

My father was also sending me a lot of reading material in those years related to his spiritual beliefs, including a longtime favorite, *Awareness Techniques* by William Swygard, and a new discovery: Dr. Bruce Goldberg's *Custom Design Your Own Destiny*. I was quite moved by Dr. Goldberg, a former dentist, who happened to be based in Woodland Hills. I even got in touch with him in order to get a tape on managing dental phobia so my father could begin to deal with his increasingly pressing need to have his teeth replaced.

It wasn't difficult to be drawn to teachings that led to greater personal happiness and success, especially when I felt so lacking in both areas. This was in the wake of the cultural phenomenon *The Secret*, after all, and everyone was talking about manifestation, especially in California. I was attracted to my father's beliefs that suggested I could create positive outcomes in my writing career, which seemed stalled, and was a constant source of stress and longing for me. I kept tutoring, and catering, used my credit cards and dog-sitting gigs to fill in the gaps, and felt grateful for Rebecca's ongoing kindness.

I had gone to Los Angeles to find an outlet for my writing and seeking, and I would stay and fight it out for as long as it took. And yet, it was hard not to be impacted by seeing my friends from Boston start to marry and settle down while I was no closer to achieving my goals. I spent hours on the phone with my dad. He believed in me. There was no doubt in his mind I would achieve everything I set out to accomplish and more.

"I fully support you getting everything you want," he said again and again.

Early in 2008, I had a lucky break, on two levels. A friend of a friend who wrote celebrity memoirs became a meditation teacher and decided to only cover health and wellness topics. She was up for a book with the bisexual reality TV star Tila Tequila. She offered the gig to my friend, and my friend offered it to me.

I was only vaguely aware of Tila at the time, but a writing job meant money, and even more important, it meant the chance to write for hire, which was one step closer to my goal of being a working writer. I sent some journalism clips and a bio, including mention of a ghostwriting job I'd done for a life coach, to the agent handling the project. Tila was intrigued by my experience writing about self-help, as she wanted the book to be genuinely useful to people. We had a phone meeting. I found her to be bright and excited to be writing a book, which charmed me, as I'd been trying to publish a book for fifteen years, and I considered it a great privilege. I got the job. I was ecstatic. My rate as a first-time collaborator, even after the agent got his cut, was more than half of what I managed to scrape together in an average year at that point.

When it came time to edit, I was thrilled to find that my editor regularly worked with the cultural critic Chuck Klosterman, a serious writer I often admired who I had once interviewed for the *Boston Globe*. Through the entire process, I learned an immense amount about every aspect of publishing, from the contract to the publicity. Every step was precious to me.

No matter that when the *Boston Globe* covered the book's release in their gossip section, "Names and Faces," the reporter who called me to do the piece razzed me, asking, "So did you hook up with Tila Tequila?"

"I would never write and tell," I rebounded coyly.

No matter that no one was taking the book seriously. I got it. The cover featured Tila in a bikini sitting near a pool and was filled with sexy photos of her. But it was a real book, one I could find on bookstore shelves and, yes, even in the Library of Congress.

The other unexpected windfall of the book came when I met the woman who had passed on collaborating with Tila. She was trying to make the bulk of her living by teaching what she called "twenty-minute meditation." This was basically an introduction to the principles of transcendental meditation, which I primarily knew of through the director David Lynch. Out of gratitude for my newfound job, I decided to sign up for the introductory workshop at her apartment in Laurel Canyon over Memorial Day weekend.

I didn't know what to expect as I nervously wound up into the Canyon, trying to feel soothed by chirping birds and the smell of eucalyptus. She was absolutely lovely, possessed of that perfect mix of energy and calm I saw in people in Los Angeles who were pursuing a healthier, more fulfilled life. I wanted some of whatever she had.

When we practiced together on that first day, I was sure I wasn't doing it right. But I kept going back, out of respect for her, and because I could sense there was something good for me there. On the final morning, as instructed, I brought offerings for the shrine and was given my personal mantra during a private ceremony. There was something gilded and precious in the moment. Raised without religion, I loved symbolism and ritual and was moved by the ceremony and the intent with which she welcomed me into an ancient tradition. After that, I began meditating every day.

My father, of course, was interested in my meditation practice, although it was hard not to feel like a dilettante for meditating twice a day for twenty minutes when he was clocking in three hours a day with his snorkel. But, for once, I let it be, and the more I meditated, the more it became a genuine passion for me, as it was for my father. As I began to step back from the frantic pace of life, even just for forty minutes a day, my practice became profoundly healing, when sometimes—not always, but enough—I felt a kind of downy cosmic bliss, a sense of being safe in the nest of a benevolent universe, much as I had when I'd used drinking to blur the edges of my experience when I'd been younger, only now it felt so much better, authentic, mine.

That year, my relationship with my father was complicated by his relationship with my sister, who he'd been conscientious about staying in touch with ever since her visit in 2005. He had saved enough money, and he was going to visit her in Munich during the fall of 2008. I helped him find a plane ticket he could afford, and he sent me a check to cover the cost so I could order it for him online. Then he nervously prepared for his trip, going to the airport to be sure he would arrive in time to go through security and catch his flight, obsessing over exchange rates, how much money he needed for the trip, and how much of this should be a gift for Asmara.

I had lived in Los Angeles for nearly two years now, and he had never considered coming to visit me, even though the flight was a third of the cost. And if he went to Germany, it would be many, many months before he would be able to afford a flight to California. I tried not to be greedy and focused on how much more time I'd had with my dad than Asmara had, and how good this visit would be for both of them.

When my dad traveled to Germany in early October, I was in Boston, doing a project for a website development company, a much-needed influx of capital. I was going over some notes in my hotel room when my phone rang. I didn't recognize the number but answered.

"Hi, this is Sarah," I said, my tone formal in case it was a work call.

"Hi, this is Dad."

"Oh, hey, how's Germany?"

"You have to find me a flight home," he said.

"Why, what happened? You've only been there two days."

He described how he'd decided to fast when he landed and was consuming nothing but green tea, sounding put out as he described how Asmara's stepfather had encouraged him to drink a Bavarian beer and eat some of his homemade German noodles. I felt for everyone involved, knowing my dad was just trying to feel in control of a situation that stressed him out, and also guessing that he had no idea how uncomfortable it would be to have a houseguest who refused to eat. The tensions had culminated when Asmara and her mother, Eva, had taken my father sightseeing to a beautiful Bavarian park. My father had been hurt by what he'd seen as my sister's aloofness. Choosing to ignore her obvious discomfort, he had pressed her to talk about several serious topics. As they hiked in the woods, she spun around on him.

"I will not be your mother!" she shouted at him.

Then she ran back to their van, and the three of them returned to the city in heated silence. Now I was jealous of my sister for a new reason: she'd had the guts to push back. I suddenly had mad respect for her and, with it, a newfound affection. She was a spitfire. I liked her. And I wanted to help her.

"You're not leaving," I said.

"What do you mean?"

"You're the adult," I said. "You're supposed to be the parent. It's up to you to be forgiving, no matter what she says or does."

"Yeah."

"This is important. This is your chance to spend time with her. I wish we'd started fixing things earlier, instead of waiting until I was twenty-five."

"I know."

My dad stayed until his scheduled flight, even though it wasn't easy for him. A few days after my sister's eruption, he was called to a family meeting in their apartment and told that they had taken a vote and decided to pay for him to move to a hotel. And then they gave him an unexpected gift, which I was ecstatic about, even if he was uncertain.

My dad had terrible, rotten, broken teeth. But every time I gently worked the conversation around to getting them fixed, he put me off by saying he didn't want any "welfare teeth." I couldn't blame him. Now, however, he'd have his own set of beautifully handcrafted teeth made for him by Asmara's Bavarian stepfather, Norbert, who made teeth for a living. As my dad described how Norbert had made a mold for the teeth, he sounded doubtful about the whole thing.

Take the teeth! Take the teeth! I thought.

"Dad, that's great! Bavarians are known for their handiwork. Those are probably some of the highest-quality teeth you could get anywhere. What a wonderful gift."

"Yeah, but I'd have to get my teeth pulled out in America and travel to Germany, without any teeth, to get them put in."

It wasn't my mouth, but that seemed like a small price to pay to repair a chronic condition that could have serious health implications if left untended.

"I'll go with you, Dad," I said.

"What I really want is to take you and Asmara on a trip around Europe," my dad said. "You and I could go to Paris to see the cafés where all the writers hung out. We'd take you to Bavaria to see where Asmara grew up. And then the three of us could go to Hungary to see where we're from."

It was a whole lot easier to plan a dream trip than a trip to Germany, without any teeth. And so I let him change the subject, and I gave him my belief in his great European adventure.

Meanwhile, my dad remained serious about rehabilitating me. He gave me "homework," to write down everything I wanted from my dream relationship, and to answer questions about my sense of self from one of his self-help books. I dutifully considered the questions, answered them as honestly as I possibly could, and mailed them to him. I wasn't just doing it for my dad, though. I needed help, and I knew it. But, as for my dad, it was often hard for me to accept assistance, even when it was offered. I wanted to grow and become strong like my sister, but fearing I'd fail to reach my constant goal—perfection—it often seemed scary to even try.

chapter sixteen

LEARNING TO LOVE THE FALL

Even though I had pushed myself and opened up my life by moving to Los Angeles, I felt stuck. My friends were buying houses, planning weddings, and I still couldn't even pay my bills without falling back on my credit cards. I was looking for help anywhere I could find it. I had become smitten with one of my dad's great passions—isolation tanks—and had written them into the first TV pilot I finished under my Los Angeles mentor's guidance. Now, as a way to support myself while I got my writing career up and running, I wanted to open a business where people could float in a spalike environment. A man had opened just such a space in a suburb of Boston, which I'd tried during one of my trips back home. I e-mailed with the owner about franchising his business in Los Angeles. At a networking event, I was talking about floating when a woman told me she went to a tank that was just a few blocks from where I was living. Not only that, but it was overseen by the son-in-law of the couple my dad often spoke of as the patron saints of flotation tanks. They had even owned a float business in Beverly Hills in the seventies.

I went to float in the tank, which was the more common "coffin"-style tank. As the body-temperature water and the toxin-clearing saline soothed me, I began to feel a rising sense of possibility. In fact, by the time I climbed out of the tank and showered off the salt, I was euphoric. It was like a postworkout endorphin rush, magnified a thousandfold, and I was sure it could be the next big thing in LA.

I found a woman with a hundred thousand dollars to invest and took her to float, convinced it was all happening, and sure I would soon be running a business that could also provide a good source of income for my dad. The investor, however, was not as convinced as I was.

And so, still searching for a way to leap into the next stage of my life, I gave my father my full attention for the latest plan he was working on; he'd become convinced—by reading Dr. Goldberg—that he had the ability to manipulate the outcome of events in his life. He, of course, decided to apply this power to horse racing. He asked me to buy him books and videos on mastering the racetrack, and he studied them carefully. He was also rereading *On the Road,* and he'd become obsessed with a moment in the book when Kerouac had intuited the winner of a race but failed to trust his instincts. Maybe because writers I admired—Kerouac and Hemingway—wrote about the track, I was still able to find the romance in it, or maybe that was my way of not fully holding my dad accountable. Whatever the reason, I needed to trust in my dad, and so I did, still avoiding the possibility that there might be a reason not to at this point.

My dad was open with me for the first time about his regular trips to the track, because now they were research, and any money lost was kind of like a business expense. His plan was to hone his intuition to the point where he could pick the trifecta at the Kentucky Derby. He thought he might have to come out to LA to Santa Anita, the big track east of the city. My faith in his plan, which had been total, wobbled slightly at this news. He wouldn't come to LA to visit me, but he would travel for the track.

No matter, though, I reasoned, his plan was for me as much as for him, so I forced myself to stay cheerful. He was going to win a hundred thousand dollars and give it to me so I could put a down payment on a property with a guesthouse where he could live. Intellectually, I knew it was a long shot, and I told almost no one about our plan. Before I dared to confess our dad-daughter undertaking to my friend Cathy, I stopped abruptly and said, "I'm going to tell you this, but you have to absolutely believe it's going to be true." In my heart of hearts, I was still that little girl at the window.

More important, I still believed in my ability to believe. I had to: how else to justify my decision to stick with my writing, seventeen years after my first fiction class? Yes, I made my living as a writer, but whether it was as a journalist or a ghostwriter, I was still telling other people's stories, when I wanted very much to be telling my own.

Being in Los Angeles was both wonderful and maddening for all of this. On the one hand, unlikely discoveries did happen: writers who'd been reduced to living in their cars did go on to sell scripts that launched lifelong careers. It gave me hope. But on the other hand, it also made me wonder when, if ever, my time would come. It only seemed fitting that my always troubled relationship with my father might bear some sweeter fruit. I had friends whose fathers had helped them with their down payments. My version of the story might look different than the norm, but that suited me just fine anyhow. I was sometimes irked at the thought of him saving enough to place a big bet, but I believed in him enough to stay loyal. And yet, the day of the derby came and went, and my dad never even said a word.

Meanwhile, my financial situation was still so perilous that I couldn't afford to rent my own studio apartment. But I did land my second ghostwriting job that fall, to write a book with the actor Todd Bridges, who had played Willis on *Diff'rent Strokes*.

As soon as I had my first payment in the bank, I took care of some necessities I'd been putting off due to lack of funds. One of these was an appointment with a gynecologist. Since moving to California, I'd been exposed to more holistic approaches to health and well-being and met women who'd also been living with PCOS. Several of them had chosen to go off birth control pills because of concern about the long-term effects of being on hormones. Given the fact that I had never completely managed to quit smoking, I figured this was probably something I should look into. Because I'd regularly had my period since going on the pill, I assumed it had cured my PCOS, but I wanted to be sure. I sprung for an ultrasound.

I was surprised to see what looked like hundreds of tiny pearls all over both of my ovaries. There was, apparently, a big difference between masking symptoms and curing a chronic condition. I told the doctor I wanted to go off the pill.

"Oh, you shouldn't go off the pill, especially if you want to have kids," she said.

"That doesn't make any sense," I said.

"Your cycle will get so out of whack without the hormones to regulate it that you'll never be able to conceive."

"But won't I have to go off the pill to get pregnant? What then?"

"We'll give you drugs to help you conceive."

The idea of putting extra drugs into my system along with a tiny fetus concerned me. It was clear that this doctor was not going to be supportive of my attempts to take control of my condition, and I've always hated being spoken to like that. I was my father's daughter, so I decided to prove her wrong.

I went off the pill around the holidays. Based on collected advice from friends with PCOS and other chronic conditions, I did a cleanse in January that was twenty-one days of no booze, no cigarettes, no caffeine, no sugar, and for the final week, all liquid foods, including endless meals of what was called "energy soup." At the same time, I attempted to repair any damage that had been done to my system by years of birth control and the antibiotics I'd taken to clear up my skin, and I adopted the Body Ecology Diet, which involves specific food pairings and eating almost no sugar—even from fruits.

The first few days were really hard. I was groggy, and the cup of hot water with lemon I had in the place of my coffee was a weak alternative. Luckily, I was in the habit of running in the morning, and that helped to wake me up. By midafternoon, I was craving some sugar, anything, even just a piece of fruit. I was allowed fresh cranberries, which at least reminded me of my childhood in Maine, and dried currants.

Many people in my life thought I was crazy, but I knew it was something I needed to do. At least I got compliments, not just about the weight I'd lost but about my skin, which was perfectly clear and radiant, as it hadn't been since I was twelve years old.

"What did you do?" friends asked me.

"I went on a cleanse," I said.

They all wanted to try it, until they learned what was involved, and that was even without my telling them about the colonics.

My dad's support was crucial. He was a devotee of fasts and juice cleanses, not just for their physical benefits but also for their mental and spiritual advantages. He was very sympathetic to both how difficult the experience was and how unwilling I was to quit before I'd reached my twenty-one-day goal. While I still had a bit of the teenager's desire to find things for myself rather than learn from my parents, I appreciated my dad's knowledge of these subjects and didn't allow myself to question how successful they had really been for him.

Even after the end of my cleanse, when I started reintroducing some items, I stuck to a strict diet designed specifically for women with PCOS. Because the condition causes insulin resistance and an inability to process sugar, this meant restricting anything that might turn to sugar in my system, including all grains, dairy, beans, soy, and corn.

I continued to drink very little, as alcohol is full of sugar. I was amused, though, by one health care provider who said it was a good idea to eliminate most alcohol but also noted that because most women with PCOS have type-A personalities, it might actually be beneficial for them to occasionally have a glass of wine to help them relax.

For me, the possibility of drinking a little bit here and there was a total revelation. I knew I had been a lush in Boston and my early days in Los Angeles, and because of my dad's family history, I'd always known there was a possibility I was an alcoholic and would have to eventually stop drinking. When I cut out drinking temporarily, I made a breakthrough almost immediately. Often, when I was out, I was bored. I didn't like small talk. I craved the transcendent. Because such extreme experiences were not always possible, in their absence I often drank a lot to make things wild and fun. Now, when I wasn't turned on by what was happening, I just went home.

On the one hand, I was profoundly grateful. I had seen too many friends and lovers struggle with substance abuse to take it lightly. I was relieved I wouldn't have to tow the line that way, and that I would still be able to have a champagne toast when I sold my first book and at my wedding. But on the other hand, just as I'd been a little miffed when I'd found out I wasn't depressed, there was a part of me that was disappointed. If I wasn't depressed and I wasn't an alcoholic, why was I so unhappy? What was wrong with me? And if I never got diagnosed with anything, then how would I ever get cured?

I was meditating regularly and taking yoga classes at my gym. Some change was evident, at least. A less-than-tactful yoga teacher who had grown up speaking Korean and did not have the English vocabulary to soften her message came up to me one day.

"I don't know what happen to you, maybe you have bad husband, but you unhappy person before," she said. "You change. You softer now."

I couldn't help but laugh, but I was moved as I thanked her.

I kept it up. I started going to an acupuncture school, where a Chinese doctor who specialized in reproductive health treated me. I had my period twice in a row—with a month skipped in between—but still, that was the most regular it had ever been.

And then it stopped. And we had no idea why. I was sticking to my diet without any cheats. I was running and meditating and doing yoga. I was monitoring my temperature and cervical fluid and charting it for the doctor. I was getting acupuncture done every week and taking the herbal formulas the doctor had mixed up for me.

In fact, it felt as if everything was getting worse. I didn't have any of the buffers I'd had before: booze, or cigarettes, or journalism dead-lines, or boys, or the bars where I was a regular and could pop in for a distraction every night of the week.

Without all of that, I felt everything, and it was awful, horrible, black. Maybe I wasn't clinically depressed, but I felt as dark as ever in a lifetime of bouts of feeling bad. Looking back over my life, it seemed as if every temporary safety I'd ever found had been wrenched away from me in the most painful way: I had a family, and then my dad had chosen gambling; I had Simon's Rock, and then Wayne Lo had gotten a gun; I had Scott, and then he didn't love me enough to make it work; I had Anthony and Judah, but they had gone on to other women, other cities, other pleasures.

And still I didn't get my period. Thirty days became sixty days.

I began seeing a homeopathic doctor who gave me the few blood tests I could afford and started prescribing me her own herbal remedies.

Sixty days became ninety days.

I tried harder to be good, to be better, but nothing helped. Even though running in the morning made me feel awake and alert all day, I preferred running in the evening when the air was cool and smelled like jasmine, and the palm trees cast pretty shadows in the deepening dusk. I ran up into the lush green foothills on the edge of Pasadena and soaked in all of that beauty and affluence, hearing the sprinklers kick on just beyond the sound of the music in my headphones. It was so beautiful, but the beauty couldn't touch me.

My entire body and soul felt like one dark bruise, a blood blister, with sick black deposits of hurt visible beneath the skin. As I ran, I began to sob, choking as I tried to catch my breath. I ran harder, but I could never run fast enough.

I was out at a local Mexican restaurant for an early dinner with a girl-friend when I saw a familiar car in the parking lot. She happened to live on the same street as Judah and had pointed out his black Jaguar on several occasions. Here, now, was a black Jag just a few blocks from where they both lived. The skin at the back of my neck prickled in a satisfying, familiar way. He was here.

He and his guitarist were seated against the far wall. My friend looked at me, her eyes wide. I managed to get into the bathroom to put on some face powder and lipstick without his seeing me. When I emerged, I drew up to his table and cocked a hip.

"Why, hello, Judah," I said.

"Why, hello, Sarah Tomlinson," he said. "How've you been?"

"Great," I said. "And you?"

"I'm still here," he said. "You live in LA now?"

"Yeah, I'm a celebrity ghostwriter," I said. "Actually I'm working on a book you'd love. He's explaining how to run girls, you know, like working girls."

He started to laugh.

"Oh, is he?" he said.

I fished into my bag and held out my new business card.

"So we can stay in touch," I said.

He took the other end of the card, and for a long moment we were both holding one end of it, our fingers nearly touching, just as we had on that long-ago Boston night.

"We're in touch right now, aren't we?" He chuckled.

A few days later, I was in my room writing when a familiar e-mail address suddenly appeared on my BlackBerry.

"Was there something you wanted me to read?" he wrote.

We flirted back and forth for a few days. And later that week I found myself once again walking up the steps to his house around eleven o'clock at night, wearing a short green dress and my mom's Frye boots from the seventies. He kissed me on the lips.

"Water?" he asked.

"Sure, that'd be great, thanks," I said.

I laughed to myself about how much had changed since my last visit there, now more than five years ago, as we sipped bottled water. We'd both quit smoking. It didn't take long for us to move downstairs to a new lounge he'd put in, where he opened a nice bottle of wine. And it didn't take much longer for me to find myself in just my bra and underwear. "Leave your boots on," he said.

During all of our many late-night phone sessions, we had talked at length about almost every sex act, and I knew exactly what he liked.

"Do you want to get fucked or do you want to come back?" he asked.

I wanted nothing more than to, finally, after all of these years, be taken upstairs to his bed. But I also didn't want this newest incarnation of our affair to end so soon, especially because there was something comforting about reconnecting with someone who had known me for so long and who still seemed to have answers I continued to seek. Although I had changed and grown in some ways, I still valued the intensity of the experience over everything else. "I want to come back," I said.

After he came, I went into the bathroom, still in my bra and underwear and boots. I looked in the mirror. My collarbones jutted out like a model's. I was maybe a little too skinny, but I knew as long as I still had hips and breasts, men found skinny sexy, and so I shook out my hair, seeing myself through his eyes, not my own.

When I left with the sun rising over the freeway, I put in a CD of classical music he'd made for me and felt my mood brightening along with the sky. I sent Judah a flirty e-mail thanking him for our night together. And, once again, I waited.

I was spending that spring working on a final revision of my first novel. Now that I was regularly working with a literary agent on ghostwriting projects, I hoped he'd like it enough to help me realize my nearly twenty-year dream of having my own book published. In order to have quiet time, I'd taken on a variety of pet-sitting gigs. I bounced from house to house, trying to focus. Instead, I composed e-mails to Judah that I never sent. On nights I felt particularly angsty about his silence, I drank red wine.

It was a relief to let myself go, to let the edges become blurry and give up on my constant bid for perfection. But I wasn't the drinker I'd once been, and in the morning I felt foggy and sick, and guilty, for possibly diminishing all of the good work I'd done—and the money I'd spent—toward trying to heal myself.

In the aftermath of my temporary, tipsy escape, the blues came back worse than ever. It felt as if everything I did was pressing on the bruise, and it hurt. I was tired of the hurting, tired of feeling crazy and sad and fucked-up.

I began to have a new fantasy that was much more pleasurable than anything involving Judah, or even selling my novel.

In the fantasy, I was in an elegant hotel room. Everything was clean and quiet and dim. I stretched out on the bed. No one knew where I was. I was alone, and this solitude made me feel safe to do what I needed to do next. I took a handful of pills, and then another. I washed them all down with expensive bourbon. As I started to drift, I lay and sipped bourbon, for the pleasure of it, until I stopped breathing, and everything was silent.

No more pain of my unending, bottomless lack.

I was filled with relief. The image made me feel light in a way I hadn't in so long, maybe not exactly happy, but the next best thing, and far better than I'd felt in months, years, even, maybe in as long as I could remember.

I didn't tell anyone about my fantasy because I knew they would try to stop me. The first step was the pills. I didn't have a regular doctor. But I knew I could convince a doctor I needed some sleeping pills, just enough to get me through a temporary anxiety about writing deadlines, and blah-blah-blah. I would supplement those with over-the-counter sleeping pills. The booze was easy. That would be a treat.

The hotel room was a safe place I went to every day in my mind. The reality of my daily existence became the background noise to this necessary escape. Even developments that would have pleased me a few months before no longer did. Judah called me from a recording session, wanting me to have phone sex with him while his band went out to get dinner, as we had done so many times before.

"I should get a thank-you on this album," I joked. "I've given you 'creative inspiration' on what, three or four albums now?"

He chuckled his great, deep laugh.

"That you have," he said. "Maybe if we do a vinyl edition."

I sighed. I was tired of the conditional maybes that never came true. What interested me more was our talk about a female musician who'd been recording strings for his new album a few weeks earlier. When she hadn't turned up for a session one day, he'd called a mutual friend. They'd gained entrance to her apartment and found her dead.

He went on to describe how he'd known she was troubled, and because they were fellow night owls, he'd gone over to her house late a few times, just to listen to music and keep her company. As he talked, I grew jealous, not because he had shown her more care than he'd shown me. Instead, I was jealous because she was dead and I was not.

I pictured the tranquillity of her apartment, the finality of the scene, and how when the intruders had entered, they no longer had any power over her. It made me more determined than ever to claim my own moment of peace. But I didn't tell him any of this. I was sure he wouldn't care. I was sure I wasn't worth even a late-night record-listening session. And so, instead, I moaned when he said moan. And when he didn't come over later that night, I cared less than I ever had before. I had a solution. It was a relief, too, because after a hundred days, I'd gotten my period, but it hadn't changed the way I felt.

Before I could put my plan into motion, I had one more dog-sitting gig in one of my favorite neighborhoods, Mount Washington, a wild snarl of narrow winding roads clotted with overgrown vegetation. I particularly loved to run there in the evening, breathing in the smell of eucalyptus, and watching the whole city twinkle and pulse below me when I crested the highest hill at dusk. The house was a great Spanish colonial mess filled with the clutter of a single mom and her young son. It was hot that summer, and only the son's room had AC, so I sweated all day, nearly hallucinating with the hazy deluge of the afternoon heat, amplified by my laptop, which cooked on my lap, and then after my run, I slept in his narrow bed amid stuffed animals in the artificial icebox chill.

It was there, sitting in the hot, cluttered living room one afternoon, that a scene rose up within me, as vivid and full of emotional resonance as any of the sense memories I had of my past. This new scene felt equally real; it was as if it had already happened, and yet, I knew it was in the future. In it, I was driving somewhere in Los Angeles in a new car, the windows down, cutting through the twilight city with confidence and calm, beautiful, strong, happy, the opposite of how I felt now, and most of all *alive*.

Somehow, I knew this vision was inside of me, which meant that it would happen if I could just hold on.

When I got back to my house, I sat on my bed and took a deep breath. I called my mom and told her everything about my hotel fantasy. She was understandably upset, but it was Craig's response that really moved me.

"You can't let that happen again, okay?" he said. "You have to tell us."

He tried to convince me I should come back east and go with them to my mom's family reunion, which was happening at Grammy's old house the next month. I told him I didn't have enough money and was worried I'd be self-conscious about my special diet. He laughed at how he and my mom had been drawing sidelong glances for being mostly vegetarian for more than three decades and that they'd pay for the ticket.

"Just come home," he said.

My father made me promise that if I ever had such dark thoughts again, I'd tell him. So did my friend Cathy. My friend Jodi cried when I told her. Even if I still had trouble wanting to live for myself, maybe I could live for them. Finally, as my period came regularly, and my Chinese doctor beamed at me each week, I started to feel better.

The Kentucky Derby had come and gone, and my dad had not won us the money for our house in Los Angeles. In fact, he had never even placed his bets the day of the race, or if he had, he'd never mentioned anything about it to me. I knew from long experience that gamblers only acknowledged their bets when they were winning, and if they didn't bring them up, it was better not to ask. Of course I was aware it had been unlikely, but I was disappointed nonetheless. Not so much that we hadn't won the money—it would have been nice, sure, but I'd never had any money, and I'd always assumed if I ever made any, it would be through my own writing. I was let down because if the plan was going to work, my father was going to have to finally believe in himself. After years of listening to him talk his big talk for a time, and then suddenly stop talking because he'd lost interest or given up, I wanted him to actually follow through on something. And after years of believing in him, no matter what, and even when he didn't believe in himself, I wanted a little payout, not specifically of the financial kind.

I knew better than to bring any of this up with my father, and so I let the topic wane. In the meantime, he had raised the possibility of moving out to Los Angeles, which I thought was a great idea. I knew the general interest in health food, meditation, and mysticism would make him feel right at home, and because he'd been approved for Section 8 housing, the move would be fairly easy for him.

"I'm just going to come out to California for a year or two," he said. "I'm going to find a tank or a hot tub and do my work there. And once been married to, and no one could figure out why she wasn't more sensitive, until they realized the girl was so young that the first marriage predated her.

"I just don't understand it," I said. "I mean, his wife is gorgeous, and she's an amazing actress, and she seems like a total badass. I can't understand why he would choose to spend his time with this woman who doesn't know anything. Sure, sex is one thing, but he still has to talk to her."

"I'll tell you why, Sarah," my dad said. "Men want control. They want to be with a woman they can control. And so the younger she is, the less intelligent she is, the less money she has, the better they feel about themselves."

As I was a single thirty-four-year-old woman, this wasn't exactly encouraging news for me, especially since I still felt like my dedication to writing had—to some degree—cost me Scott. But at least my dad was in the trenches with me. That Christmas when I went home for my annual visit, my dad met me in Cambridge. We had lunch and, still talking animatedly about cinema and the feature script I was writing, and meditation, and Asmara, we went for a walk around the neighborhood. There's a kind of high I get from a really good conversation, all of my synapses firing just right, surprising connections blooming as topics morph and grow, and that feeling of intense well-being that comes from connecting deeply with another person. I had it that day, and as the midafternoon sun warmed the winter air and softened the snow, I felt uplifted and very happy.

My father and I stood facing each other. I looked at him in his brown winter coat and his black winter hat, which he kept neat to make them last, and because he was the grown-up version of the teenage boy in the Trenton projects who'd had his clothes hand tailored. He smiled at me, and I saw his broken brown teeth before he reflexively closed his mouth, covering them quickly.

"I love you," I said.

He looked at me, his face wide open in surprise.

"I love you, too, Sarah."

then I'm going to find a place in the woods. Maybe in Vermont or New Hampshire. Maybe even get a piece of land. What I'd really like is to build my own house. There are some books I'd like you to look up."

As I listened to him happily plan for just the kind of healthy, DIY life in the woods that he'd opted out of when I was a baby, I waited for the moment when he realized the irony of this, how sad it was that, thirty years too late, he finally wanted and felt capable of the choice that would have allowed us to remain a family. And then I realized he'd never get it. He was so used to thinking only of himself, that's how it'd always be. And so I would have to learn to think of myself first, too.

"Sure, Dad," I said.

I could hear him shuffle papers on the other end of the line.

"There's one called *Back to Basics,*" he said.

"We had that book when I was growing up."

"You did?" he asked, simply pleased with the synchronicity.

"Yeah, it was a pretty iconic book for the back-to-the-land movement."

"Oh, far out, well, if you could see how much it would cost to get a copy, that would be great."

Dad continued to be obsessed with film, and he loved to hear stories of my adventures in Hollywood. When an indie actor who'd just gotten his big break on a popular network sitcom took me on a date, my dad watched all of his movies, even many that I'd never seen. A few months later my dad gingerly raised the subject.

"I have to ask, since you haven't mentioned him, do we still like him?"

"We still like his movies, but we don't like him as a person," I said. "He never called me for a second date."

My dad laughed, and that's how it went.

Another time, I told him about a friend who was working on a film with a major Hollywood actor who had his young mistress on the set with him, even though everyone knew he was married. The mistress had happily gone on and on about how much she liked a woman he'd

It was the first time I could remember either of us saying the words to each other out loud. But I left the momentousness of the occasion unspoken. It felt too tender to examine.

I hugged him, and he hugged me back, and maybe I wasn't really a little girl anymore, but he was still big enough to feel like my dad.

That spring, I had a whirlwind three-month romance with a pedal steel player, Leo, who warned me not to fall for him and then took me to honky-tonks and home to meet his mom for Shabbat dinner. I'd gotten my own bungalow with an extra room I could use as an office. Leo helped me to move in and took me back to his place because I had no bed, vowing to come back and help me set up my bed frame. Although we e-mailed or spoke on the phone every day, updating each other on his recording projects and my writing gigs, he began to avoid making specific plans, as he'd once been eager to do.

I had bought a bottle of Veuve Clicquot to toast my new apartment, and I opened it with the forced air of a bon vivant during one of our phone calls, as I asked him to come help me with my bed, once again. I hated my nagging tone, hated myself for not just going into the bedroom and putting my own fucking bed together. As I listened to his excuses, I walked to the sink and poured out the glass of bubbly I was drinking, and then the entire bottle of expensive champagne. He was leaving me. I had no control over that. But I had control over everything else. I knew I had to stop drinking at the very moment I wanted it most, or else this new heartbreak might pull me under. Ten years after my breakup with Scott, I had given away my heart, again to someone who didn't want it.

We'd only dated for three months, but I had given myself to it completely, and I was bereft. I went to see a shaman in Topanga Canyon. She laid her hands on me and told me that I had never really let Scott go, even though he'd moved on years ago, and that beneath that heartbreak was the sadness of the little girl I'd been.

I had just been asked by a friend to write a piece for a reading about a book that had impacted me deeply because I'd either loved it or despised it. I surprised myself by writing about Donna Tartt's *The Secret History*, which Claire had given me years ago in the wake of the shooting, and the piece became about the shooting itself. I stood up in front of a small group of friends in a supper theater in Hollywood and shook and spoke Galen's name out loud through a nearly closed throat for the first time in years.

Now, alone in my two-bedroom bungalow, I felt all of this, each layer of sadness calcified into its own unique patterns and built upon the one below, and for once, I just allowed myself to be sad. I didn't drink. I didn't rush out and find another boy to kiss and make me forget about the one who had just broken my heart, or the one who had broken my heart so badly I'd hid it away for nearly a decade.

I was so sad it scared me. I didn't think about dying like I had the summer before. But this was no way to live. That's when it hit me: I'd been drunk for nearly twenty years, since my falling-out with my dad when I was fifteen, since the shooting, and in the wake of my breakup with Scott, and this was the first time I'd let myself feel everything I'd pushed back with all that booze. I went to a sweat lodge, because my friends in LA encouraged self-exploration through such means, which made me hope I'd eventually fix myself. When the spirit animals came and I was allowed to ask my question, I asked about my father, and the shaman told me that sometimes when things are too hard for us to do them for ourselves, we do them for someone else, and that when repairing my relationship with my father got too hard for our sake, then we could heal ourselves for others—for the children I would someday have, who would be free of the legacy of addiction and abandonment. Someone on the other side of the fire from me pointed at my shirt. "Look, you sweated in the shape of a heart."

I looked down. There was a giant heart in the center of my chest. I smiled.

During all of this, my dad stayed close beside me, even though he was far away. There wasn't much he could do, but he never left me alone, and that was something, particularly for him. We always had our weekly call scheduled in advance. But on days when I was really sad and lonely, I broke down and called him on his cell phone.

"I don't have many minutes left," he said. "Let me go into town and call you from a pay phone."

An hour later, my phone rang. He had left his apartment, walked two blocks to the main street, taken a bus to the subway, taken the orange line to Downtown Crossing, transferred to the red line, and ridden out to Alewife station, the only pay phone left of the many from which he used to call me. Once there, he stayed for as long as I needed to talk, even if there was nothing really to be said. The world was very black and white for him when it came to me. He wanted me to be happy. "I fully support you getting everything you want," he said to me, again and again and again.

But he also cited a book he'd recently reread, Carolyn Cassady's *Off the Road,* about her relationship with Neal Cassady and her affair with Jack Kerouac.

"If you want to talk about unconditional love, I can't think of a better example than how Carolyn felt for Neal," he said. "She accepted him for who he was, and she loved him anyhow. I mean she didn't try to change him at all. I think it was a result of the spiritual work they were doing, and you can see in her writing how it really helped her."

He sent the book to me and pointed out particular passages he thought would be useful. I had mixed feelings about my dad's advice. When he advised me to emulate a woman who put aside her own needs to love a man who was exceptional, yes, but who was also clearly a selfish, narcissistic womanizer who was maybe a little crazy, I felt that my dad was telling me to love him, no matter how he had let me down or might do so again. And sometimes I resented this greatly, especially because the closer we became, the harder it was for me to understand how my father could have been capable of abandoning me so completely for all of those years.

And I had a new concern now. For decades, I had thought my dad was the key to all of my unhappiness, and having a real relationship with him would heal everything. But I felt just as rickety as ever. How would I ever go from intellectually understanding the ways in which my relationship with my dad had created negative patterns within me to actually changing those patterns?

My father had said I could ask him anything—say anything—to him. One day, I screwed up my courage while sitting in my living room.

"Dad, I have to ask you something," I said.

"Okay, Sarah."

"I think it would just be really helpful for me to know, all of those times when you said you were going to come see me, and then you didn't, what were you thinking?"

"What do you mean?" he asked.

"When you called me to cancel, what were you thinking? Was it because it was too much for you to handle? Or your back was bothering you? Or you didn't have enough money? I mean, did you dread calling me, or did you not even think about it?"

"I can't remember, Sarah," he said, his voice cold. "That was a long time ago. And you're a grown woman now. Don't you think it's time you started taking responsibility for yourself instead of blaming everything on me?"

"Okay," I said.

But I got off the phone with him as quickly as I could, afraid I might cry. I knew the past was as painful for him as it was for me, but he had never spoken to me like that before. I was shocked. And then I was mad. He had fucked up for the first twenty-five years of my life, and now he was going to put a time limit on how long I was allowed to take to heal? I called bullshit on him, at least in my own mind, where it was safe. Even as angry as I was, I wasn't going to risk pushing him away again.

The pain forced me to deal with stuff I would probably have put off under sunnier circumstances. I sought answers, or at least solace.

I read Eckhart Tolle and was moved by his words about trauma and how a person's wound magnetizes the pain of every negative experience, making it worse than it would be for someone with a sturdier foundation. I went with a newly sober friend to Al-Anon meetings and felt deeply comforted by the premise that we are allowed to be in pain for as long as it takes us to heal. A friend became a disciple of an Eastern religion, Johrei, whose practitioners do public service by clearing the energy of those who go to their temples. I had my energy cleared again, and again. I had moments of happiness and peace, and then, more sadness.

One day that summer, I was driving in LA while talking with my father. In the midst of one of his endless, endlessly entertaining monologues, he brought me up short.

"You're a good girl," he said.

Just like that, tears pressed hard against the backs of my eyes, threatening to spill.

Something strange happened inside of me, like the moment a wall of icicles melts, setting off a cascade of falling ice that's beautiful to behold.

"You've always been a good girl. Even when you were running around with Judah, you were a good girl. And you're a good girl now."

My tears came on hard. I wasn't crying because it was something I'd always needed him to say to me. I was crying because I was finally able to believe him. My dad's constant presence in my life for the past nine years, and the loyalty my friends—old and new—had shown me during my bleakest hours, had been the foundation from which I had launched my growth. But something in the wild adventure itself, in my new life in Los Angeles—and my ability to weather all of the hardships it had precipitated, and the ones I had finally attacked related to my own sense of lack—couldn't help but make me begin to feel more confident, and more worthy, and it was such a relief.

chapter seventeen

DADDY ROLLIN' IN YOUR ARMS

That fall, one of my favorite musicians, Conor Oberst, was playing one of my favorite venues, Pappy & Harriet's, out near Joshua Tree. I booked a room at the Pioneertown Inn, just behind the venue. I filled my car with my computer and notebooks, the zebra throw Marya had given me, mineral water, and snacks. At the last minute, I threw in a bottle of red wine, just in case, even though I'd mostly been sober all summer.

Like my father, I loved to drive, and I loved road trips, and usually my spirits lifted as soon as I got away from the traffic that encased the city. But on this day, I didn't feel my usual sense of adventure. Instead of being inspired by the amusing signs and offbeat businesses in the small towns along the way, I was brought low by all of it. I couldn't imagine living in any of these towns. I couldn't imagine living any-where, really. It was all futile, the endless repetition of day-to-day life, with people all alone in their houses, eating junk food and watching TV. I couldn't see any point in any of it. As I approached the turnoff for my motel, I passed a gun shop. Ever since the shooting, I could hardly stand to look at the facade of a gun shop, let alone think about entering one. This time, I craned my neck, curious about what was inside. I could go in there and get a gun, and I could take it to my motel, and I could shoot myself in the head, and all of this would be over, and I wouldn't feel so sad or be so fucking pathetic all of the time.

By this point, I was a quarter mile past the gun shop. I considered turning around and going back. I could feel how cold the muzzle would be against my temple, could feel the relief of the moment, the total calm. I knew I could do it. But I forced myself to keep driving. I checked into my hotel, charmed as always by the porch swing and the view of the horse paddocks and the vast desert, which seemed so clean and empty and inviting. When it was time for the show, I got dressed up in a pretty blue dress and a pair of vintage country boots.

But as I entered the crowded venue, my mood darkened again. I felt the futility of it all, of trying to think or feel or do anything original in a world clotted with people. I pictured my hotel room and wondered whether I could hang myself in the closet, or whether I was too tall or the bar wouldn't hold my weight. If it came to that, there would be time. But first, I was here for the show. I looked around at all of the other kids who had driven out from Los Angeles with Bright Eyes in their gazes. I sighed and gave up: I went to the bar and ordered a Cazadores tequila with lime. As I sipped the booze, I felt the tension leak out of my neck and shoulders, and I stepped up to the edge of the throng in front of the stage. Conor came on, backed by the Felice Brothers. Seeing him wince at the catcalls from female fans with crushes, and rush his lyrics, seemingly because he hated it when everyone sang along, I felt a little better. Here was someone who had released a half dozen albums in the years since I'd interviewed him at a booth at the Life Diner in New York's East Village. His songwriting had improved with every one. He had earned more money than most indie-rock musicians dared to dream of, and without ever having to compromise his vision or make nice. And he was totally uncomfortable with everything—his fans, his fame, his own existence, really—except for the music itself.

And yet, he had gotten up this morning and put on his boots and gotten on with it. I thought of his song about waking up in the hospital with his father beside his bed, and how his father had made him promise it would never happen again. He sang about the great pain some of us are in, and the pain we cause those who love us. Just as I'd never been able to make it better for my father, or any of the other men I'd loved. The bloodletting we do to alleviate this pain, just enough to survive—in prose, in film, in art, in song—is probably the most beautiful thing about being alive, because it can't lie.

I pushed through the crowd and ordered another tequila. Instead of holding on so hard to my need for control, I let go of everything—fixing my father, making Leo love me, making it big in Los Angeles, being perfect in every way possible. I let life blur a little around the edges, and I let the music be my interior world in place of my own feelings, which had become such a burden. At the end of the show, I went back to my hotel room, the music still in my veins, the sound of drunken revelers shouting back and forth to their friends outside, and I didn't go out and join them and get drunk, and I didn't tie a noose and drape it over my closet. I took a coffee mug down from the mini kitchen, and I filled it with a few fingers of red wine, and I pulled out the new novel I'd begun, and I gave myself over to it completely. Caught up in the safe bower of words, I felt a sliver of light crack through the darkness inside of me: I was happy. When I was writing, I was happy. And if I could be happy when I was writing, then maybe I could find happiness in my life. My love of the act of writing, my one steady companion during all of these years, brought me back from the brink. I survived the night.

When I loaded my car in the clear desert air, I felt just the tiniest bit better, but I knew I had to once again climb out of the abyss. As I drove back to Los Angeles, I thought about calling my dad and the friend I had promised I would alert if I ever became suicidal again. I knew they would probably try to get me to come home, to maybe check into a clinic. I didn't want to do anything to make my world small. I wanted to crack it wide open.

Four days later, I was again behind the wheel of my car, this time on my way to Nashville to see my friend Traci, who was also going through a rough time. On my first day's drive, I saw seven rainbows. I listened to nothing but Conor Oberst for four days as I traveled across the country, indulging myself because there was no one else there to complain.

While I was driving, my dad called me. "Sarah, I don't want to worry you, but I read this article in the newspaper today about rest-stop serial killers."

"I know, Dad, I saw it. I never pull over at rest stops anyhow."

"I know but I saw this horror movie once where the woman was driving alone, and she needed cigarettes, so she got off the highway in this small town."

"Good thing I don't smoke anymore," I said. "Don't worry. I'll be fine."

Instead of getting irritated at my dad for worrying about me, I felt good about it this time. It felt like having a dad who cared. Maybe I could get used to it, after all.

From the moment I arrived in Nashville, I was in heaven. I loved the drowsy, honeysuckle-dusted humidity and the lazy drawl of everyone who greeted us everywhere we went, and the pork belly, and the music, oh the music, and the moonshine. As I relaxed and let myself have fun, I understood that maybe my perfectionism was my most dangerous compulsion of all, and that enjoying myself a little bit here and there might be better than running and meditating and eating mostly healthy and not drinking every day. A female musician taught me how to play spoons outside the club where she'd just performed—and where I'd seen a dozen pedal steel players and fiddlers and banjo players remind me that no matter how many times I had my heart broken, there'd always be someone new to come along and give me something to sing about. Drinking moonshine by the fire pit behind Traci's house, sitting outside with my computer on my lap, working on my novel in the dulcet Tennessee sunshine—it was like a Band-Aid for my soul. My agent called to tell me that I'd landed a new ghostwriting job in Los Angeles. I got into my car and made the long drive back to the best home I'd found so far, feeling wobbly but restored.

During my first week back in Los Angeles, I met a bookishly charming guy, Robert, at a friend's birthday party and talked to him all night. I didn't give him my number, but he found my contact info and sent me an e-mail that weekend asking me out. Here, finally, as multiple friends reminded me, was the kind of guy I should be dating—a writer who managed an independent bookstore and came from a close-knit family. And he seemed to really like me. We e-mailed throughout the week leading up to our first date, and he was thoughtful and clever. When I sent him a line from a screenplay, he responded with a song and a poem that expanded upon the theme. I was cautious after having just pulled myself out of my first major heartbreak in a decade, but excited going into the weekend.

After dinner, Robert took me to see his great-uncle play show tunes at an old-school restaurant with a supper club vibe. When Robert stood to use the men's room, he put his hand on my back and held it there a long moment. I felt something that made me ask: What would it be like to belong to this man?

When we got back to my house, I went with my instinct.

"I'm going to go inside and have a cup of tea," I said. "And you're welcome to come in, but I'm really just going to have a cup of tea."

"You're inviting me in?" he asked, his voice lifting with happiness, his hand already pulling the key out of the ignition.

I laughed and led him inside.

On my little maroon love seat, mug of tea in his hand because there was nowhere to put it down, he took a deep breath.

"I have to tell you something," he said.

My insides shifted with anxiety.

"When I was a teenager, I was a really bad drug addict," he said. "Like I didn't have a plan for my future. I thought I'd be dead. When I was seventeen, my parents put me in rehab, and I was sober for eighteen years. I used to do the speaker circuit and everything. I used to say, 'My mom told me to find something I was really good at and do it a lot. I was really good at being drunk.' When I was thirty-five, I felt like I could try drinking again. I talked to my therapist about it, and he agreed. And for a little while, I went wild. I mean I was really wild. But now it's just something I do sometimes."

That wasn't so scary. In fact, that sounded pretty great to me. He'd done the work to be healthier, to be happier. He'd made changes that had improved his life. He'd assessed the outcome of those changes and changed again. That sounded like growth, like how I was trying to live my life.

"I guess I should tell you that I have some abandonment issues," I said. "My dad and I were estranged for ten years. We've been repairing our relationship, but it's a work in progress. And I can be a little passive-aggressive sometimes. But I'm trying not to be. And I'm always open to being called on it, because I know that's how I can change."

He didn't seem any more put off than I'd been by his revelation, and we were both a little giddy with that high of having revealed our worst secrets and finding that they weren't dark or scary enough to scare the other person away. He used the term "emotional intelligence," which was one of my catchphrases, the real quality I was looking for in a man. I felt myself swoon a little even before he leaned over and kissed me, and the kiss opened up and lasted until nearly dawn. When we agreed that he should leave for the night, I made him inscribe the book he'd brought me. As he sat at my table, I stood close to him. He wrapped one hand around my hip and wrote with the other while I ran my fingers through his hair and examined the particular flavor of my fear.

Really, truly, I'm afraid he's going to break my heart. But he seems like a nice guy, and like he'd probably do anything in his power to make me feel comfortable enough to date him. So what if I got him to promise me that he wouldn't break my heart?

As he stood, and I walked him to the door and kissed him good-bye on the little front porch of my bungalow, I was still mulling over the idea in my head, which felt gauzy and light from all of that good conversation and kissing. In the morning, I woke up to find an e-mail from Robert with the link to a song: a gorgeous lo-fi gem by Dion with a pulsing drum, a throbbing intensity, and an apt title, "Daddy Rollin' in Your Arms." All morning, as I listened to the song and got my new script ready for a table read that week, I contemplated my solution. I decided to write a contract, laying out everything I hoped to give and receive:

> *I promise to behave with integrity, humility, and grace to the best of my ability at all times. I promise to be generous and kind. I promise to listen. I promise to be honest, even when what I have to say might be unpopular or uncomfortable because it is better to cause a small pain in the moment than to allow untruths to fester. I promise to ask for help, and when I don't understand something, to ask for clarification, rather than to assume. I promise to not hide behind past disappointments and hurts, but to embrace the pleasure and possibility of a new beginning. I promise to take responsibility for myself, my needs, and my writing. I promise to compromise without resentment. I promise to be a sweet sweetheart.*

As I read the final version of what I'd written, I realized that I was not just terrified of being abandoned again, which was how my system registered each breakup, but of doing something unkind to Robert. I knew that if Leo were to want me back, even for one night, I would be powerless to resist him. I knew that all of the ambition and self-interest that had caused me to put my writing before Scott was even more present as I'd gotten ever closer to my dream of succeeding as a writer.

When Robert called me the day after our first date to ask me about an e-mail I'd sent him, admitting I felt "raw," I tentatively mentioned the contract.

"I'm not going to have to sign it in blood, am I?" he joked.

"No, of course not, that would be crazy," I joked back.

While he seemed a little uncertain about my methods, he was intrigued enough to bring up the contract when he came over for our second date. When he read the contract, he was moved. He signed it and suggested we each hang a copy on our refrigerators.

It was a grand romance. I loved reading the contract on the fridge every morning, either at Robert's house or my own, because it seemed like such a strong example of clarity. But honesty is a funny thing. You can focus so much on the need to speak hard truths that you neglect to consider the importance of the things left unsaid.

In the first month, during which we reveled in the giddy joy of having found each other, we also established a pattern born out of my inability to ask for what I needed. I was good at big gestures—letters, contracts, gifts—but I had trouble with the small, everyday negotiations that make up a relationship and a shared life. Because Robert worked forty hours a week at a bookstore, and I worked as many hours as I needed to each week at home, our schedule became shaped by his work obligations. Every night, I waited to see whether Robert would call me. He always did, so I knew intellectually that the question itself was my own insecurity.

But no matter how many evenings in a row he got in touch with me, I always doubted him. And when he did, as he told me about his day and checked in with mine, I waited anxiously for his decree about whether or not he would be coming over that night. I always wanted to see him, always wanted him with me, but I felt that it wasn't up to me, and I resented what felt like my powerlessness.

On the nights when he had band practice or dinner with his parents or just wanted to go home and have a drink and read a book on his own, as he was telling me his other plans, I began to shrink back from him, tender with disappointment. Because we weren't going to see each other that night, he tried to coax more out of me about my day or my plans for the evening. I tried to act nonchalant, but my misery bled onto the phone in long, tense silences and clipped responses.

"Well, I guess I'll go then," he said.

"Okay."

"Have a good night."

"Yep."

As soon as I hung up, all I had been holding back erupted, sometimes in tears, sometimes in profanity. I knew I was being crazy. I didn't want to be the kind of woman who spent every minute with her boyfriend. I had work and friends and my own writing, all of which I enjoyed greatly and was fed by. But, still, there remained a huge, fraught gap between what I knew to be true and what I felt to be true: that there was not enough love and would never be enough love, and I would always be the one who was left lacking. But, of course, I didn't tell Robert about this, fearing he'd think me needy and immature. I was trying to lead with my strong suits in the early days of our relationship. As if I could hide the insecurity from him. Honesty really is a funny thing.

After we'd been dating for about three weeks, during one of these tense calls, Robert mentioned he had a work event at a bar that night. I was already armoring myself to get through the rest of the call when he surprised me by inviting me to meet him there. I wasn't feeling well, really. My skin was broken out, and I felt stressed about my ghostwriting project, which I was behind on because I was spending all of my time with Robert or thinking about Robert. But I was pleased to be invited, and I put on some lipstick and a short, flirty skirt and went to meet him. I savored being introduced to his coworkers as his girlfriend, as much as I had when Scott had first said it to his bandmates in Portland. He and I sat close at the bar, talking, our hands on each other's thighs, as the group made merry at a booth behind us. Still feeling close, we went back to my house and lay on the living room floor, making out, sprawled on the rug.

"I love you," Robert said.

"What?"

"I love you."

"Oh, I love you, too."

We had sex for hours that night. And in the morning we woke up and were both moved to tears, and we had sex again, and it was all a big ball of giddy happiness, talking, and laughing, and tears seeping out, and everything pulsing and beating like birds on the wing, that first-flush feeling of love. We stayed in bed all day and then went out to lunch so late it was basically dinner, going back to the barbecue restaurant where we'd had our first date. Only, this time, we sat together in a booth, both on the same bench because we couldn't stand to have even the distance of the table between us.

The next week, Robert was due to go away to San Francisco to see friends, a trip he'd planned before we'd met. I'd done that new-relationship thing of letting my regular healthy habits—daily meditation and runs and lots of salads and little booze—give way to indulging and being indulged by my new love. Although my period had remained regular since my epic health odyssey of 2009, and I had every reason to believe my PCOS was a thing of the past, my system remained very sensitive to sugar and junk food, and after a few weeks of being off my routine I felt fat and gross, no matter that Robert had told me that being with me was "like dating a Playboy Bunny with a brain." And so I was looking forward to this time apart as a way to get back onto my routine a bit and also, more important, get caught up on my ghostwriting project, which was due in early January, but which I planned to finish in advance of the holidays. At the last minute, in the flush of our new love, Robert invited me to go along to San Francisco with him. I declined, trying to be strong and independent. But then I missed him terribly, and the one night he didn't call me, I fretted and fumed at his indifference and cried myself to sleep. So I felt pretty shabby the next day when he told me he hadn't called because his friends had gone to sleep early and he'd stayed up late reading my script.

By the time Robert returned to LA, a day early, to hasten our rendezvous, I was feeling more like myself. As excited as I was to see him, and as pleased as I was that he invited me over right away, when I stepped across the threshold of his bungalow, I felt my old fears surface. I had trouble looking him in the eye, and all of the love and intimacy I'd felt just days before was now murky with insecurity. He felt like a stranger to me. When he kissed me, I smelled booze, not fresh booze on his breath, but old booze coming out of his pores, the result of his vacation indulgences. I pulled back, just a little, but enough for him to notice. "What?" he said.

Tension flickered between us.

"Nothing," I said, leaning in and kissing him harder because I was afraid to speak my true reaction, because I didn't want to embarrass him, because I didn't want to make a big deal out of what was probably nothing. So I'd stayed home and been a nerd while he'd been out in the world having a good time, so what? He offered me a glass of wine, and even though I'd enjoyed how clear I'd felt all week, I agreed, hoping everything would just relax and ease up between us. And it did.

In the morning, while we were still in bed, Robert sat up against the pillows.

"I need to talk to you about last night," he said.

"Okay," I said, trying to sound mature and adult, even though I felt like running from the bed.

"It's really important for me to feel wanted by you," he said. "And when you act like that, it's really hard for me to want to be close to you."

I felt awful. I loved him. I didn't want to hurt him and make him feel bad.

"I'm sorry," I said. "You know, it's not easy for me to trust, and being close is hard for me sometimes."

I felt shaky throughout the conversation, but by the end I was glad he'd said something. And I was excited to be with someone who was so capable of identifying a problematic moment in the relationship and bringing it up in a neutral conversation. It felt like we were building something with real potential.

We spent Thanksgiving alone together, even as his family, who he was close with, celebrated together up in Santa Barbara. He brought over a bottle of bourbon with the remaining ingredients for dinner, and he poured us drinks and kept me company while I cooked. Tipsy, working through the multitude of steps in Marilyn Monroe's elaborate stuffing recipe, I chopped my finger badly. Queasy at the sight of blood and unable to look at the carnage full-on, I let Robert doctor and soothe me while I cried from the shock of the cut and the pain, comforted by his steadiness in a crisis.

The following weekend, he took me up the coast to meet his family, who were the kind of lovely, real people it's so easy to forget live in California alongside the stars and aspirants. They made me feel very welcome, and I was flush with good feelings as Robert took me out to an upscale bar afterward to celebrate what was also our one-month anniversary. I was still on my superstrict diet, but I hadn't wanted to put his sister-in-law out, so I hadn't eaten much at dinner, and I was starving now. When the food came, Robert picked up the knife and fork and cut the food into tiny pieces, and then he handed me the fork. I felt cared for, and I leaned in closer to him and took a bite.

"I want to talk to you about what our future might be like," he said. "Now that you've met my family, I want you to be close to me."

I swooned at his assuredness and his openness to discussion. Here, finally, was a secure future with a man I loved deeply. We spoke about places we might want to live, and about our thoughts on marriage. He promised me a forty-five-year honeymoon. I felt as if we were already building a shared life, even though we'd only dated for a month.

Robert was clearly besotted, and I was deeply in love, but the night before I left to go home for Christmas, my old daddy issues reared their grizzled heads. After years of toil and aborted hope, I'd had my first feature script go out to producers, and I had a meeting in the morning with a hotshot producer who'd scored a big hit in the indie world and had told my agents she'd loved the writing enough to want to meet me. Given the pressure I was feeling to make a good impression, and the fact that I had to then get on a plane to fly home for two weeks, I'd suggested that Robert stay at his house that night so I could wake up rested and have plenty of time to get ready in the morning. He'd taken me to dinner and then come over, and we'd had a nice night in which I'd felt well taken care of and close to him.

When it was time for him to leave, I was already in bed. He got dressed and leaned down to kiss me good night. I was consumed by a wrenching sense of loss. He was going to walk out that door, and although he was driving me to the airport, I wasn't going to sleep next to him again for two long weeks. I felt as if I would never see him again. I squeezed my eyes shut and buried my head in his neck, soaking up his familiar scent of rose and musk. Hot tears punched their way out of my lids, and my body jackhammered with sobs. He squeezed me tighter, but I just cried harder.

"Hey, hey, it's okay," he said. "You have a big meeting tomorrow. And then you'll be at home. And the time will go by before you know it."

"I know," I choked out. "But I'm going to miss you so much."

"I'm going to miss you, too. But it'll be all right. You'll see."

He climbed into bed with me and held me close. But no matter what he said or how long he lay next to me, I couldn't stop crying. I could tell he felt awful, even though he knew he hadn't done anything wrong, and that he was confused and a little scared. I was, too. Intellectually I knew that this was fucked up. But emotionally I was hemorrhaging grief and loss, and I couldn't stop. It was almost midnight, and it became clear I wasn't going to stop crying. Robert unclenched my arms from around his neck. I curled up in a fetal position.

"I love you," he said. "I'll see you tomorrow, okay? Try to get some sleep."

"I love you, too," I choked out.

Through tear-clogged eyes I watched him put on his coat and step out the door. I heard him turn the lock behind him. I heard his car start up and drive away. My tears kept up for another thirty minutes after he was gone. Clearly having a loving boyfriend wasn't going to heal my issues any more than reconciling with my dad had.

When I flew back into Los Angeles a few days after Christmas, Robert was at work, but he stopped at the grocery store to buy essentials and then came over. This was not just a thoughtful gesture on his part. One of my clients hadn't paid me thousands of dollars the previous year, and the contract for the book I was about to hand in had been delayed. My credit cards were literally charged to the max. Robert was barely keeping up with his expenses, but he told me that he had some credit available that was all mine if I needed it. I couldn't take his money, but I appreciated his keeping me in food and drink and, even more important, books. I had missed him just as much as I expected to and was ferociously glad to see him. We instantly stitched our schedules back together, but the seams were visible.

We left my friends' New Year's Eve party early and went home, where I was abuzz with bliss. As we sat together at my table, Robert's mood didn't match mine.

"That's the first time I haven't had anything to say to your friends," he said.

"Oh," I said. "I'm sorry you didn't enjoy yourself more. They're all really nice. They've known each other forever. I'm sure next time will be more fun for you."

I moved on to what I really wanted to discuss.

"I think we should talk about next year."

"What, like New Year's resolutions?" he asked.

"Sort of, more like what we want to do together, like it would mean a lot to me if you could come home with me."

"Um, maybe in the fall," he said, sounding less excited than I'd hoped.

"It's so beautiful in New England in the fall," I said, fighting to stay perky. "I'll ask my mom and Craig when would be best for foliage."

But what I really wanted was a little bigger than a vacation.

"And I really want to buy a house next year," I said.

I prattled away happily about neighborhoods and fixer-uppers and how Craig could come out and help us do work on the place. Robert didn't exactly run away with the conversation, but he didn't shut me down either.

The next day, Robert started to feel weird, queasy and tense, and that deflated further into him being distant and a little cross. I was already restless, and the more he pulled away from me, the more anxious I got, and the more I wanted to be closer to him. I put on my sneakers to go for a quick run. I returned feeling energized and inspired, but Robert was feeling worse than before. Later that night, he confessed he was having a hard time; feeling anxious lately. By this point, I was feeling so far away from him, it was as if I were staring at him across a vast silent library, instead of sitting next to him on my tiny love seat.

Our conversation became a subtle sortie of defensive moves. I tried to feel out how bad it might get and how much help he was willing to enlist. He tried to manage his anxiety, which wasn't being helped at all by my probing.

"You make it sound like this is a deal breaker, or something," he said.

"Of course it's not," I said, shocked he'd made such a vast leap. "I'm just trying to figure out what I can do to help you."

By the time we went to bed that night, I was crying. I felt so very alone, and I felt guilty for demanding anything from him during his time of need. Instead of being better in the morning, things flatlined as they were, and even got a little worse. Robert faced off against his anxiety attacks and waged a steady war against increasingly severe neck and back pain. Socializing was out, but I didn't care. I was happy to drive up to his apartment.

Feeling helpless in the face of his unhappiness, I wanted to be near him, to try to lighten his mood. I slid into a sheer pink nightgown and twined flowers in my hair, and then pulled on my black trench coat against the January chill. I put lamby, my stuffed animal from childhood, in my bag, and when he opened the door, I held lamby aloft, an amulet against bad feelings. Once inside, I slid off my coat and showed him his other present. He laughed.

I stretched across his bed and talked him through his anxiety as he packed to go to a conference for work. But after he left for his business trip, the tempo of our lives suddenly changed. I was just finishing the book I'd started the previous fall. And I was hired to ghostwrite two other books and edit a third, starting immediately. I left for Las Vegas with a new client on the day I was supposed to pick Robert up from the airport. Her book was due in six weeks, and I had promised I could meet the deadline. The day I flew back from Las Vegas, I didn't have enough cash to take a cab from the airport, and only one of my credit cards had enough credit left to cover the fare. But I had a big check in my bag. I went immediately to the bank, feeling everything lighten. It was the first time I hadn't been worried about money in nearly two years. I drove back to the airport to pick up my friend Cathy, who'd flown in to celebrate my birthday, but really, she'd come to meet Robert.

"I've never heard you talk about a guy like this before," she said.

The only problem was Robert was now sick with a bad cold and bowed out of all of my invitations to meet us for dinner or sightseeing. One night, on the verge of a meltdown, I dropped Cathy off at my house and drove up to see Robert, desperate just to be near him. It had been nearly two weeks since we'd seen each other. I climbed into bed with him and took off all of my clothes. Afterward, we lay together talking quietly, and it was if a great weight had been lifted from me, just like at the bank.

It seemed that Cathy might not meet Robert at all, until the last night she stayed with me, on the eve of my birthday, he joined us for dinner and a show at the Magic Castle. The next morning when Robert and I woke up alone in my house, he immediately began secret birthday maneuverings. He'd snuck stuff into my refrigerator the night before, and he now got up and cooked me eggs with special steak he'd tracked down for me. At my place setting was an antique souvenir book from Niagara Falls inscribed with a beautiful, romantic letter, and a birthday card that echoed a vow he'd been making to me since we confessed our love, the promise of a forty-five-year honeymoon. Nothing scared me when I knew we were both in it for the long haul. This was how relationships got broken in, this was how people got to know each other, this was how families worked, right?

The day after my birthday, I went back to work, and I only saw Robert for a few hours here and there after that. When we were together, I was still fielding e-mails from my clients, whether it was two in the morning on a Wednesday or two in the afternoon on a Sunday. I could feel the chill emanate from him every time I picked up my BlackBerry. "I'm sorry," I said. "Is it bothering you that I'm working so much?"

"No, no, it's your work, I get it."

But his posture told a different story. By Valentine's Day, I was convinced we were going to break up, and was floored when I arrived that evening to find he'd lit candles throughout his apartment and yard and put on a suit jacket and greeted me with as much romance as ever. I was temporarily reassured and too busy and tapped out to really investigate beyond the surface. And when we did get to spend time together, it was still so easy for us to connect.

During a conversation with Robert about my dad's gambling and the books I'd bought him to help him master the racetrack, Robert paused and looked at me.

"Well, you know your dad is mentally ill, right?"

I was shocked. My dad wasn't mentally ill. He was cool, bohemian—eccentric, yes, but in a good way.

The possible truth of Robert's words bloomed in my mind: the untreated gambling addiction, the depression, the narcissism that my new therapist had basically diagnosed when she'd recommended all of those books on narcissism to me. It wasn't that I cared, really, about any of this. I certainly had plenty of my own issues. What unsettled me was the possibility that my father had raised me in a complex fantasy where he was the infallible king, and I his most loyal subject. If I woke up from the enchantment, what would happen? Who would I be and in what world would I live?

I didn't ever make a conscious decision to change my behavior, but after that moment, I started to pull back from my dad. I didn't talk with him about Robert the way I had about previous relationships. Even though Robert and I were both having a difficult winter, as far as I was concerned, we were still moving toward getting married and starting a family, so maybe it was right for me to push my father off his pedestal and become an adult. My dad even seemed to agree. One day when we were discussing my life—Robert, my ghostwriting, my script—he paused.

"You're almost done," my dad said, sounding a little sad that I might not need his support as I had during the early years of our reunion.

Even as blissed-out as I was in my surety that I'd finally found the one, work deadlines consumed me. I was distracted and exhausted. Robert protested up and down that everything was fine, but that did not stop him from growing more distant as the winter progressed, which only made me cling harder. When we did see each other, with booze in our bloodstream, we had sex like we had in the beginning. In the morning, I woke feeling bleary and bruised and went back to my computer, where I stayed for days at a time.

When I opened the file for the book I'd been hired to write, I lost myself in the story I'd been told by my client, whom I genuinely liked, and the sheer joy I felt when I got caught up in the puzzle of moving prose around on the page. It was a welcome respite from the seemingly bottomless longing I felt, which never seemed to alter in any measurable way, even if the men I was longing for changed.

In the first few months of our relationship, Robert had sent me his schedule every week, so I could go to events with him, and we could plan to hang out on his days off. Now, when I asked him about the week ahead, he ran through the plans he had already made for his free time. I sat, staring at him, frozen with fear and dread.

"So you're not going to see me at all next week," I said.

"Well, you've been so busy," he said.

At the end of one such exchange, he was sitting in a wingback chair at his house, impassive and closed off. I ended up kneeling by his chair, my arms around his waist. I knew I was clinging, literally, but if I didn't move toward him, there would be nothing left of our relationship for me to reconnect with after my deadline.

"We'll talk about it after your book is done," he said.

"Talk about what?" I asked. "I don't understand what's going on."

"Everything is fine," he said. "Just get your book done."

For the last week of my deadline, I slept six hours a night and spent literally every other waking moment working on the manuscript. When I handed it in, a week late because of the client's last-minute changes, Robert and I went to Malibu for a night away, which I'd planned carefully and then postponed. I wanted to have sex. He wanted to have adventures. When he reached for a napkin in my glove box, he found there were none.

"How do you expect to be a mom if you don't have paper towels in your glove box?" he asked.

Instead of defending myself, I made a mental note to get some napkins.

I'd bought a Frisbee and a kite for our weekend away, and as he tossed the white disc to me on the beach, he laughed.

"Maybe you'll be a good mom after all," he said.

I stared at him in disbelief but held my tongue.

When we got back to his house, I was supposed to go to a friend's birthday party, and he wanted to bow out and spend the night at home. Even though we'd just spent twenty-four hours together on a supposedly romantic getaway, I felt farther away from him than ever. I melted down, sobbing and shuddering on his bed.

He drove me to the party and remained cheerful throughout, but I didn't feel victorious. It hadn't been a battle or a point I'd been trying to prove. I regularly drove to Texas and Tennessee by myself and had no problem going to a party alone. What I was fighting for, clumsily, was something much deeper and harder to get at than that. I wanted closeness from him, and I did not feel it simply because he was standing in the same room with me, or sleeping in the same bed. Every good moment we spent together was evidence I stored up to ward off this feeling of lurking trouble, but the shadows persisted.

In mid-April, Robert came over on a Friday night. This was usually our date night. But he didn't ask me where I wanted to eat or grab his keys to head out the door. Instead, he sat heavily on my love seat, and he didn't move at all.

"Sarah, I have to tell you something. I haven't been honoring the contract."

"Okay," I said. I felt my mouth go dry.

"I haven't been honest with you," he continued. "I've been feeling distant from you, and our relationship, and I have been for some time. I kept thinking it was me, but it's been a month, and so I have to assume that it's not."

We talked for hours, with Robert getting up to bring me glasses of water, none of it enough to quench my thirst. We lay down on my bed, which he knew made it easier for me when I was emotionally stressed. He held me, and I cried. He was the man I was going to marry and have children with. He was the man who had promised me a forty-five-year honeymoon. But, as I told him almost immediately, if he needed to go, he had to go. He wouldn't say he wanted to leave. But he wouldn't let me back in, either.

A week later, I pushed him to admit he wanted out. Despite looming deadlines, I managed about four hours of work a day. Around one in the afternoon, I forced myself to get up and go into the kitchen to make tea and eat an apple with almond butter, one of the only things I could force down. I sat at my dining room table and looked at the postcard of Marilyn Monroe I'd hung there when I'd first moved in—before Robert had bought me all of those books about her, before I'd made us her stuffing for Thanksgiving—and I'd think about how unlucky in love she was, and how unhappy. She'd spent her whole life fearing she'd end up crazy like her mother, and I thought about whether or not Robert had been right about my dad. And how Robert had gone away, and now it was only my dad who had stayed.

chapter eighteen

GOOD GIRL

I was still on the outside of everything I wanted, feeling like it was other people who had the power to give me value—all of the lovers, editors, and experiences I had given myself over to for years, rather than owning myself. Never seeing that I had been at the center of my own big life all along.

I was sad because Robert and I had broken up; because my dear friend Marya had just been diagnosed with brain cancer; because the script my film agents had been sure would sell had not; because feeling like my life had fallen apart at thirty-five was that much worse than feeling like my life had fallen apart at thirty-four. There was one circumstance that was better now. For the first time ever, really, I had money.

This meant I actually had health insurance that wasn't given to me by the state (thank you, Oregon and Massachusetts!). I went to see a gynecologist and got another ultrasound. The good news was my PCOS was gone. The other news, which he announced just as matter-of-factly, was that I had five years of fertility left.

"I think I probably have seven years left," I said to the doctor.

"You have five," he said. "Meet a nice guy and have a baby."

He was lucky I didn't start crying right there. I waited until later in the day when I was home alone and my tea and wine were not far away.

The therapist I'd found in the last weeks of my relationship with Robert to help me save the relationship, and who was now helping me handle the breakup, encouraged me to maintain appropriate boundaries with my dad: not letting him talk to me about his porn habits or make me feel guilty for not enabling him. And to get angry: at him, at Robert, at Leo, at anyone who had made promises to me he hadn't kept. I wouldn't say I succeeded at getting angry. But I found I was different in moments that sometimes surprised me. When Robert began e-mailing and texting me to check in, I e-mailed back and said I wasn't ready to be his friend. It was a small but crucial step. Slowly, I began to feel better.

No matter how much I changed and grew, it seemed as if my father was capable of spinning out in the same few areas indefinitely. There were times when he disappeared for a week or two. When I eventually coaxed him onto the phone, he revealed it had struck him how much went into raising a kid—the cost of shoes, the constant need to teach and love—and how completely he had failed my sister and me. His bottomless regret had made him feel so lousy that he'd dodged my calls. We had already had this conversation many times, and as much as I wanted his patience during my healing, I was incredibly frustrated that his guilt about having been absent from my life in the past had caused him to be absent from my life again. Most of all, he seemed incapable of seeing the pattern. It was hard to stay mad at him, though. Sometimes he came out with the loveliest assessments of our relationship, like "Sarah, I'm sorry I couldn't be a better father to you, but I've had my own head so far up my own ass my entire life." Other times, he'd been silent because he was worried about his health. He confessed that he'd been having trouble with his prostate and was obsessed with the fear that it was cancer. Eventually, he'd begin circling a topic that had become fraught between us.

"I know we haven't talked about it in a while, but I was wondering if you'd given any more thought to me coming out there," he said. "You used to want me to come."

It wasn't that I didn't want him to move, it was that I had no idea whether I'd stay in Los Angeles, or for how long, and I didn't want him or anyone else to be reliant on me. Always, I feared hurting his feelings or driving him away. But I knew, this time, I had to be honest.

"I don't think it's a good idea right now," I said. "I need to focus on my own life. I might want to have a kid. I need to put my energy there. I need to take care of myself."

He let the topic drop then, but he returned to it again and again. Finally, I got fed up.

"I won't have this codependent relationship with you anymore," I said. "I'm working really hard to be healthy, and I just won't do it anymore."

He waited a beat.

"I have cancer," he said.

"You don't have cancer," I said. "You haven't had the test yet. You might have cancer. Well, I might have cancer, too."

I couldn't believe he'd played the cancer card like that, especially when he knew about Marya's diagnosis. But, then again, I could completely believe he'd used cancer in this way. That was exactly why my therapist had written down that list of books about narcissism and kept reminding me about the importance of healthy boundaries.

I was frustrated with my dad, but I was also concerned. I knew my dad was scared. I felt for him, especially because he could be self-aware in this particular way that made his plight more sympathetic.

"I've always been a hypochondriac," he said. "I remember when I was a kid, we used to go swimming in the river, and they said if you swallowed the water you would get polio. One day I swallowed a whole mouthful, and for years, I was sure I had polio."

"Just wait and see what the tests say," I said.

My dad did have cancer. Prostate cancer.

I tried to remain upbeat and patient as I called him after each of his doctor's appointments and asked him a series of small, neutral questions in order to try to extract all of the information he'd been given that day. It was during these calls that I was struck by what a classic addict my dad was. For many addicts, the secrets they build around their bad habits are as succulent as the verboten substance or behavior itself. My dad was in the habit of withholding information and only giving up small nuggets at moments when he felt the revelation could be beneficial for him, often to manipulate. It didn't help that he was naturally distrustful of all doctors as extensions of the epic global conspiracy that was keeping us all ignorant and poor and isolated, and maybe, even, taking our lives.

"All of the doctors came in and gave their spiels because they all think their treatment method is the best," he said. "The surgeon, he tells you that surgery is the best option, the only option. And then, no, the radiologist says that radiation is the best. And then, no, it's chemotherapy that's the best."

I tried to ask him about side effects and outcomes, anything concrete I could hold on to, but there was nothing like that to be gotten from him. He did confess that there was one question he really wanted to ask his doctor: "Well, I just want to know if it's possible, because I think I gave myself the cancer with my marathon masturbation . . ."

I missed the rest of what he said.

I never pushed for one treatment option or another, simply waiting to see what he would decide. And when he told me he'd found a book by a man who'd cured his prostate cancer with diet and herbs, I was encouraging and supportive. When he told me that he'd asked his doctor for six months to try out this approach before he decided about any of the traditional methods, I remained positive. I wasn't particularly surprised. He'd always said that when his time came, he wanted to go out into the woods and die alone. I'd supported this option in theory, and I'd always believed that everyone had the right to live and die with dignity, whatever that meant for them. But that had all been in the abstract. Now that my dad really did have cancer, and his mortality was on the horizon, we were forced to have some hard conversations.

Our candor didn't make it any easier for me to look on as my dad adopted the health regimen that was supposed to cure his cancer and then neglected to stick to it. Even though I was supposedly done being codependent, I hadn't been able to resist going to Erewhon, the Los Angeles mega–health food store where I'd sought advice and support when I'd waged my holistic health campaign against PCOS. I'd asked a woman in the supplements department what she would recommend for prostate cancer. She told me that one of the most important things my dad could do for his prostate health was to bring down his weight. He knew this. He was supposed to be on a special diet. And yet, he kept bingeing on hummus and peanut butter.

"You don't know what it's like, Sarah," he said. "You're disciplined."

"Only because I almost starved when I started out, so I had to write every day, and it became a habit. Only because I know I'll go crazy if I don't run and meditate."

I knew it was his own battle to fight, and there was nothing, really, I could do to change its outcome. Just as I had when I was a little girl, I listened and encouraged without registering my own opinion.

"I can see all of the shit I've been running from my whole life coming down on me, and if I don't deal with it, I'm going to die," he said.

He was scared. I was scared for him. And I was frustrated with him, too. I struggled to help where I could without destroying carefully constructed boundaries. My sister moved to America for four months that summer and took a college internship in Fullerton. Picking her up at the airport and driving her out to her new home, I could tell from the first few minutes that she was going to be miserable there.

I drove down to have lunch with my sister, trying to be supportive, even though I felt I was barely keeping myself functioning. I invited her up to my apartment for the night. As we sat eating the snacks I'd put out, I gently mentioned something about our dad's cancer. I didn't want to upset her, but I also needed to talk about it with someone who could really grasp what we were dealing with, not just with the disease but also with his response to it.

"You mean you know?" she said, looking shocked.

"Yeah, he told me when he was diagnosed," I said. "Why?"

"He made me promise I wouldn't tell anyone," she said. "And I told him I couldn't do that because I tell my mother everything. But I didn't think you knew."

We stared at each other, not in disbelief, exactly, but with a new understanding of what we were up against. Here it was, again, the addict's mind at work, thinking he could control the outcome of the situation and our reaction to it, thinking he could make himself powerful if he released the information to us in small doses.

Our conversation lingered on our father's behavior. I wasn't sure how much she knew about his past because she'd had so little exposure to him.

"Do you know why your mother left our father?" I asked her.

"Because of his gambling, and because she wanted to go back to Germany to be closer to her mother," she said.

"Yes," I said. "My mom left him because of his gambling, too."

"For school, in Germany, the government pays, but I had to get proof of John's income to show that he didn't have any money, and so I know how little money he has."

I knew the specific figures weren't important. If a gambling addict had a nickel, he'd risk it. If he didn't have any money, he'd gamble whatever else he had, even his life.

The conversation opened up to the subject of men in general, and the men we'd dated. Asmara was in America because she'd fallen in love with a young American man who lived in New York City, and she was going to be with him in the fall when her internship was over. I told her about my recent breakup, and about the many needy men, recovering and otherwise, who'd found a place in my heart.

"I don't understand," she said. "They're sick men. How can they be a husband? How can they be a father?"

"I don't think of it like that," I said. "For me it matters that people are working on themselves, like I'm working on myself."

She shook her head, as if maybe I were the lost cause. I didn't take it personally.

We also talked about travel and fashion and friends and vowed to make a trip around Europe together soon. We were both profoundly moved by the experience of suddenly having a sister. We both came from small families and had yet to start families of our own.

By the end of the weekend, I was grateful for the time we'd spent together and the way it had helped me to see her as more than a competitor for my father's love. When she left the next day, I felt exhausted and washed out in that clean, worn way, as if my insides were made of sea glass. It was a feeling I was becoming increasingly familiar with as I began letting go of more old pains and misconceptions, finding a way to be at peace with the faint scars they left behind. Scars, I was finding, didn't preclude clarity or healing.

I was so desperately unhappy for so many years, and I tried so many different remedies to make myself feel better—particularly coming out of my suicidal summer and many romantic woes—that it's hard to say what helped and how much. I was seeing a clairvoyant, a body worker/yoga instructor, and a therapist, all with the intention of releasing the trauma and pain I'd stored in my body and my self, and building a new, stronger, and healthier foundation for that self. Ever the perfectionist, I'd always assumed that doing this kind of emotional restoration was like cleaning house, and if I worked hard enough, I'd eventually get to the bottom of my pain and release it all completely. My energy healer and two different therapists broke it to me in the lingo of their different disciplines that it doesn't quite work that way.

My relationship with my father, or my lack of relationship with my father during my childhood, was a trauma that was embedded in my core self. It was never going to go away completely. It would always be a part of who I was. But maybe that was okay. Maybe that was even a good thing. All of me—troubled and not—had contributed to my writing, and to the friendships I'd formed, and to the amazing life and adventures I'd been privileged to have.

Maybe I didn't want to get rid of any parts of who I was. Instead, the healers and friends in my life helped me enhance the positive sides of that self, increase my tolerance for pleasure and happiness, and reinforce my boundaries so I didn't let my father—or anyone like him— take more than I really wanted to give.

And slowly, remarkably, it started to come together.

I poured my heartbreak into a new novel. I did a lot of yoga. I didn't drink so much. And just as I was pulling myself up, I was visited by three men who'd flitted in and out of the past nine years of my life—Judah, Anthony, and Leo. Over the course of a month, I spent a night with each of them, talking about our histories, appreciating the genuine affection that existed between us after so many years.

But I also had relapses. One night I ended up at the home of a very cute man I'd met at a party, very drunk, so drunk I shouldn't have been driving, so drunk I shouldn't have been there at all. He'd talked vaguely about his daughter and his "baby mama," who was out of town. It was only when I was already on my knees in front of his chair that what he said reached me.

He pulled back, alarmed. "I have a girlfriend. We have a daughter."

"What am I doing here, then?" I asked, embarrassed, angry.

"Having a drink?" he said.

"Oh, come on," I said. "You know that's not what's happening here."

We looked at each other for a long moment. He kissed me. Having decided to be bad, we indulged ourselves fully. In the morning, he woke me up very early because he had to go pick up his daughter from her grandmother's house. As I dressed, hangover-sick, I fully registered what I'd avoided the night before: all around me were pink toys and dolls and the whimsical drawings of his little girl, a little girl much like I'd been. Only now, I wasn't the little girl anymore, I was the interloper who threatened her entire childhood realm, her future happiness, even.

Instead of wanting anything more from him as he walked me to the door, I had only one thought: *Please be a good dad to your little girl.*

As I drove home, I broke it down. It was time to stop fucking around. I didn't like the woman I'd been the night before. I made a vow to never be her again. Over time, with vigilance, it got easier.

My dad and I grew closer again, but not too close. He told me about the time in his life right before we'd reconciled, and how he'd finally been able to take the risk and do the work to be a father to me. When I'd first moved to Boston for grad school, he was so consumed by his gambling that he'd been spending all of his disability check at the track each month and paying for his basic expenses by collecting cans. It had dawned on him that I might see him digging in a trash can some day, recognize him, and be horrified and embarrassed. When he thought about being back in my life, he worried that I'd introduce him to one of my friends and they would recognize him as the man they'd seen around the city gathering cans for money. He couldn't stand the thought of either of these scenarios, but he wanted, badly, to have a relationship with me. And so he began rehabilitating himself, getting his gambling and his finances under enough control—with the intention of reuniting with me—so that when my letter of invitation arrived, he was able to respond fully. I'd had no idea his life had gotten so dark, and I was deeply moved at the effort he had made to turn things around so he could sit across from me and begin our new relationship.

I struggled to keep tabs on his cancer care but not control it, and to enjoy his presence in my life but not give more power to him than was appropriate. I was writing a lot of personal essays, particularly about my dad, and performing them more and more, but there was one I couldn't bring myself to read aloud; it was about a conversation I'd recently had with my mom.

"That family sure has a lot of crazy in it," she said. "I hope you didn't get too much of it."

"I probably got enough," I said.

"Well, but you've done such good work, with your therapy, and your writing, and everything," she said quickly, trying to regroup.

The conversation lingered with me long after I wrote the piece it inspired. Was my dad really mentally ill? How much of it had I gotten, and how would it play itself out? What if my dad really did die because of his decisions about his cancer treatment? Had we really done all of our work? And what about the rest of my life? Would I ever have a healthy relationship, make it as a writer? Even though two of the books I'd ghostwritten had been successes at this point, I'd never spoken with my own voice.

As I struggled to simply live with the fact that these questions weren't answerable—would always be works in progress, just as my wound would never be completely erased, and it was all a part of my life's labor—I kept on living.

My father still fell back into some of his old patterns in our relationship, but I worked on tamping down my irritation at his behavior. He had cancer. I couldn't get mad at him.

My dad wasn't worried about my being angry, though, he was worried about my being sad. Whenever he didn't want to answer a question about his cancer, his treatment, or his fear his cancer had worsened and spread, he gave me the same reason:

"I don't want to upset you," he said.

He didn't want to upset me, as if he were staying alive for my sister and me, when of course, the only person he was facing off against was himself. That's when I realized something I'd never understood before.

My father was still talking, but I was only half listening to him. Instead, I was circling this new thought, wondering whether it could possibly be true. And even though I knew that *yes, yes, it was true,* I wondered whether I could say it to him.

I wanted to say it. I needed to say it.

But I couldn't.

That's how we were. It was how we'd always been, and it was how we still were, no matter how much work we had both done, collectively, and how much work I'd done to heal myself and this relationship with the man who was my father, for better or worse. But this was it, this was quite possibly the end of it all, after which there would be no more chances. I had to be sure or, as my father said, "get clear" on what I believed and how I behaved. Again, it hit me: I already was clear on how I felt and how I wanted to behave. I just needed to be brave enough to say it. When my father paused in his rumination on his illness, I took a deep breath.

"You have my permission to die," I said. "I don't want you to, and I'll be sad when you eventually do. But we've done our work. We've had all the conversations we needed to have, and we've healed our relationship. And I'm incredibly grateful for that."

"Thank you, Sarah."

"Thank you, Dad."

But my dad wasn't dying. He was living. It seemed that his cancer was slowly getting worse, but it hadn't spread, and now that he'd brought his weight down, he actually had periods when he felt better than ever. He was striving to adopt a health regimen known as 80-20, which he took to mean eating eighty percent vegetables and fruits, with the twenty percent comprised of a little bit of bread with hummus or peanut butter, and he was taking herbs he'd been prescribed by a prostate cancer expert in New York City. But the herbs were expensive, so he'd found some herbs on the Internet that would cure his cancer immediately. Bits and pieces of these developments came up in conversation, amid our regular talk of movies, my sister, and my writing projects. I always listened with interest but tried to maintain some degree of distance. My father had chosen not to treat his cancer with traditional methods. He'd admitted to being sporadic in his own self-care. I knew I had to do my best to remain optimistic and supportive, while being okay—as I'd said I was—with the outcome.

One day, he began circling around the topic of the herbs in a familiar way. He wanted something but was afraid to ask, fearing a no.

"I don't know if you read the information I sent you or not," he said. "But I need to borrow a thousand dollars to buy three months' worth of the herb I found on the Internet."

"What happens after three months?" I asked.

"After three months it will have knocked the cancer out of my body," he said.

I wanted to believe this was true, wanted to believe if I gave my dad a thousand dollars he wouldn't immediately take it to the track. I circled his request again and again in my mind, feeling uncertain. I was scheduled to visit with him the next week, and when I entered his studio apartment, he immediately handed me printouts about his diet and the herbs, pitching me his plan as a way to avoid hearing my answer.

"I'm sorry, Dad, but I can't give you the money," I said. "I've supported your decisions about how to handle your cancer. And I don't want to jeopardize a relationship we've worked very hard to repair, when you're sick, by taking on too much responsibility for your treatment."

We talked of other things, and then it was time for me to go.

"Are we cool?" I asked my dad.

"Do you want me to be honest?"

"Yeah, be honest."

"Well, I'm disappointed. I feel like you're showing me a side of yourself you never showed me before."

"It's because that side of me wasn't there before, Dad," I said. "It's the result of a lot of therapy and a lot of hard work."

He didn't acknowledge my therapy, or my hard work, or the reason I'd needed so much of both in my life, and he didn't seem particularly happy about this new side of myself, especially in terms of what it meant for getting what he wanted. But then he smiled.

"You're still my best friend," he said.

As I left, I was surprised to find I was elated. I wasn't worried about getting knocked down, by my dad or by anyone else. I wouldn't lose it all and have to start all over again. I knew my own mind, and I didn't need my dad, or anyone, to think for me or to complete me. Finally, I was free, not to do everything, or to chase the big life I'd pursued to give me external value. But to do the one thing I really wanted, the one thing that was really me: to be my true self, to write, to live as I believed, and to be happy. I could be the good girl of my own choosing, whatever that meant, and the woman she had finally become.

A year after I said no to my father, I was back on the East Coast for a writer's retreat and to visit with family and friends. I drove up to the land and stayed a full week, listening to the crickets' and bullfrogs' cacophony in the deepest darkness, a total blackness still not penetrated by a single light beyond my family's home, the neighbors' houses obscured by the thick leaves of the summertime trees; smelling the infinite shades of green abloom in a humid afternoon; appreciating, finally, the purity and the peace.

Alone in the house one morning, I faced the big windows I had haunted as a child. I looked out at the driveway where I'd waited for my father's cab to appear on so many days that the waiting became my constant state, who I was. I looked at my parked car, which I had driven from Los Angeles, crossing the country, visiting friends, doing my best thinking on the road, just like my dad. Finally, I'd come to enjoy all I'd longed for as a little girl, my power of volition, my ability to choose. And now that I did have the choice—had been across the country and back a half dozen times—I knew I would always return to this land, and I would always go away again, taking this refuge with me, but making my home wherever I found myself in the world. Whether I was here or there, with others or alone, a writer, a mother, a wife, a good girl, or the best woman I could be, I wasn't waiting anymore. I had arrived at the heart of my big life. It had been with me all the time, and always, it had been no one's but mine.

acknowledgments

My dad, who showed great valor in his willingness to help repair our relationship, and who inspires me with his curiosity and always supports my happiness.

Craig, who was a dad to me long before I could see it, and taught me the value of hard work and showing up for family in the simple ways that really matter.

My wonderful extended family including all of the Tomlinsons, Trouwborts, and Rands, who nurtured me and championed me, no matter what.

My brother, Andrew, for enduring my sullen teenage years, for being my companion at so many Bright Eyes shows, and for being the musician I always wanted to be.

My sister, Asmara, for being my sister, and for great examples of strength and grace.

All of those on the land, who were like members of my big, extended family.

So many fantastic teachers: Mrs. Fallagario, Mrs. Meyers, Hal Holloday, Pat Sharpe, Benjamin LaFarge, Laurel Leff, and especially Peter Sourian, whose kindness and belief in my writing came at a crucial moment in my life.

So many brilliant editors and mentors: Laura Miller, Haley Kaufman, Steve Morse, Scott Heller, Matt Ashare, Carly Carlioli, David Daley, Sarah Hepola, Whitney Joiner, Laura Sinberg, and especially James Reed, who never fully succeeded in teaching me how to use a semi-colon, but who has always been a good friend and a source of joy.

Kirby Kim, who believed in me early, and throughout mergers, moves, and celebrity meltdowns, my writing is better and my work life is more fun thanks to you.

Jen Bergstrom, such a dear mentor and friend, whose belief in me and this book literally changed my life; I wouldn't have wanted to write it for anyone else.

Trish Boczkowski, for essential edits and helping me to find the strongest, clearest version of my story.

Kate Dresser, for tireless enthusiasm and support and for encouraging me to go back in one last time and make the manuscript as good as it truly could be.

Louise Burke, Kristin Dwyer, Melanie Mitzman, Jennifer Weidman, and all at Gallery Books who have welcomed me to the family and helped me to share my story.

Carrie Thornton, Farrin Jacobs, Jeremie Ruby-Strauss, Kara Cesare, Zachary Schisgal, Marc Gerald, Patrick Price, Jan Miller, Nena Madonia, Andy McNichol, Brant Rumble, and everyone in my celebrity ghostwriting life who has taught me so much about publishing and storytelling and made the job so enjoyable.

All of my ghostwriting clients, who have invited me to tell their stories, and by doing so, taught me so much of value when it finally came time to write my own memoir.

All of the writers who have critiqued my work or sat in conversation with me, especially Ellen Dorr, Monica Drake, Erin Almond, Liz Barker, Edan LePucki, Patrick Brown, and Josh Levine.

Cathy Elcik, for talking me off more ledges than I can count and being a true friend to me, a patient listener, the person willing to tell me the things I didn't want to hear, and a tremendous source of inspiration and solace in both the trenches of writing and life. Thank you, especially, for your tremendous service to me during the writing of this book. It would not exist in this form without you.

Beth Cleary, who saved me from myself so many times, taught me so much about music and food and wine, devoted endless hours of her life to some of my most important conversations and nurtured and spoiled me during nearly every chapter of my life. Everyone should be so lucky to have a friend like you.

Jodi Jackson, source of sparkle and wisdom in equal parts, a huge instigator in so many adventures, not least of all my California life, and whose straight talk and kindness have both been so dear to me on so many occasions.

Marya Janoff, for teaching me about the best ways to wield intelligence with ease and grace, for giving me so much to look up to and admire, and also for being so smart and interesting and just so much fun.

Sarjan, although we don't see each other as much as we should, the fantastic and inspiring conversation between us feels like it's continually ongoing.

Cracker, a true friend on so many occasions, thanks for providing essential support and distraction during the time I lived in Brooklyn and wrote this book.

Rebecca Berman and Chris Fagot, the most generous and supportive patrons a writer could ask for, and the core of my wonderful West Coast family.

Mark Mallman for being an artistic inspiration and true friend and for the best musical voice mail messages, ever.

Karina Briski, for inspiring conversation and sweet friendship during the writing of this book and for being one of the best gifts of my move to New York.

Rachel Egan, my Canadian soul sister, for dear friendship and the loveliest pep talks.

Jill Soloway, the most generous and encouraging mentor imaginable, who helped to grow me as a writer and person, and told me what to wear to meetings.

Richard Stein, for being a crucial sounding board and support during the final work on this book and for being the home I came out to on the other side. I love you so.

For their friendship, belief and support over the years: Kyle Purinton, Erica Swift, Brianna Bateman, Tori Bunker, Cory Costello, Tan Twhigg, Liz Hottel, Galen Gibson, Mark Harmon, Amanda Touchton, Sonja Gshosshman, Emily Mann, Zack Lipez, Josh Balog, Ben Bertocci, Daphna Kohn, Whitney Blank, James Sparber, Mishka Shubaly, Matt DeGenero, Nicole DeJesus, Benji Bogin, Zach Brockhouse, Kitty Diggins, Dawn Henshel, Ryan Puckett, Meredith DeLoca, Christine Celli, John Frutiger, Erin King, Iwalani Kaluhiokalani, Tara Julian, Rachel Legsdin, Amy Wallenberg, Anthony Rossomando, Damian Genuardi, Jared Everet, Carter Taunton, Darcy Scanlon, Joseph Sadar (and Nabile and everyone at the Middle East), Deanne Devries, Whitney Blank, Greg Dulli, Lucinda Williams, Janet Fitch, Joshua Grange, Traci Thomas, Sera Timms, Laurel Stearns, Steffie Nelson, Piper Ferguson, Caroline Ryder, Jodie Wille, Sanae Barber, Valerie Palmer, Amelia Gray, Fiona Dourif, Sabra Embury, Brett Fenzel, Pascal Vincent, Melanie Lynskey, Misha Rudolph, Jessica Amos, Rachel Melvald, Donna Coppola, Allison Linaman, Camille Hines-Parker, Azniv Bozoghlian, Arrica Rose, Benj Hewitt, Brooke Delaney, J. Ryan Stradal, Joshua Wolf Shenk, Matthew Specktor, Summer Block Kumar, Todd Zuniga, Jim Ruland, Cecil Castellucci, Steven Salardino, Robin Schwartz, Heather Crist, Tracy Scott, Imaad Wasif, Kristina Kite, Tracy McMillan, Sean H. Doyle, and Laura Feinstein.

The many writers whose books, advice, and friendship supported and inspired me during the creation of this manuscript: Dani Shapiro, Alysia Abbott, Leigh Newman, Wendy C. Ortiz, Jillian Lauren, Jen Sincero, Jennie Ketcham, Liz Prato, Sara Lippmann, and Darrin Strauss.

The communities where I learned so much and honed my writing, including GrubStreet, the Community of Writers at Squaw Valley, Writing Workshops Los Angeles, and Wellspring House.

To the many people I didn't have the space to name who also helped to get me here.